Places of interest Nos. **64-160**:

Areas covered by the plans: *see map inside back cover*

PRESTEL
CITY
GUIDE

Munich

by
Lillian Schacherl
and
Josef H. Biller

Prestel-Verlag

This guide contains 471 illustrations, 386 in color,
17 colored and 20 black-and-white plans.

Front cover:
Theatine Church of St. Cajetan,
with lion in front of Field Marshals' Hall.

Back cover:
Detail of the Maria-Hilf altar by Ignaz Günther
in St. Peter's Church.

Page 2:
The heart of the Old Town. From top to bottom:
Cathedral, Marienplatz with New City Hall,
St. Peter's Church, Old City Hall, Church of the Holy Ghost.
(Reproduction permit no. G 42/371 of the Government of Upper Bavaria)

Translated from the German by John William Gabriel,
with David Britt and Graham Lack.

© 1987 Prestel-Verlag, Mandlstrasse 26, 8000 München 40,
Federal Republic of Germany
The concept, format, and layout of this book have been
developed specially for the series "Prestel City Guides."
They are subject to the laws protecting intellectual property
and may not be copied or imitated in any way.
Registered with the DBGM.

© of works illustrated: the artists, their heirs and assigns.
Works by Wassily Kandinsky: copyright 1987 VG Bildkunst, Bonn;
works by Paul Klee: copyright 1987 COSMOPRESS, Geneva.

© of all other illustrations: see Photography Credits, p. 239

Distribution in the U.S.A. and Canada by
te Neues Publishing Company, 15 East 76th Street,
New York, N.Y. 10021

Offset Lithography: Karl Dörfel GmbH, Munich
Maps and plans: Astrid Fischer, Munich
Paper: Phöno matt, Papierfabrik Scheufelen, Lenningen
Composition, printing, and binding: Passavia Druckerei GmbH Passau
Printed in Germany

ISBN 3-7913-0838-6

Contents

Munich at the foot of the Alps – the Bavarian capital as it can be seen on the kind of clear day produced by the *Föhn* wind. The view extends from the Schwabing district in the north to the city center.

On the right, the picture is dominated by the mighty Gothic Cathedral [No. 47], with its characteristic Renaissance tower caps, and by the Baroque Theatine Church [No. 27], with its Italianate cupola and elaborate towers. The Triumphal Arch in the foreground [No. 89] marks the entrance to the historic Old Town. In the middle distance one sees the long roof of the Residence [No. 18] on the far left and, behind it to the left, the National Theater [No. 17]. The sequence of towers begins on the far left with the Church of the Holy Ghost [No. 5] and, to its right, the Neo-Romanesque church of St. Maximilian [p. 204]. Further to the right, one encounters the tall, slender tower of St. Peter's Church [No. 6], the Neo-Gothic tower of New City Hall [No. 2], and, just left of center, the north tower of St. Ludwig's Church [No. 87].

In the Alps, which begin about thirty-five miles south of Munich, the cleft of the Isar valley is clearly visible to the left of center. The highest chain of mountains to the left of the valley is the Karwendel range. Stretching across to the right are the Wetterstein mountains, which culminate in Germany's highest mountain, the Zugspitze (unfortunately, not included in the picture – see p. 228).

Reactions to Munich have differed radically among both Germans and foreigners. Here is a representative selection:

A dissipated, licentious nest.
GOTTFRIED KELLER

Munich was the place where I felt most at home.
THOMAS MANN

Munich is a pompous town.
FRANK WEDEKIND

How I would like to be right in the middle of Munich!
JOHANN WOLFGANG VON GOETHE

Things look bad in Munich:
a sea of petty souls.
HEINRICH HEINE

I like being here.
WOLFGANG AMADEUS MOZART

It is extraordinarily boring, with a terrible climate.
HANS CHRISTIAN ANDERSEN

Munich has become a second home to me.
HENRIK IBSEN

I hate Munich art.
D. H. LAWRENCE

This town is a German heaven on earth.
THOMAS WOLFE

Reactions to this guide will probably differ just as radically. If you like it, tell your friends (and enemies); if you don't, tell the publishers (and the authors).

7

Above:

Munich's Airy Spirit,
a tormentor and a charmer,
a magician who brings distant things
suddenly closer and wraps nearby things
in an almost unendurable radiance.
Stranger, who is he?

As any local will tell you,
it's the *Föhn,* that warm, dry wind
that blows whenever the air pressure
on the northern side of the Alps
falls below that on the southern side.
In many people, it induces lethargy,
headaches, sleeplessness,
and irritability; in others,
it stimulates activity and euphoria.
But be consoled: newcomers
to Munich often remain immune
to its effects for several years.

Munich
Month-by-Month

New Year's Call

The New Year doesn't really begin in Munich until the brass band plays from the tower of St. Peter's at 12 noon on New Year's Day.

Debutants' Ball

Coming-out balls at the Hotel Bayerischer Hof and elsewhere give a shimmering elegance to some of the month's long nights.

Fasching Enthronement

Carnival time – called Fasching in Munich – begins with a "solemn" enthronement of the Fasching Prince and Princess in the Deutsches Theater, after which the motley assembly appears in crazy mood on Marienplatz.

Dance of the Market Women

Customers on Viktualienmarkt join the stall owners in an uproarious dance on Shrove Tuesday, the last day of Fasching.

Fasching in Giesing

The Giesing district has celebrated its own carnival for the last thirty-five years, and still puts on the traditional parade on Shrove Sunday.

Silly Knights Ball

One of Fasching's highlights is the eccentric *Ball der Damischen Ritter,* held in medieval costume in the Löwenbräu-Keller.

Strong Beer Season

Beer feeds the stomach – this old monks' rule for coping with Lent is followed with relish at the Salvator-Keller, where the first strong beer (*Starkbier*) of the year is tapped.

Dancing World Cup

After Fasching has passed, the world's most accomplished ballroom dancers compete in standard and Latin American dances during the annual world cup competition at the Deutsches Theater.

Botanical Garden

Spring comes into its own at the Botanical Garden, whose ornamental garden is transformed into a sea of daffodils, tulips, and hyacinths.

April: Spring Cleaning

Flea Markets

The bizarre collections of objects at the large flea markets on Theresa Meadows and in the Ramersdorf district seem to come from a collective spring cleaning.

Spring Festival

Watched over rather sternly by the Bavaria statue, this two-week fair on Theresa Meadows culminates in a splendid firework display on the final day.

Illuminations

Munich puts on nocturnal makeup in readiness for its visitors: the tourist season is about to begin!

May: Outdoor Pleasures

Carriages in the English Garden

Starting at the Chinesischer Turm, you can take the air the way your grandparents did by joining one of the horse-drawn tours through the English Garden.

May Bock Beer

In Munich the blossoming of the chestnut trees means but one thing: the season of May bock beer has arrived. Waitresses carrying up to eight liter glasses (*Mass*) at a time are the goddesses of Munich's beer mythology.

Brewers Parade

Every two years at the end of May Munich's breweries celebrate their own "labor day" with brass bands, dancing, and free beer. The festivities culminate in a procession to Viktualienmarkt.

June: First Summer Days

Raft Trip on the Isar

Starting at Wolfratshausen (about twelve miles south of Munich), groups can enjoy a six-hour trip down the Isar, accompanied by music and dancing, and including a lunch break on land.

Concerts in Nymphenburg Palace

Chamber music of all kinds is performed in the opulent Rococo surroundings of the Great Hall in Nymphenburg Palace.

Corpus Christi Procession

The history of this impressive event, which is organized by the Cathedral parish on the Feast of Corpus Christi, goes back to the Middle Ages. Smaller processions take place in various parishes on the following Sunday.

Opera Festival

A must for all lovers of opera and festive occasions, the Munich Opera Festival is one of the oldest in Europe and a meeting place for opera buffs from all over the world.

Concerts in Schleissheim Palace

Concerts of mainly Baroque music are given in the sumptuously festive setting of the palace that Elector Max Emanuel intended to be a Bavarian Versailles.

Jakobidult

Held since 1310, the Jakobidult (Jacob's Fair) is Munich's oldest fair and the second of three that take place in the Au neighborhood every year. Those looking for rare antiques or second-hand books seldom go away empty-handed.

Kleinhesseloher Lake

Schwabing's "own" lake in the English Garden, with its nearby beer garden and restaurant, is a good place to relax after a day spent in the full heat of a Munich summer's day.

Beer Gardens

Beer gardens are Munich's paradise on earth. They are not just a place to sit and drink beer: they are a philosophy of life!

Bavarian Derby

If it's too hot to undertake much yourself, you can always sit and watch others exert themselves! At the races, for example. The climax of the German horse-racing season takes place at Munich's racecourse in the Riem district.

Großer
Amdahl-
Deutschland
Pokal

September: Oktoberfest

Opening

Tradition decrees that the *Oktober*fest begin on the third Saturday in *September*! Preceded by a festive parade, it opens its doors to the public when the first keg of beer is tapped at 12 noon.

Parade

The magnificent parade on the second day of the Oktoberfest transforms the entire city into a forum for traditional costumes from all over the world.

At Night

The largest and most famous of all public festivals, the Oktoberfest rages for sixteen long days and sixteen short but spectacular nights. Seven million visitors consume a total of five million liters of beer.

October: Auction Time

Dealers' Auctions

Everything from medieval books of hours to avant-garde paintings are up for sale at the fall auctions of Munich's leading art dealers.

Antique Fairs

The German Art and Antiques Fair in the Haus der Kunst, the antique fair in the Regina Haus, and dealers' displays in the Pschorr-Keller and Salvator-Keller transform Munich into an antique hunters' paradise.

Colorful Fall Messengers

Their baskets full of herbs, women from Franconia and the Palatinate regions of Bavaria come to Munich in the fall to ply their wares from market to market and house to house.

November: Mixed Delights

Roast Chestnuts

No sooner have the cold days arrived than sellers of roast chestnuts appear on Munich's streets. A bag of roast chestnuts is a good substitute for gloves left at home!

Music-in-the-Home Festival

During the *Tage der Hausmusik* chamber and folk music are performed by up-and-coming musicians in the Music College, in various restaurants around town, and in the "Closing Time Concerts" that take place at 6.15 in the Gasteig Arts Center.

Six-Day Bicycle Race

Munich is "Europe's Capital of Six-Day Racing" with this event in the Olympic Hall. Actually, the days are nights: the competition takes place between six in the evening and one o'clock in the morning. Accompanied by music and showgirls, the spectacle is enjoyed by 91,000 visitors every year.

December: Winter Warmth

Christkindlmarkt

This colorful Christmas market, with its mulled wine, roast chestnuts, gingerbread, and trinkets in all shapes and sizes, has been a Munich institution since the fourteenth century.

Christmas Mass in St. Peter's

The Christmas celebrations culminate in the midnight mass held on Christmas Eve, performed ceremoniously in the city's large churches and more intimately in the former village churches on the outskirts of town.

A Winter's Night on Marienplatz

Munich's cosy winter beauty can be experienced nowhere better than in the very heart of the city.

History, Art, and Culture:
An Outline Chronology

Henry the Lion, the founder of Munich. Tomb in Braunschweig Cathedral, c. 1250.

Emperor Ludwig the Bavarian. Sculpture from the former Trade Hall in Mainz, c. 1330.

1158 Foundation of Munich: Duke Henry the Lion destroys the bridge over the Isar at Oberföhring, moves the river crossing to Munich, and establishes a market and a mint here.

1175 Earliest ring of fortifications.

1214 Munich first referred to as a city.

1240 Munich passes from the rule of the bishops of Freising to that of the House of Wittelsbach.

1255 Munich becomes the seat of government of the Duchy of Bavaria-Munich, one of the four parts into which the Duchy of Bavaria is divided.

1285-1315 A second ring of fortifications is laid out around the city, which has grown to five times its former size.

1294-1347 Duke **Ludwig IV, the Bavarian,** King of Germany from 1314, Holy Roman Emperor from 1328. Munich becomes a center of European culture, with the Englishman, William of Occam, as its leading philosopher.

1324-50 The regalia of the Holy Roman Empire are kept in Munich. In consequence, the heraldic colors of the Empire, black and gold, are adopted as those of the city.

1340 Emperor Ludwig the Bavarian awards Munich the status and privileges of a major city.

1429 An outer ring of fortifications is built in response to a threat of attack by the Hussites.

1467-1508 **Duke Albrecht the Wise.** Flowering of Late Gothic art in Munich, with the architect Jörg von Halsbach, the sculptor Erasmus Grasser, and the Polish painter Jan Polack. The great age

The oldest view of the city, from Schedel's Chronicle of the World, *1493.*

*Bird's-eye view of Munich: Model of the city by Jakob Sandtner, 1572
(original in the Bavarian National Museum, larger copy in Munich City Museum).*

of the armorer's art in Munich; ceremonial armor is made here for the French kings.

1483 Two musicians of the English Chapel Royal, Conret Smith and Peter Skeydell, found the Munich *Kantorei.*

1505 The duchies are reunited, and Munich becomes the capital of Bavaria.

1516 The Bavarian Purity Law for beer, the first modern food legislation, is passed. The Munich mathematician Nikolaus Kratzer goes to England, where he becomes Astronomer Royal to King Henry VIII and his portrait is painted by Holbein.

1541-73 Hans Mielich illuminates magnificent Renaissance manuscripts.

1550-79 **Duke Albrecht V, the Magnanimous.**
Albrecht V promotes the Counter-Reformation and the art of the Renaissance. The Netherlandish composer Orlando di Lasso is brought to Munich to direct the musicians of the Court Chapel. In 1569-71 the Antiquarium (Hall of Antiquities), the largest secular building of the German Renaissance, is built to house the duke's collection of antique sculpture. This is the first museum building in Germany.

1568 Italian actors bring the *commedia dell'arte* to Munich.

1579-97 **Duke Wilhelm V, the Pious.**
Munich becomes a center of German Renaissance culture. The first flowering of Munich bronze casting, with Hubert

17

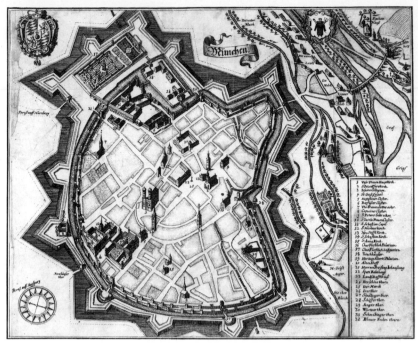

Munich fortifications, 1645-1791: Medieval inner ring (1285-1337), late medieval outer ring (1429-72), and Baroque moat and ramparts (1619-32 and 1638-45).

Gerhard, Hans Krumper, and Hans Reichle. Netherlandish artists are brought to the Court: Friedrich Sustris, Peter Candid, and Nikolaus Gerhaert.

1578-90 The Netherlandish miniaturist Georg Hoefnagel active in Munich.

1578-79 Vincenzo Galilei, father of the Italian astronomer, works in Munich as a musician.

1583-97 Construction of the Jesuit church of St. Michael's, the largest Renaissance church in northern Europe.

1593-1620 The Netherlandish poet Aegidius Albertinus is working in Munich.

1597 English actors perform English plays in Munich for the first time.

1597-1651 Duke **Maximilian I,** Elector of Bavaria from 1623.
Beginnings of the Baroque style in art and literature. Much building activity. "Munich Circle" of poets; Munich Tapestry Manufactory.

1601-18 Rebuilding of the Residence. The largest palace complex of the age, it

Maximilian I (1597-1651).

The city coat of arms, c. 1560.

View of Munich in 1761. Painting by Bernardo Bellotto in the Residence.

includes northern Europe's first monumental stairway, the Kaisertreppe.

1607-31 The musician Michele Galilei, brother of the Italian astronomer, is a member of the Court Chapel.

1609 The Catholic League is founded in Munich.

1619-45 Construction of a new ring of fortifications.

1628 The first newspaper is published in Munich.

1632 King Gustavus Adolphus marches into the city upon its surrender to the Swedes. The occupation lasts until 1634.

1651-79 **Elector Ferdinand Maria.** High Baroque period; strong Italian influences, promoted largely by Electress Henriette Adelaide of Savoy. Among others, the Court employs the architects Agostino Barelli and Enrico Zuccalli, the stucco artists Giovanni Perti, Giovanni Brenni, and Carlo Brenneti Moretti, and the musician Ercole Bernabei.

1679-1726 **Elector Max II Emanuel.**

1692 Max Emanuel becomes governor of the Austrian Netherlands.

1701-14 War of the Spanish Succession. Bavaria allies herself with France against Austria and England.

1705-14 Munich under Habsburg rule.

1705 "The Bloody Christmas of Sendling": peasants and townspeople rise up against Austrian occupation.

1706-14 Max Emanuel is outlawed by Imperial decree. Exile in France and the Netherlands.

1715 Max Emanuel returns from exile in France. Under French influence, art in Munich rises to a leading position in Europe, with such figures as Giovanni Antonio Viscardi, Karl Effner, and the

Elector Max Emanuel (1679-1726).

Napoleon's entry into Munich at Karlsplatz in 1805.

Asam brothers. The Frenchmen François de Cuvilliés and Guillaume de Groff settle here. Palaces and mansions in and around Munich are designed by the French architects and landscape gardeners Jacques-François Blondel, Robert de Cotte, André Le Nôtre, and Dominique Girard.

1701-22 The French composer François Loeillet is a member of the Munich Court Chapel.

1726-45 **Elector Karl Albrecht,** as Charles VII Holy Roman Emperor from 1742. The great age of Rococo art in Munich, with Johann Michael Fischer, Johann Baptist Straub, Johann Baptist Zimmermann, François Cuvilliés, and others. From 1736 onwards, Bavarian art is increasingly characterized by rocaille ornament; in the congenial setting of Bavaria, French Rococo reaches new heights of perfection.

1729 Introduction of street lighting.

1742-45 War of the Austrian Succession; Karl Albrecht allies himself with France. Munich occupied by the Austrians, 1742-44.

1745-63 **Elector Max III Joseph.** Last phase of Rococo art, with artists such as Matthäus Günther, Franz Anton Bustelli, François Cuvilliés, and others.

1754-63 The Italian artist Franz Anton Bustelli designs *commedia dell'arte* figurines for the Nymphenburg porcelain factory.

1759 Bavarian Academy of Sciences founded.

1777-99 **Elector Karl Theodor.** Bavaria and the Palatinate are united.

1777 A language teacher by the name of Robespierre dies in Munich; his son Maximilian will become famous as a French revolutionary leader.

1748-98 The Bavarian army is reorganized by Colonel Benjamin Thompson, Count

Rumford, an American from Massachusetts, who also promotes social reforms and founds the English Garden.

1791 Munich ceases to have the status of a fortified city.

1798 Alois Senefelder invents lithography, the technique which made modern offset printing possible.

1799-1825 Elector Max IV Joseph, as Max I Joseph King of Bavaria from 1806.

1800 Munich occupied by French revolutionary forces.

1803 A general decree of secularization leads to the dissolution of all monasteries in Munich.

1805 Napoleon enters Munich, as an ally.

1806 Munich becomes a royal capital. The sciences flourish. The optical industry is founded by Joseph von Fraunhofer, Georg von Reichenbach, and Joseph von Utzschneider. Munich becomes a center of Romantic philosophy when Friedrich Wilhelm Joseph von Schelling accepts an invitation to come here.

1810 A horse race held to celebrate the wedding of Crown Prince Ludwig (later Ludwig I) to Therese of Saxe-Hildburghausen leads to the tradition of the Oktoberfest.

1812 King Max I Joseph allies himself with Russia, England, and Austria against Napoleon.

1814 Joseph von Fraunhofer discovers the solar spectrum.

1817 Franz Xaver Gabelsberger develops shorthand. Karl Friedrich Philipp von Martius and Johann Baptist von Spix set out on their famous expedition to Brazil.

1818 Bavaria becomes the first German state with a written constitution. The Bavarian parliament, the Landtag, sits in Munich, which is also the seat of the new archdiocese of Munich and Freising.

1824 Second great period of bronze casting, with Johann Baptist Stiglmaier and Oskar von Miller.

1827 Charles de Coster, author of *Uylenspiegel,* born in Munich.

1825-48 King Ludwig I.
Munich becomes a major artistic center again. High point of Neoclassicism and onset of Gothic Revival. Artists include Leo von Klenze, Friedrich von Gärtner, Peter Cornelius, Johann Friedrich Overbeck, Karl Rottmann, and Bertel Thorwaldsen. Writers in Munich include Joseph von Görres, Heinrich Heine, Clemens Brentano, Friedrich Hebbel, and Gottfried Keller.

1826 The University of Landshut is moved to Munich.

1832 Prince Otto, son of Ludwig I, becomes king of newly independent Greece, where he embarks on the creation of a modern state.

1835 The Scottish astronomer John Lamont becomes director of the Munich observatory.

1838-39 First experimental photographs taken by Carl August von Steinheil and Franz von Kobell (anticipating Daguerre).

View of Marienplatz, c. 1830. Lithograph by the English artist Samuel Prout.

King Ludwig I (1825-48).

1839 Opening of the first railroad from Munich.

1841 The world's first society for the protection of animals is founded in Munich.

1846 Population reaches the 100,000 mark.

1848 Political unrest (March risings) and scandal involving Ludwig I's association with the dancer Lola Montez. Ludwig I abdicates.

1848-64 **King Max II.**
Scientists, scholars, and writers from northern Germany (the so-called *Nordlichter*) are welcomed to Munich, among them Justus von Liebig, Wilhelm Heinrich Riehl, Friedrich von Bodenstedt, and Paul Heyse. Development of the Maximilian Style in architecture.

1855 Bavarian National Museum founded.

1861 Munich receives its first public transport: the horse omnibus.

1864-86 **King Ludwig II.**
Music and the decorative arts flourish. Richard Wagner in Munich (1864-65): world premieres of several of his music dramas.

1868 Technical College founded.

1868-70 The Czech composer Bedřich Smetana lives in Munich.

1873 First Carnival procession.

1875-91 Henrik Ibsen writes six plays in Munich.

1876 Horse tramway service started.

1882 International Electricity Exhibition includes the world's first demonstration of electrical power transmission.

1880-95 Albert Einstein in Munich.

1886-1912 **Prince Regent Luitpold.**
Brilliant period in architecture, painting, decorative arts, literature, and theater.

1887 Foundation of the Esperanto movement.

1892 Foundation of the Munich Secession.

1896 The periodical *Jugend* inaugurated; Munich becomes one of the main centers of *Jugendstil,* the German version of Art Nouveau.

1897 Wassily Kandinsky settles in Munich. Kathi Kobus opens her bar, the Simpl, which becomes a famous haunt of artists.

1898 Rudolf Diesel demonstrates the first diesel engine in Munich.

King Ludwig II (1864-86).

1899 The world's first car license-plate is issued in Munich.

1900 Population reaches the 500,000 mark. Literary life at the turn of the century features, among others, Thomas Mann, Stefan George, Rainer Maria Rilke, Max Halbe, Heinrich Lautensack, Frank Wedekind, Carl Sternheim, Karl Wolfskehl, and Ernst von Wolzogen.

1900-02 Vladimir Ilyich Lenin in Munich, where he edits two revolutionary journals.

1900-03 Literary cabaret at the Elf Scharfrichter (Eleven Hangmen).

1905-09 The Italian 'Metaphysical' painter Giorgio de Chirico studies in Munich.

1906 Foundation of the Volkshochschule, providing adult education through evening classes. The Munich Playhouse opens in the Augustenstrasse.

1910 Wassily Kandinsky paints the first abstract picture.

The world's first demonstration of electrical power transmission by Oskar von Miller and Marcel Deprez during the International Electricity Exhibition in Munich's Crystal Palace, 1882.

1911 First exhibition of The Blue Rider, the pioneer modern art group which includes Wassily Kandinsky, Franz Marc, and Paul Klee.

1913-18 **King Ludwig III.**

1916 In the course of the First World War Munich comes under air attack just once, when French aircraft drop three bombs.

1918 Revolution. The Spartacist Federation is founded in Munich. Kurt Eisner proclaims the People's Free State of Bavaria. The king flees.

1919 Bavaria becomes, briefly, an independent soviet republic (*Räterepublik*). Kurt Eisner is murdered.

1923 Adolf Hitler mounts a Putsch from a Munich beer cellar against the Bavarian

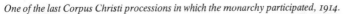

One of the last Corpus Christi processions in which the monarchy participated, 1914.

23

Chamberlain, Daladier, Hitler, and Mussolini after the signing of the Munich Agreement on September 29, 1938.

cabinet and the central government of Germany under Chancellor Strese-mann. The insurgents march to Field Marshals' Hall, where they are forcibly dispersed by the police.

1925 Otto Falckenberg becomes producer at the Munich Playhouse.

1929 Ernst Henne creates the first absolute world motorcycle speed record in Munich: 134.68 miles per hour.

1933 Thomas Mann, Lion Feuchtwanger, Oskar Maria Graf, and other leading Munich writers leave Germany.

The Bürgerbräukeller after the unsuccessful attempt on Hitler's life in 1939.

The destruction of Munich during the Second World War: View of St. Peter's Church in 1945.

1934 Röhm Putsch: in the "night of the long knives" Hitler rids himself of the last remaining rivals within his party.

1935 Munich is proclaimed "Capital City of the [Nazi] Movement."

1937 Modern art is pilloried in the exhibition *Degenerate Art.*

1938 Signing of the Munich Agreement between Hitler, Chamberlain, Daladier, and Mussolini over the German occupation of Czechoslovakia.

1939 An unsuccessful attempt is made on Hitler's life in a Munich beer cellar.

1943 The "White Rose" resistance movement.

1944 Munich suffers extensive bomb damage.

1945 US troops arrive on April 30.

1946 New Bavarian constitution. Munich becomes capital of the Free State of Bavaria.

1948 Bavarian Academy of Fine Arts founded.

1955 The first Max Planck Institute is founded in Munich.

1957 Population reaches the 1,000,000 mark.

1958 Celebration of the city's 800th anniversary. Nuclear research reactor in operation in the Garching district.

1960 The Eucharistic World Congress takes place in Munich.

1963 The rebuilt National Theater opens it doors to the public again.

The start of the 1972 Olympic Games.

1980 The European Patent Office is opened.

1983 International Garden Exhibition in Munich. Sir Colin Davis becomes Chief Conductor of the Bavarian State Radio Orchestra.

The European Patent Office, built in 1975-80.

The nuclear research reactor at Garching.

1971 Opening of the first subway.

1972 The XXth Olympic Games are held in Munich.

1979 The Romanian Sergiu Celibadache becomes Chief Conductor of the Munich Philharmonic Orchestra.

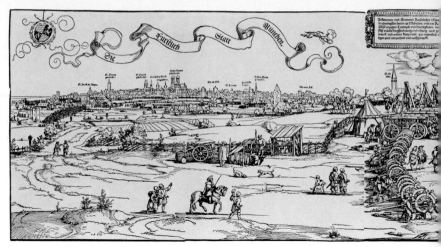

Visit of Emperor Charles V, 1530: Welcoming outside the city walls. Woodcut by Hans Sebald Beham.

Illustrious Visitors

1473 Emperor Frederick III.

1489 and 1491 King Maximilian (Holy Roman Emperor from 1508).

1530 State visit of Emperor Charles V (Charles I of Spain).

1580 Michel de Montaigne passes through Munich on his way to Italy.

1619 Emperor Ferdinand II.

1653 Emperor Ferdinand III.

1658 Emperor Leopold I.

1680 The Italian composer Arcangelo Corelli works in Munich at about this time.

1684 Prince Eugene of Savoy (later to fight alongside the Duke of Marlborough in the War of the Spanish Succession: Battle of Blenheim, 1704) comes to Munich for Carnival.

1690 Emperor Leopold I and his son King Joseph I, later allies of England in the War of the Spanish Succession.

1722 The Italian composer Tommaso Albinoni visits Munich.

1762 Wolfgang Amadeus Mozart's first visit to Munich; he returns in 1774-75, 1777, and 1780-81.

1781 Emperor Joseph II.

1782 Pope Pius VI passes through Munich on his way back from Vienna to Rome.

1786 Johann Wolfgang Goethe stays in Munich on his way to Italy.

1796 The Duc d'Enghien, with the forces of the Prince de Condé, passes through Munich on his retreat from the advancing French revolutionary armies.

1814 Emperor Franz I of Austria and the Tsarina of Russia.

1823 The eleven-year-old Franz Liszt plays in Munich.

1829 Nicolò Paganini plays in Munich.

1833 The Danish writer Hans Christian Andersen stays in Munich for the first time; he returns in 1840, 1851, 1852, and 1854.

1839 State visit of Tsar Nicholas I and Tsarina Maria Alexeyevna.

1866 The French writer Alphonse Daudet visits Munich.

1869 The French painter Gustave Courbet makes the first of three visits to Munich.

1907 and 1922 Jean Giraudoux in Munich; he describes his experiences in *Siegfried*.

1917 Franz Kafka visits Munich to give readings from his works.

1925 The Russian bass Feodor Ivanovich Chaliapin sings in Munich.

1928 The American writer Thomas Wolfe visits Munich.

1957 Igor Stravinsky and Darius Milhaud conduct concerts organized by Musica Viva.

1962 State visit of President Charles de Gaulle of France.

1965 State visit of Queen Elizabeth II of England and Prince Philip.

1973 State visit of King Olaf V of Norway.

1976 State visit of President Anwar al-Sadat of Egypt.

1979 State visits of King Carl Gustav of Sweden and his Munich-born consort Queen Silvia; President Sandro Pertini of Italy; and the leader of the Chinese Communist Party and Government, Hua Goufeng.

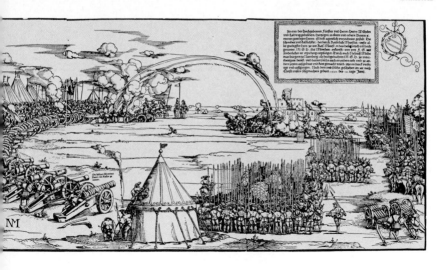

1980 Pope John Paul II in Munich.

1987 Pope Paul II in Munich to mark the Beatification of Father Rupert Mayer, the "Apostle of Men" who was persecuted by the Nazis.

*The city coat of arms
in its two current official forms,
full and simplified.*

Statistics, Etc.

Name: München (Munich) derives from *Mönch,* the German word for "monk."

Importance: Apart from the city-state of Hamburg, Munich is the largest and most densely populated city in the Federal Republic, its major center of higher education and its second largest industrial city. It is the capital of the Free State of Bavaria and the seat of the Bavarian government.

Position: Latitude 48° 8' 23" N, Longitude 11° 34' 28" E. Average height above mean sea-level: 1,379 feet. The highest point (in the south of the city) is 1,896 feet; the lowest (in the north) is 1,568 feet.

Area of city: 119.84 square miles.

Local time: 13 minutes and 42 seconds behind Central European Time, which is the official time.

Population on 1 January 1986 (projection): 1,282,645. Highest population figure ever recorded, in 1972: 1,338,924. Proportion born in Munich: approximately 30%. Foreign residents: 203,953 or 15.8%.

Transport network: Streets, 1,387 miles; tramways, 54.3 miles; subways (U-Bahn), 25.4 miles; suburban railways (S-Bahn), 310 miles, including 5.4 miles underground.

Motor vehicles: 589,122, of which 89.2% are cars.

Buildings: 144,027, including 114,129 residential buildings with 604,769 dwellings.

Economy: City Council budget for current expenditure 4,833,200,000 DM, for capital expenditure 1,594,500,000 DM.
Total gross product of Munich economy: 182.7 billion DM.
Total of persons in employment: 775,000, including 105,000 foreign workers.

Beer: 7 breweries producing 130,704,280 gallons annually.
Lager beer: original wort 11-12%, alcohol 3.5%. Strong beer: original wort 18-19%, alcohol approx. 5.5%.

Administration: City Council with 80 members and 3 mayors. City area divided into 41 districts.

Colors: Black and gold (yellow).

Coat of arms: A monk, habited, with a prayer book in his left hand. (The *Münchner Kindl,* or "Munich Infant," is a modern trivialization.)

Patron saint: St. Benno (secondary patron saint St. Cajetan).

Sister cities: Edinburgh, Bordeaux, Verona, Sapporo (Japan).

Postal code: 8000

Telephone area code: 089.

I Marienplatz with St. Mary's Column

A lovely square with splendid architectural views and vistas. The geographical center of Bavaria, St. Mary's Column serves as the state's main surveying point.

The old square, Marienplatz, is at once an open-air living room for Munich residents and a promenade for visitors; an auditorium when the glockenspiel sounds at eleven o'clock and a forum for political meetings; a space to roll out the red carpet for celebrities and a bazaar at Christmas time. It is not difficult to imagine the opulent royal parades and popular festivities that took place here during the Middle Ages – nor, for that matter, the grisly executions.

A marketplace for salt and grain, then known as Schrannenplatz, this early commercial nucleus of Munich was located on the main East-West trade route and intersected by two North-South roads, a coordinate system still visible in the streets of today. In 1310, further building on the square was prohibited. The arcades of narrow houses gave the marketplace its characteristic appearance until the second half of the nineteenth century. The famous Herb Market was once held in the eastern part of the square, and the Fish Market to the northeast. You can still see the

Marienplatz, with St. Mary's Column, Old City Hall, and tower of Church of the Holy Ghost.

Sculptures on St. Mary's Column: The Virgin Mary (above) and (left) a putto fighting a snake (an allegory of the struggle against unbelief).

Fish Fountain into which butchers' boys made their traditional headfirst dive upon finishing their apprenticeship, and where pious citizens still rinse out their empty wallets on Ash Wednesday. The fountain was restored by Henselmann in 1954, using figures by Knoll (1862-65).

The focal point of the square – indeed, the heart of Munich – is the "sacred domain" of **St. Mary's Column.*** During the Swedish occupation (1632-35) Elector Maximilian pledged a donation to the city if it managed to regain its freedom, and in 1635 he had the column erected in thanks. It was dedicated in 1638, on the anniversary of the Battle of White Mountain.

The Corinthian column on a marble base bears the most graceful of all the city's symbols, a statue of the Virgin Mary as Queen of Heaven★. Created by Hubert Gerhard in about 1590, the figure was originally located in the Cathedral. The armored putti★ around the base are vanquishing a dragon, lion, snake, and basilisk, symbols of famine, war, unbelief, and pestilence. The designer of these superb allegorical figures, which already breathe the Baroque spirit, is unknown, although he was probably one of the three great Bavarian-Swabian sculptors in metal, Hans Krumper, Georg Petel, and Hans Reichle. They were cast by Bernhard Ernst in 1638. The Munich column inspired numerous similar monuments in Austria, Bohemia, and further east.

Münchner Kindl, *atop the City Hall tower.*

2 New City Hall – *Neues Rathaus*
Marienplatz 8

A strikingly monumental Neo-Gothic structure attesting to civic pride at the turn of the century.

Although this outsized and elaborately decorated building in the Flemish Gothic style is not exactly indigenous to the region, the people of Munich have a very soft spot for it. Gothic Revival was all the rage when Hauberrisser, an architect from Graz, designed and built the City Hall in three

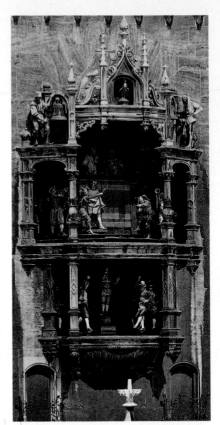

Glockenspiel with two scenes: Tournament at the Prince's Wedding, 1568 *and* Coopers' Dance. *Below: Royal Loggia on City Hall, with statues of King Max II and King Ludwig II.*

phases from 1867 to 1908. The brick and ashlar complex, with its 260-foot-high tower, is built around six interior courts, among them the ornate **Prunkhof** with a spiral-staircase tower. Sculptures representing historical figures adorn the main facade, which is over 300 feet long.

Marienplatz with New City Hall, St. Mary's Column, and Cathedral towers in the background.
Left: Summer garden of the Ratskeller, in the ornate Prunkhof of New City Hall.

Every day at eleven o'clock, the **glockenspiel** in the tower oriel commemorates events that took place on Marienplatz – a tournament held to celebrate the marriage of Wilhelm V and Renata of Lorraine in 1568 and the Coopers' Dance (*Schäfflertanz*) to avert the plague, a tradition dating from 1683. At 9 p.m. the Night Watchman of Munich and the Munich Infant (*Münchner Kindl*), blessed by an angel, appear on the seventh storey. (The bells sound again at 12 noon and 5 p.m. from May to October.)

3 Old City Hall – *Altes Rathaus*
Marienplatz 15

A fine example of the simple Bavarian Gothic style. Formerly the dominant building on Marienplatz, it remains one of its outstanding features.

Replacing an intricate complex of still older civic buildings, the Old City Hall was built in 1474 to the plans of Jörg von Halsbach, called Ganghofer, Master Builder of the Cathedral. It originally comprised a Gothic vaulted hall with a tower converted from one of the city's gates. Often altered and rebuilt over the centuries, particularly when tunnels were dug beneath it in 1877 and 1934, the building was largely destroyed in the Second World War. The hall was restored in simplified form from 1953 to 1958, and in 1972 the tower was reconstructed by Schleich on the basis of its appearance prior to 1474.

The interior furnishings included such gems as the *Morris Dancers* by Erasmus Grasser, a masterpiece of Late Gothic sculpture in Munich (1480; replicas on view here, originals in the Stadtmuseum). A painted frieze with the coat of arms of the artist and poet Ulrich Fuetrer (1478) and Grasser's carved arms and emblems heighten the medieval aura of the **Council Chamber and Dance Hall.** The bronze girl adorning the south face of the tower comes from Verona – Shakespeare's delightful **Juliet,** a gift from Munich's partner city south of the Alps. She may often be seen heaped with flowers, brought there by lovers.

Dancing couple, c. 1900.
Toy Museum in the tower of Old City Hall.

4 Toy Museum – *Spielzeugmuseum*
Old City Hall tower

A childhood world hidden away in the busy pedestrian zone.

A more charming use for the reconstructed tower of the Old City Hall could scarcely be imagined: toys from top to bottom, collected by filmmaker and caricaturist Ivan Steiger, and installed there in 1983. Two hundred years of children's playthings, from the naive to the highly sophisticated, unfold before the eyes of the visitor as he descends the winding staircase. There are toys of wood, paper, and metal; steam-engines, carousels, and magic lanterns; the world of dolls' houses, knights' castles, the Wild West, and menageries; and finally, the model railways, automobiles, airplanes, and ships that marked the innocent beginnings of contemporary playroom technology.

Church of the Holy Ghost: Neo-Baroque facade.

5 Church of the Holy Ghost
Heiliggeistkirche

Tal 77

The oldest Gothic hall church in Munich, gracefully decorated in the delicate style of early Rococo and containing valuable items from the original furnishings.

Although its tower has long been a downtown landmark, when the Holy Ghost infirmary, pilgrims' hostel, and chapel were founded in 1208 they lay well outside the city walls. The Gothic **hall church,** completed in 1392, received a Baroque and Rococo interior from Ettenhofer and the Asam brothers in 1724-30. The harmonious rhythms of its **facade** are pure Baroque Revi-

Church of the Holy Ghost: view toward the high altar (above) and angel adoring the tabernacle (right).

val, dating from 1885, the time at which the infirmary buildings were torn down and the church extended to the west by Friedrich Löwel. Reconstruction work led to a happy merger of surviving and restored elements.

The frescoes in the ceiling vaults, originally by C.D. Asam and authentically restored, depict the founding of the infirmary. Outstanding works include a large-winged Rococo angel★ on the high altar, created by Greiff in 1730; the *Hammerthal Madonna* on the Altar of the Virgin in the north aisle (c. 1450); and the bronze tomb★ of Duke Ferdinand of Bavaria, made after 1608 to designs by Krumper, flanking the main entrance.

33

St. Peter's: Exterior from the southeast (above) and view of the nave (below).

6 St. Peter's Church
Rindermarkt 1

The oldest parish church in Munich. Its Renaissance tower, nicknamed "Old Peter," is one of the city's traditional emblems. The church harbors masterpieces by Grasser, Straub, Günther, and Asam.

St. Peter's is both one of the most venerable and one of the most popular of Munich's churches, and its tower affords a marvellous view of the Alps, particularly during the south wind known as the *föhn*.

Even before the founding of the city, a chapel occupied the hill known as "Petersbergl." It formed the core of the first church on the site, a Romanesque building of the early eleventh century, which was followed in the thirteenth century by a new Gothic structure. At the end of the fourteenth century the twin-tower facade made way for the single tower, and at the beginning of the seventeenth century Schön and Pader renovated the church in the early Baroque style. It received its Rococo appearance in the mid-eighteenth century at the hands of I. A. Gunetzrhainer, Zimmermann, and others. Severe damage during the Second World War necessitated rebuilding work that lasted until 1975.

The **interior** of the Gothic basilica is clad with stucco and gilded figures in a delicate and airy Rococo. The high altar★ (**1**), an inimitable *mise en scène* designed by Asam and executed by Stuber, provides a dramatic setting for the noble seated figure of St. Peter★ by Grasser (1492) and the Four Church Fathers★ by E. Q. Asam (1732). Angels (1804) by Franz Jakob Schwanthaler flank the tabernacle. Polack's paintings of St. Peter, part of the Late Gothic high altar (1517), now hang on the walls of the choir. The fine Rococo choir stalls are the work of Günther (**2**) and Dietrich (**3**).

Like the choir, the entire church contains important works of art from many periods. The Gothic era is represented by the

Right: St. Peter's, high altar with Grasser's statue of St. Peter and Egid Quirin Asam's Church Fathers.

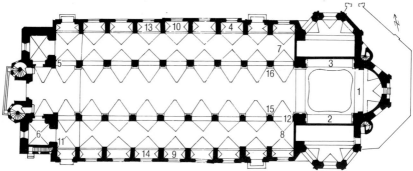

St. Peter's: Schrenck Altarpiece, *c. 1400.*

Cattle Market with "Old Peter" and Lion Tower.

7, 8, 9 Cattle Market Fountain, Lion Tower, Ruffini Buildings
Rindermarkt

A slice of Old Munich, combining historical monuments, authentic reconstruction, and effective modern accents.

The Rindermarkt, probably even older than Marienplatz, was once the city's central cattle market, a function commemorated by Josef Henselmann's **fountain** of 1964 with its herdsman and cows drinking at the terraced basins.

In the course of postwar rebuilding and redesign of the square the old **Lion Tower** (Löwenturm) was again revealed to view. Although it looks like part of the ancient town fortifications, it actually served as a water tower for a park on this site.

The block of **Ruffini Buildings** at the western corner of the square, with its elaborate

Enjoying the sun at the Cattle Market Fountain.

Schrenck Altarpiece (**4**), a rare sandstone retable of about 1400 with a depiction of the Last Judgment★, and by Grasser's vivid *Aresing Epitaph* (**5**) of 1482, with St. Peter, St. Catherine, and the donor. A Renaissance master, the sculptor Krumper, created the font in the baptistery (**6**). Ignaz Günther's elegant Rococo dominates some of the aisle altars, for example with sensuous girl angels and expressive putti (**7, 8, 9**), a moving *Holy Family*★ on the St. Sigismund Altar (**10**), and two superbly carved epitaphs (**11, 12**). The *St. Anne* (**13**) and *Three Kings* altarpieces (**14**) are by Günther's teacher, Straub. Zimmermann's frescoes above the oratory windows have survived only partially; most of them have been repainted to the original designs. The pulpit, with its angel blowing a trumpet, and the large figures of the apostles were carved by Prötzner in 1750, with the exception of St. Paul (**15**) and St. Andrew★ (**16**), which are by Greiff and Faistenberger. These gilded figures high on their columns lead in festive procession to the high altar.

Ruffini Buildings, a picturesque example of turn-of-the-century revival architecture.

facade decoration consisting of reliefs on a colored ground, appears historic despite its late date of 1905. It was created by Gabriel von Seidl, an architect who devoted himself to a revival of the old Munich style of domestic building.

"Weinstadl," with Renaissance facade painting.

10 Weinstadl
Burgstrasse 5

The oldest surviving example of a Munich town house, largely in its original form, with Renaissance facade decoration. Now a tavern.

If any excuse is needed to enjoy a glass of fine wine, this solid Late Gothic house certainly provides more than one. Not only the superb paintings of 1552 by Hans Mielich on the facade, but also the arcaded courtyard, spiral tower, and vaulted rooms inside deserve a visit. Typical Munich features are the gabled dormers projecting from the roof and, in the interior, the "Jacob's ladder," a narrow stairway extending straight from ground floor to attic. This building was once the residence of the town clerk and scribe. Next door, at No. 7, Mozart composed his opera *Idomeneo* in 1780-81. Thirty years earlier, working across the street at No. 6, the lawyer Wiguläus von Kreittmayr extensively codified German law for the first time, while the Rococo architect François Cuvilliés lived and died at No. 8.

Loggias in the courtyard of the "Weinstadl."

The Old Court with tower gate and "Monkey Turret."

II Old Court – *Alter Hof*
Burgstrasse 8

An imposing example of a fortified medieval residence, center of imperial administration under Emperor Ludwig IV. The atmosphere of the courtyard, with its murmuring fountain, is particularly idyllic after sundown.

The Old Court, the first ducal castle of the House of Wittelsbach, was erected at an unknown date at what was then the northeast corner of the town as protection against enemies from without and within. A royal

Statue of Emperor Ludwig the Bavarian.

residence from 1253, its heyday was under Emperor Ludwig the Bavarian, who reigned here from 1328 to 1347. By the time Duke Sigismund came to live in the Old Court over a hundred years later, the main residence had moved to the New Castle (Neuveste), of which no traces remain [see p. 44]. The building has been renovated most picturesquely, particularly on the courtyard side. Its surviving original sections are easily recognized: to the south, the castle wing with tower gate and charming oriel turret; and to the west, the keep, which also contained the ladies' chambers (all dating from 1460-70). Outside the new gate to the north is the mighty **Equestrian Monument to Emperor Ludwig** by Hans Wimmer (1967).

I2 Hofbräuhaus
Am Platzl 9

Munich's most popular attraction, a tavern celebrated like no other in song and story.

This world-renowned institution owes its establishment to a boycott of imported beer issued by Duke Wilhelm V, who in 1591 declared that his court would drink only the products of the brewery he had built at the Old Court. The Royal Brewery – Hofbräuhaus – moved to a building on the Platzl in 1644; but it was not until 1830 that ordinary citizens were able to enjoy their tankard there. They came in such droves that the brewery was soon compelled to relinquish the premises entirely to the tavern and its growing clientele. The present **building,** in the old Munich style of domestic architecture, dates from the turn of the century (1896, by Littmann and Maxon). Over 10,000 liters of beer are now served daily in the Schwemme, Trinkstuben, Festsaal, and beer garden.

I3 Former Central Mint and Mint Court
Hauptmünzamt, Münzhof

Hofgraben 4

One of the earliest and most beautiful of all Renaissance arcaded courtyards in Germany.

An architectural gem hidden in a side-street: this **courtyard★**, with three-storied arcades whose Italianate origin is not belied by their stocky Bavarian proportions, was created by Court Architect Egkl in 1567. The **facade,** added in the Neoclassical period by Andreas Gärtner (1809), has in its pediment three female personifications of gold, silver, and bronze by Franz Jakob Schwanthaler, which allude to the building's function. Originally accommodating the Royal Stables and, above them, Albrecht V's *Kunstkammer* (Cabinet

Right: Outside the Hofbräuhaus, on the Platzl.

Arcaded courtyard of Duke Albrecht V's Cabinet of Curiosities, now known as Mint Court.

of Curiosities), it was used from 1809 as a mint (coinage mark: D). It is now the seat of the Bavarian State Department of Public Monuments.

I4 Central Post Office – *Hauptpost*
Residenzstrasse 2
Main facade on Max-Joseph-Platz

A monumental facade of noble Italian derivation, perfectly complementing the Residence and a dominating element in the Neoclassical design of the square.

If Max-Joseph-Platz has a Florentine air, it is thanks to the **arcade**★ with frescoes of horse-tamers on a red ground, erected by Klenze in 1835 for the Central Post Office (now Post Office I). During the eighteenth century the building, designed by the Gunetzrhainer brothers, was the palace of the dukes of Töring. Its Baroque entrance has been incorporated into the main hall, while two large Rococo figures by Straub stand in the lobby.

I5 Eilles Court – *Eilles-Hof*
Residenzstrasse 13

One of the last arcaded courts in Munich to have survived almost unchanged from the sixteenth century.

Standing in this courtyard one gains some idea of what Munich must have been like in late medieval times. Built about 1560, it perfectly exemplifies the residential architecture

Female Allegory *by Johann Baptist Straub in the lobby of the Central Post Office.*

North facade of the Central Post Office, a key work of Munich Neoclassicism based on Florentine Renaissance models.

of the period, though of course it has not survived completely intact. The loggias, with their open brickwork parapets, have been carefully restored; the glazing is naturally a modern addition. Eilles Court is part of a series of arcades, lined with elegant shops, which run from Residenzstrasse to Theatinerstrasse.

16 Max-Joseph-Platz

A spacious Neoclassical square, manifesting the pomp and power of a royal seat and capital city.

Conceived in the first third of the nineteenth century by Leo von Klenze and Karl von Fischer, the great rectangle of the square is flanked by the Neoclassical facades of the National Theater [No. 17], the King's Tract of the Residence, and the arcade of the Central Post Office [No. 14], which are delightfully complemented by the facades of the houses along the west side.

Accentuating the center of the square is a **Monument★** to Max I Joseph, the first king of Bavaria, who in 1818 gave the state a constitution, the first in Germany. The memorial was not unveiled until 1835, ten years after the monarch's death, for he had refused to be immortalized in a seated position. The overall design, by Klenze and the sculptor Martin von Wagner, enhances figures and reliefs by the great Berlin sculptor, Christian Rauch, which were cast by Stiglmaier. The scenes on the base of the monument depict key events in the reign of Max Joseph.

Eilles Court: old Munich domestic architecture with interior arcading.

41

Max-Joseph-Platz with National Theater and Monument to Max I Joseph, first king of Bavaria.

17 National Theater
Max-Joseph-Platz 2

An important Neoclassical building, monumental in effect and gloriously furnished, the home of an opera company with one of the richest traditions in the world.

Deciding that Munich needed a national theater comparable to the Odéon in Paris, King Max I Joseph launched a competition. The winning design, by a young professor at the Academy, Karl von Fischer, was this austere, Greek-inspired temple of the arts. The theater was opened in 1818, only to be destroyed by fire five years later – divine retribution, people said, for building it on the site of a Franciscan monastery that had been torn down during the period of secularization after 1802. Fischer having died in the meantime, Klenze restored the opera house, making only slight changes to the original design, and by 1825 it was again ready to receive opening-night guests. The Second World

National Theater: Stairway to the foyer (left) and auditorium with Royal Box (above).

War left only its outer walls standing. Despite protests from advocates of a modern-style substitute, the National Theater was rebuilt for the third time, by Gerhard Graubner and Karl Fischer, and completed in 1963.

A broad flight of steps leads up from the square to a **colonnaded portico** topped by a double pediment – the essence of classical decorum. The lower pediment has stone figures of Apollo and the Nine Muses by Georg Brenninger (1972), the upper a glass mosaic representing Pegasus with the Horae, based on a design by Ludwig Schwanthaler. The elegant curve of the **auditorium★**, with its five tiers and Royal Box, is accentuated by

43

King's Tract, the Residence: modelled by Klenze on the Pitti and Rucellai palaces in Florence.

caryatids and colossal orders. It seats an audience of about 2,100; unusual for a royal theater of that period, it was open to the general public.

That Ludwig II occasionally indulged in the luxury of private performances given for his benefit alone was already considered rather eccentric at the time. Yet it was Ludwig who made the National Theater a Wagner house, with world premieres of *Tristan and Isolde, The Mastersingers, Rhinegold,* and *The Valkyrie.* Franz von Dingelstedt and Ernst von Possart were the theater's most famous directors in the nineteenth century, when it also staged plays with major stars of the German stage. Ibsen's *Nora* touched off a scandal when it received its world premiere here in 1880.

Richard Strauss experienced the first success of his opera *Salome* here in 1906, at a time when it was still banned elsewhere. His *Friedenstag* had its first performance at the National Theater in 1938, and his *Capriccio* in 1942, both under Clemens Krauss. Krauss was only one in a long line of great conductors who made the Munich Opera famous – Franz Lachner, Hans von Bülow, Hermann Levi, Felix Mottl, Bruno Walter, Hans Knappertsbusch, Georg Solti, Rudolf Kempe, Ferenc Fricsay, Joseph Keilberth, and its present Musical Director and General Manager, Wolfgang Sawallisch. Highlight of the season is the annual Opera Festival.

18 The Residence – *Residenz*
Max-Joseph-Platz 3;
Residenz-, Hofgarten-, and Marstall-strasse

The seat of the Wittelsbach rulers until 1918.
An imposing complex developed phase by phase
through four centuries – a memorable testimony
to courtly culture in Europe.

When the town had spread beyond their first fortified residence [No. 11], the Wittelsbach family built the New Castle (Neuveste) at the northeast corner of the old town wall in 1385. Continual expansion, to which the New Castle itself eventually succumbed, led to the palace complex as it stands today. Building activity began in 1571 with the Hall of Antiquities (Antiquarium) and reached a peak under Maximilian I, who commissioned the four wings surrounding Emperor's Court (to 1620), a structure King Gustavus Adolphus of Sweden reputedly wished to put on wheels and roll back to Stockholm. A second great expansion came with Ludwig I, who in the mid-nineteenth century added King's Tract, the Festival Hall Building, and the Court Church of All Saints. Largely destroyed during the Second World War, the Residence was rebuilt at great expense of time and effort, and finished in 1980.

Lion at the west entrance to the Residence.

The interior of the Residence is largely coincident with the premises of the Residence Museum [No. 19]. A stroll around the complex is perhaps the best way to gain a general impression.

The main facade can be seen from Max-Joseph-Platz: the Neoclassical **King's Tract** (Königsbau) was designed by Klenze and built in 1826-35. Its entrance provides access to the Residence Museum. Earlier, the main facade was that of **Maximilian's Residence★** on Residenzstrasse, a Renaissance structure of 1611-19 by an unknown architect. Its central axis is marked by a niche containing a vivaciously girlish statue of the Virgin, *Patrona Boiariae★*, by Krumper (1616). Two triumphal portals with allegories of the four cardinal virtues by Krumper and flanking lions by Pallago lead to Emperor's Court (Kaiserhof; not always accessible) and Chapel Court (Kapellenhof).

Passing through the narrow lane of Chapel Court one emerges in **Fountain Court★**

Northwest gate of Maximilian's Residence.

Wittelsbach Fountain in Fountain Court, the Residence.

45

West facade of The Residence: Patrona Boiariae.

Hercules tapestry in New Hercules Hall.

tian Art [No. 22]. Its colonnades and arches, topped by figures by Schwanthaler, are further distinguished specimens of Klenze's Neoclassicism (1832-42). The former Throne Hall (Thronsaal) of the **Festival Hall Building** (Festsaalbau)★, now used for concerts, is known as New Hercules Hall (Neuer Herkulessaal) after its tapestries with scenes from the Hercules legend.

At the eastern end of the Residence

(Brunnenhof), whose elongated octagonal space makes a wonderful open-air concert hall in the summer. At its center is the *Wittelsbach Fountain*★, with gods of antiquity, for the most part by Hubert Gerhard (c. 1600), gathered at the feet of Otto of Wittelsbach. Accessible from here are Foyer Court (Foyer-Hof), outside the Cuvilliés Theater [No. 21], and Apothecary Court (Apothekenhof), whose pavement design gives an idea of the groundplan of the former New Castle.

The Court Garden (Hofgarten) side of this tract abuts on the State Collection of Egyp-

Klenze erected his only ecclesiastical building, the **Court Church of All Saints** (Allerheiligen-Hofkirche) of 1826-37, now a war ruin that still awaits restoration. Another of Klenze's additions has been rebuilt, however – the exterior of the **Royal Stables**★ (Marstall, 1820-25), Marstallplatz 5, a grandly imposing building whose arched portal carries superb busts of Castor and Pollux by Klenze and whose facade is decorated with bronze reliefs by J.M. von Wagner. Part of the spacious interior now serves as an experimental stage for the State Theater, the "Theater im Marstall."

Festival Hall tract of the Residence.

Royal Stables, facade with portal.

Hall of Antiquities, the largest secular Renaissance interior in northern Europe.

Perseus Fountain in Grotto Court, the Residence.

19 Residence Museum

Max-Joseph-Platz 3

One of Europe's finest palace museums, whose interiors and individual collections record the development of court art in Munich.

Removed to safety during the Second World War, the art treasures, furniture, and wall-hangings of the Residence largely escaped destruction, and may now be seen in the restored rooms of which they are an integral part. Space does not permit a complete listing of the museum's contents, so only outstanding rooms and collections will be mentioned here (a detailed guide in English is available at the entrance desk). Those who feel daunted by the museum's size and diversity may join the guided tours, held mornings and afternoons (except on Sundays, when there is a morning tour only). Apart from a few overlaps, the two tours follow different paths through the palace.

Morning Tour (the numbers refer to the plans, next page): (**1**) Vestibule in the Green Gallery tract, by Cuvilliés, 1733. (**4**) *Ancestral Gallery★* with 121 portraits of members of the Wittelsbach family. Stucco by Zimmermann, 1730. (**5**) *Porcelain Cabinet,* designed as a treasury by Cuvilliés, 1733. (**6**) *Grotto Court★*, a Renaissance garden by Sustris, 1581-86, with the *Perseus Fountain★* by Gerhard, c. 1595. Mannerist grottoes, made of tufa and shells, in imitation of natural for-

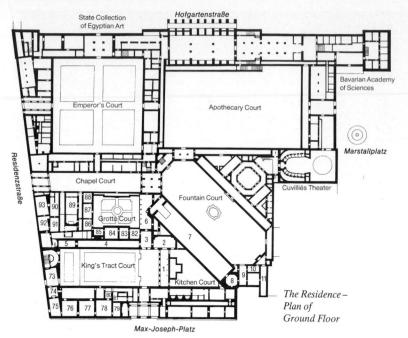

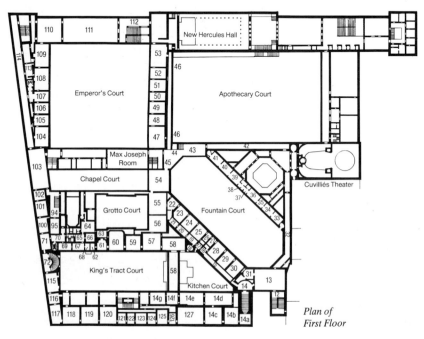

1 Vestibule of King's Tract Court. **2** and **3** First and Second Garden Rooms. **4** and **5** Ancestral Gallery and Porcelain Cabinet. **6** Grotto Court. **7** Hall of Antiquities. **8** Octagon. **9** Gateway. **10** Room with Hercules Relief. **11** Passage to staircase up to Black Hall. **12** and **13** Stairway to Black Hall, and Black Hall. **14, 14a-14g** Rooms in King's Tract. **14** Yellow Staircase. **14a-14c** Campaign Rooms. **14d-14g** Porcelain Cabinets (19th century). **15-21** Rear Elector's Rooms with Gallery of Far Eastern Porcelain. **22-31** Elector's Rooms. **32** All Saints Passage. **33-37** Former Court Garden Room. **38** Passage. **39-41** Charlotte Rooms. **42** Charlotte Passage. **43** and **44** Vestibule and Broad Staircase. **46-53** Emperor's Court tract. **54** Hall of Knights of St. George. **55-62** Ornate Rooms with Green Gallery. **63** Chinese Cabinet. **64** and **65** Cloakroom and Passage. **66-71** Papal Rooms and Cabinet of the Heart. **72** Queen Mother's Staircase. **73** and **74** Gateway to King's Tract Court and vestibule. **75-79** Nibelung Halls. **80** and **81** Passage and main staircase, entrance hall, King's Tract. **82-88** Porcelain Cabinets (18th century). **89** Court Chapel. **90** Lower landing of Chapel Staircase. **91-93** Liturgical Vestment Rooms. **94** Chapel Staircase. **95** Reliquary Chamber. **96** Court Chapel Gallery (Room 89). **97** and **98** Anteroom and Ornate Chapel. **99** Antler Passage. **100-102** Silver Rooms. **103** Hartschier Room. **104-109** Stone Rooms. **110-112** Room of the Four Grays, Emperor's Room, Emperor's Staircase. **113** Passage. **114** Theatines' Passage. **115-122** Queen's apartments. **123-127** King's apartments.

Court Chapel, the Residence.

Ornate Chapel, lantern.

mations. A gilded *Mercury*★ by Giovanni da Bologna, c. 1580.

(**7**) *Hall of Antiquities*★, the largest secular Renaissance interior north of the Alps, built for the sculpture collection (vaulted hall) and library (former upper floor) of Duke Albrecht V, by Egkl, 1571. Over 100 views of Bavarian towns by Donauer, 1588-96. Sculptures, many antique. Room now used for official state receptions.

On to the first floor: (**13**) Black Hall, with ceiling fresco of *trompe-l'œil* architecture, 1602. (**14**) Yellow Staircase: *Venus Italica* by Canova, 1812. (**14d-g**) *Porcelain Cabinets*★ of the nineteenth century, with French, Nymphenburg, and Berlin porcelain. (**15-21**) Col-

lection of Far Eastern Porcelain★, primarily seventeenth and eighteenth century. Also, seventeenth-century Persian carpets, known as "Polish Carpets" since they formerly belonged to the Polish wife of the Elector Palatine. (**22-31**) *Elector's Rooms*★ of Max III and his wife, decorated by Cuvilliés, 1763. (**32**) *All Saints Passage,* with eighteen Italian landscapes by Rottmann, 1830-33, originally installed in the Court Garden arcades. (**33-41**) *Charlotte Tract with Court Garden Rooms* and apartments of Princess Charlotte Augusta, daughter of King Max I Joseph. Parisian furniture and works of art. (**46-53**) *Trier Room*★ of Emperor's Court tract, built to plans by Duke Maximilian I under Krum-

Upper landing of Emperor's Staircase and antechamber of Emperor's Room, Maximilian's Residence.

Princess Elector Henriette Adelaide's Cabinet of the Heart, detail of ceiling.

49

Two exquisite pieces from the Liturgical Vestment Rooms: detail of a chasuble (left), and an infula (right) from the "Polling Vestments," 1730-40, from Polling Monastery, near Weilheim, Upper Bavaria.

Pieces from the Residence Museum porcelain collection: Apple Girl *(left), Nymphenburg; and water-pot from a Meissen gold-ground service (right).*

Green Gallery, a major work of Munich Rococo, by François de Cuvilliés.

per's supervision, completed 1616. Named for Elector Clemens Wenzeslaus of Trier, who often stayed here. Ceiling paintings by Candid, on the subject of the ruler's duties. Tapestries from the First Munich Manufactory (1604-15), with allegories of the months (designed by Candid). (**54**) Hall of Knights of St. George, with tapestries from the Second Munich Manufactory (1730-70) showing scenes from the history of Bavaria's dukes (by Balthasar Augustin Albrecht, based on paintings by Werle). (**55-62**) *Ornate Rooms*★, begun under Elector Karl Albrecht after the Residence burned down in 1729. Cuvilliés's Rococo decor is sheer perfection. Stuccowork by Zimmermann, wall carvings by Pichler, Dietrich, and Miroffsky. High points:

Green Gallery★ (**58**), display of royal painting collection and hall for festivities, with splendid facade onto the King's Tract Court; *State Bedroom*★ (**60**) and *Cabinet of Mirrors*★ (**61**). Now a suite for official guests, who have included Queen Elizabeth II of England and General de Gaulle. (**66-71**) *Papal Rooms*, named for a visit of Pope Pius VI, 1782. Italian Baroque style, completed in 1667. Residence of Henriette Adelaide, wife of Elector Ferdinand Maria. *Cabinet of the Heart*★ (**68**), with Baroque allegories of love.

On to the ground floor: (**75-79**) *Nibelung Halls* in King's Tract. Decoration based on designs by Klenze. Monumental scenes from the *Nibelungenlied* by Schnorr von Carolsfeld, Olivier, and Hauschild (1827-34 and 1843-67).

Afternoon Tour (parallels morning tour in Rooms 1-5, 55-71, 72-81; see above): (**82-88**) *Porcelain Cabinets*★ with eighteenth-century European porcelain from the Royal Household: English, French, and German, including Meissen, Frankenthal, and Nymphenburg. (**89**) *Court Chapel*★, two-storey interior built by Krumper in 1601, under Maximilian I. Superb stuccowork in nave (1614) and choir (1630) on the theme of the Lorettine Litany. Rococo side altars in stucco, with paintings by Zimmermann (1748). (**91-93**) *Liturgical Vestment Rooms,* ornate liturgical robes from the seventeenth and eighteenth centuries.

On to the first floor: (**95**) *Reliquary Chamber,* with reliquaries by Augsburg and Munich goldsmiths, sixteenth to eighteenth century. (**98**) *Ornate Chapel*★, exquisite private oratory of Maximilian I, probably by Krumper, dedicated 1607. Unified work of art from the late Renaissance, superbly restored. Multicolored marble paving, marbled stucco walls with scagliola panels, richly ornamented and figured. Cupola reliefs of gilded terracotta; stained glass windows in the tambour. Altar of black ebony with chased silver reliefs. Elaborate organ. (**100-103**) *Silver Rooms*★ and *Hartschier Room*

Furnishings of the Ornate Rooms saved from war damage: part of the State Bedroom (left), a carved door panel (right), and detail of a Paris chest of drawers by Charles Cressent (below).

with 3,500 pieces of table silver owned by the House of Wittelsbach, eighteenth to nineteenth century. (**104-109**) *Stone Rooms*★, like the Trier Rooms (**46-53**) part of the Emperor's Tract of Maximilian I, named for their decoration in marble, marbled stucco, and scagliola. Elaborate door frames and chimney pieces. Original ceiling frescoes by Candid restored by Trubillio, Gumpp, and Rosa (to 1696). Subjects: Maximilian's conceptions of the sacred and profane. Fine sixteenth-century tapestries from Paris and Brussels, and from the First Munich Manufactory (1604-15), made to Candid's designs and illustrating the deeds of Count Palatine Otto of Wittelsbach. Ornate furniture, bronzes, easel paintings. (**110-112**) *Room of the Four Grays, Emperor's Room, Emperor's Staircase:* Important late Renaissance rooms by Schön and Krumper (reconstructed) with ceiling frescoes and tapestries by Candid and his school (some original). Iconographical program: (**110**) the planets and their deities, (**111**) allegories of world rule guided by wisdom and the virtues. On the mantelpiece, original of the *Tellus Bavarica*★ by Gerhard [see p. 59]. (**112**) Niche figures and busts of Maximilian I's Wittelsbach ancestors.

"Hall of Treachery," one of the Nibelung Halls in King's Tract decorated by Schnorr von Carolsfeld.

(**115-127**) *Apartments★ of King Ludwig I and his wife* in King's Tract. Design of entire interior by Klenze. Unique ensemble, restoration completed in 1980. Murals in the Queen's Rooms (**115-122**), based on poems by Wieland, Goethe, and Bürger and painted by Kaulbach, Foltz, and others. Only partially restored, as are the wall paintings on classical themes by Schwanthaler, Schnorr von Carolsfeld, and others in the King's Rooms (123-127).

20 Residence Treasury
Schatzkammer der Residenz

Max-Joseph-Platz 3

One of the great European treasuries, a first-rate collection of secular and ecclesiastical objects spanning three centuries.

The foundation for the present collection was laid in 1565, when Duke Albrecht V declared in his will that the Wittelsbach "Household

Residence Treasury: Crucifix of Queen Gisela (after 1006, below left), ciborium of King Arnulf (c. 890, below right), and St. George statuette (between 1586 and 1597, opposite).

Jewels" be unsaleable. Elector Karl Theodor enlarged the collection at the end of the eighteenth century with the acquisition of the Palatine Treasures from Heidelberg, Düsseldorf, and Mannheim. Ecclesiastical treasures requisitioned from churches and monasteries in 1802-03, together with the insignia of the monarchy proclaimed in 1806, formed a further significant addition. Not opened to the public until 1939, the collection was removed during the war and survived undamaged. Including the works in the Ornate Chapel, the Residence contains about 1,200 treasury items of supreme artistic value.

Sequence of Rooms

Room I: Goldsmiths' work of the Early and Late Middle Ages, including Prayer Book of Emperor Charles the Bald, ninth century; Rhemish ciborium of King Arnulf of Carinthia, ninth century; crown of Empress Kunigunde, c. 1010-20; so-called Heinrichskrone, c. 1280; and crown of an English queen, c. 1370-80.

Room II: Sacred objects of the Late Gothic and Renaissance periods, from Germany, Flanders, and Italy, including a Burgundian portrait medallion, c. 1440; the so-called Holbein Bowl, c. 1540; and the Rappoltstein Goblet, c. 1543.

Room III: Elaborate equestrian statuette of St. George★, presumably designed by Sustris and executed by Augsburg and Munich goldsmiths between 1586 and 1597.

Room IV: Ecclesiastical art of the sixteenth to the eighteenth century, including the earliest "sun" monstrance in existence, c. 1600; domestic altarpiece of Duke Albrecht V, 1574; and ivory carvings by Georg Petel, seventeenth century.

Room V: Insignia and medals, including royal insignia of the Bavarian kings, made in a Parisian workshop, 1806.

Rooms VI and VII: Gem carving, including cut crystals from the renowned workshops of sixteenth-century Milan and from the seventeenth-century court workshop in Prague, as well as works in agate, jasper, and lapis lazuli.

Room VIII: Ornate goblets, jewellery, and goldsmiths' work of the Renaissance, primarily by Reimer and Jamnitzer.

Room IX: Goldsmiths' work, tableware, jewellery, and statuettes of the Baroque, Rococo, and Neoclassical periods, including travelling tableware set of Empress Marie Louise, Paris, 1810, and seventeenth-century Augsburg clocks.

Room X: Exotic artifacts from Turkey, Persia, Ceylon, and Central America. Sixteenth to eighteenth century.

21 Old Residence Theater Cuvilliés Theater
Altes Residenztheater

Residenzstrasse 1

The loveliest Rococo theater in Europe, created by the finest artists then active in Munich – Cuvilliés, Straub, Zimmermann.

Cuvilliés Theater: Putti on the central box (above), and the auditorium (opposite).

Residence Treasury: Royal Bavarian Crown, 1806.

With the building of this theater in 1751-53, François Cuvilliés the Elder, a Royal Dwarf who became Royal Architect, brought Munich Rococo to its brilliant climax. Commissioned by Elector Max III Joseph in 1750, the "New Opera House" was one of the last theaters built for court society before the decline of absolutism.

Since the members of court, rather than events on stage, were the real center of attraction, everything in the design revolved around the **auditorium★**. The floor could be raised to create a ballroom, while the four horseshoe-shaped tiers lead the eye to the two-tiered Elector's box in the center, with its ornate carvings, and to the proscenium

boxes flanking the stage. Strict hierarchy reserved the orchestra boxes for patricians, the first tier for the higher nobility, the second for the lesser nobility, and the third for court officials.

Lavish ornamentation in red, white, and gold floods across the architecture, concentrating in the areas of the first tier and the three large boxes. Underlying the abundance of carved atlantes, heads, cartouches, putti, and emblems is a pictorial program devoted to variations on the themes of nature (the seasons, agriculture, horticulture), the arts (music and drama), and mythology (gods of antiquity). The major ornaments were created by Straub, with the assistance of the carvers J. and M. Dietrich, while the stucco

State Collection of Egyptian Art: Bekenchon, high priest of the god Amun, c. 1200 B.C. (above) and detail of gold ornament of Queen Amanti-Shaheto (c. 25-10 B.C., below).

and the original ceiling fresco are the work of Zimmermann. Cuvilliés the Younger, Lespilliez, and Giessl collaborated on the architecture, while Gaspari was responsible for stage technology and decoration.

A direct bomb-hit reduced this Rococo jewel to rubble in 1944. The removal of its priceless furnishings beforehand enabled rapid rebuilding in 1956-58 – in the Apothecary Tract of the Residence, since the New Residence Theater had been erected on the original site in 1951.

One of the greatest events in the annals of the Cuvilliés Theater was the world premiere of Mozart's *Idomeneo* on January 29, 1781. Soon, German operas, and then plays by Shakespeare and others, were added to the repertoire, which has continued to expand – right down to today's experimental drama. But is is still with Mozart that the theater's renowned "harmony of decor, drama, and music" reaches the peak of perfection.

22 State Collection of Egyptian Art
Staatliche Sammlung Ägyptischer Kunst

Hofgarten 1

One of the finest collections of its kind in the world, the Egyptian museum is also one of the city's least ostentatious – which makes it all the more attractive to lovers of ancient art.

An obelisk marks the entrance to the collection, whose holdings were distributed among several museums before being united in 1960 and installed in the Festival Hall Building of the Residence in 1972. The collection is as old as the Residence itself, reaching back to Duke Albrechts V's Chamber of Curiosities in the Hall of Antiquities, which already contained a number of small ancient Egyptian sculptures of deities. Systematic collecting began during the reigns of Max I Joseph and Ludwig I, both of whom acquired large objects for the Academy of Sciences and the Glyptothek. As early as 1818, the imposing throne of the high priest Bekenchon, dating from c. 1220 B.C., came to Munich through the efforts of Ludwig's agents.

The collection provides an excellent survey of the classical styles of the Old Kingdom (2670-2160 B.C.), the Middle Kingdom (2040-1660 B.C.), and the New Kingdom (1550-1075 B.C.), with its golden age of Amarna art. Only a sampling of renowned pieces can be mentioned here. There is the powerful double statue of King Neuserre, a godlike image of man from the Old Kingdom. The Middle Kingdom is represented by a compelling portrait of Amenemhet II, the upper part of a statue which, despite its small scale, is truly monumental in effect, and by

View across the Hofgarten to the Theatine Church with Temple of Diana; left, northwest tract of the Residence; right, south wing of the Bazaar on Odeonsplatz. Below: Tellus Bavarica *atop the temple.*

the well-known faience hippopotamus and a bronze crocodile.

Highlights of the extensive New Kingdom collection are the kneeling figure of Senenmut, with its vividly shrewd expression; a golden figure of Tiy, revolutionary in its realism; the fragment of a head of Amenhotep IV, with sensuous mouth and chin; and the portrait head of an old man.

Equally significant are the pieces from the early and late periods of Egyptian art, particularly the elegant and enigmatic late period statuette of the Falcon God. A speciality of the Munich museum is art of the outlying regions of the Egyptian Empire, among the most superb examples of which is the Golden Treasure of the Queen of Meroe in the Sudan (dating from about the beginning of the Christian era).

23 Court Garden – *Hofgarten*

One of the finest royal gardens of its time north of the Alps. A true refuge in the midst of the city, embedded in a harmonious architectural setting.

Superbly combining the gracefulness of art with the grace of nature, the **Court Garden**★ was laid out on an open plot of land in the

northern part of town in 1613-17. Inspired by gardens of the Italian Renaissance, Duke Maximilian I had its rectangular area divided by axial and diagonal paths, centered around a circular temple and ornamentally planted in a blaze of color. Postwar restoration followed this original scheme, retaining the surrounding avenues of trees planted during the nineteenth century and adding graceful fountains at the corners. A finely composed architectural ensemble, whose arcading likewise dates back to Maximilian I (and even earlier), lends the garden the intimacy of an interior. To the south lies the Festival Hall tract of the Residence, whose loggia echoes the forms of the garden temple, and to the west and north, are arcades with art galleries and outdoor cafés, all overlooked by the dome and towers of the Theatine Church.

The octagonal **temple** at the midpoint of the Court Garden is crowned by a bronze figure of Diana★ by Hubert Gerhard (1594), which Hans Krumper transformed into an allegory of the Bavarian Soil – *Tellus Bavarica* – when the region became an electorate in 1623. This imposing goddess, with her plumed helmet and attributes symbolizing treasures of the land (salt cellar, deerskin, weir, sheaf of grain, and orb), is a replica – the original statue can be seen in the Residence Museum. The putti on the pedestal are also copies of Krumper's originals.

The gateway from the garden to Odeonsplatz is a delicately proportioned Neoclassical triumphal arch – the **Court Garden Gate**, Klenze's first work in Munich (1816-17). He followed it with a renovation of the western arcades. The history paintings flanking the gate, commissioned by Ludwig I, were begun by Cornelius and finished by his pupils in 1829. On the west side is a lovely, pensive

Bernhard Bleeker, The Dead Soldier *(detail).*

bronze **nymph** by Ludwig Schwanthaler. The northern arcades, converted into picture galleries as early as 1781, are now graced by murals of Greek landscapes by Seewald (1963).

A sore spot in this architectural setting are the ruins of the **Bavarian Army Museum,** a domed structure of 1906, which await integration in an extensive construction project that cannot help but disturb the harmony of the whole. Located in front of this building is a **war memorial** of 1925, dedicated to the men who lost their lives in the First World War. The monolith over the vault bears a bronze casting of *The Dead Soldier* by Bleeker.

Design for The Magic Flute, *Theater Museum.*

24 German Theater Museum
Deutsches Theatermuseum

Galeriestrasse 4

The oldest theater museum in Europe, with a fine collection illustrating the international history of the theater to the present day.

The northern section of the Court Garden arcades, built in 1781 to house the art collection of Elector Karl Theodor, is now the home of the German Theater Museum (since 1953), the Munich Art Association, and several art galleries.

Founded in 1910 with a bequest from Clara Ziegler (1844-1909), an actress at the Royal Theater, the Theater Museum has developed into a highly significant collection, now financed by the State of Bavaria. Its holdings comprise more than four million documents on the dramatic arts of all periods and nations; designs for stage sets and costumes; role portraits; paintings and photographs of

Field Marshals' Hall with monuments to General Tilly (left) and General Wrede (right).

performances; props; an archive with directors' scripts, programs, reviews, and 50,000 autographs; and a large reference library. The museum's Wagner collection, the largest outside Bayreuth, is particularly noteworthy. Special exhibitions are held several times a year.

25 Field Marshals' Hall
Feldherrnhalle

Odeonsplatz

An open vaulted hall based on a Florentine model: a significant Neoclassical building between Theatiner- and Ludwigstrasse.

It was a brilliant piece of town planning on the part of Friedrich von Gärtner to set a great architectural accent at the beginning of Ludwigstrasse, in the area between the Residence and Theatine Church which Klenze had designed as a square. The model for this elegant, three-arched monument was the Loggia dei Lanzi in Florence. Dedicated in 1844, the iron statues on the left and right (sculpted by L. Schwanthaler and cast by F. von Miller) commemorate General Tilly, who vanquished the Swedes at the Battle of White Mountain in 1620 and was Field Marshal of the Catholic League, and General Wrede, who defeated the French in 1814. On

the rear wall is a memorial to the Bavarian army, by von Miller (1882). Flanking the steps in front are two stone lions, vivid studies by Ruemann (1906) which looked on unmoved as Hitler's 1923 march on Field Marshals' Hall and his attempted *putsch* failed. The event was subsequently glorified

Lion in front of Field Marshals' Hall.

26 Preysing Mansion
Preysing-Palais

Residenzstrasse 27

The most beautiful early Rococo town mansion in Munich, with ornate stucco facade and spacious staircase open to the public.

The noble classicism of Field Marshals' Hall contrasts with the grace of its next-door neighbor, Preysing Mansion, whose richly articulated **facade** is adorned with playful Regency stuccowork. This first building by Chief Court Architect Effner was erected in 1723-28 for Count Maximilian of Preysing-Hohenaschau. Well worth seeing is the ornate **staircase** inside, three flights of steps that extend upwards through two stories, supported by caryatids and decorated with stucco garlands. Their beauty is marred only by the knowledge that the stairs, together with the building's three facades, had to be rebuilt (by Schleich) as a result of war damage. Exclusive shops line the ground floor and arcade.

27 Theatine Church of St. Cajetan
Theatinerkirche St. Kajetan

Theatinergasse 22

A majestic Baroque church with a grandiose air – a slice of Rome in Munich.

The elaborate **cupola** and the **towers★** of St. Cajetan's, with their swelling volutes, have long been a symbol of Munich, and it is easy to see why – such *grandezza* is rarely found north of the Alps. Rome and Venice provided the models. When Henriette Adelaide of Savoy, wife of Ferdinand Maria, gave birth in 1662 to a long-awaited heir, Prince Max Emanuel, she founded the church and monastery in gratitude to the Theatines, whose mother church was in Rome. Supervision of construction, after a heated dispute with the Bolognese architect Barelli, was assumed by Zuccalli of the Swiss Grisons and by the Theatine Provost Spinelli. The building was largely completed by 1688. Finishing touches in Rococo style were added to the facade in 1768 by the Cuvilliés, father and son.

Firmly planted and expansive, yet soaringly vertical in emphasis, the richly articulated **facade★** abounds with tense, sharp rhythms. Its sculptural decoration, including figures of the Church Fathers, was created by Boos, while the splendid coat of arms in the pediment was designed by Ignaz Günther.

Unusual in the context of Munich art is the pathos of the **interior★**, a quality elsewhere typical of the courtly style of High Baroque. Its high, barrel-vaulted nave with domed side chapels, its short transept, its tambour cupola pierced to admit light, and its massive engaged piers are profusely ornamented with

Preysing Mansion: Facade on Residenzstrasse (above) and view of staircase (below).

in a commemorative plaque on the Residenzstrasse side, watched over by a guard of honor whom every passer-by had to salute. Those who had no intention of raising their arm took a detour through the narrow Viscardigasse behind Preysing Mansion, earning it the nickname Shirkers' Lane.

Facing page: Theatine Church of St. Cajetan, view of dome.

Facade of the Theatine Church, built in the Italian Baroque style and completed in Rococo.

white stucco (including heavy acanthus motifs), large putti, and statues. Moretti, Brenni, and Perti were the Italian stucco-workers who created them, and their style

Theatine Church: Coat of arms in the pediment.

was not without influence on their German colleagues at Wessobrunn in Upper Bavaria, just as the entire structure stimulated many buildings of the type known as "congregational church with dome."

Another unusual feature for Munich is the high altar which, in accordance with Theatine custom, is divided into an altar wall and the altar proper (restored). The gable figures represent ecclesiastical dignitaries of the House of Savoy; the painting of The Virgin Enthroned is by de Crayer, a pupil of Rubens. Most of the other altar paintings are works of Italian and German artists of the Baroque. The massive pulpit★ is a masterly achievement by Faistenberger, dating from 1690.

In the **Royal Sepulcher** (entered from the right transept) lie the remains of twenty-five members of the House of Wittelsbach.

The former **monastery** adjoining the church to the south was partially restored after the war, and partially replaced by new buildings. Today it houses the Bavarian State Ministry of Education and Culture.

28 Church of Our Savior

Salvatorkirche

Salvatorplatz 17

A typical example of Bavarian "brick Gothic," elegant for all its unadorned simplicity.

The church building, with its spire and bare brickwork, is a smaller version of the Cathedral, having originally served as its cemetery chapel. It was built in 1494 by Lukas Rottaler, an architect of the Landshut school who also collaborated on the Cathedral. Buried in the cemetery, which was closed in 1789, were such well-known citizens as the composer Orlando di Lasso, the painter Hans Mielich, the architect François Cuvilliés the Elder, and Maximilian Robespierre, father of the French revolutionary, who lived here in penury as a language teacher. Since 1829 the church has belonged to the Greek Orthodox community, and is furnished accordingly. Remains of Late Gothic frescoes may be seen on the northeast side.

Church of Our Savior (Greek Orthodox since 1829).

29 Portia Mansion – *Palais Portia*

Kardinal-Faulhaber-Strasse 12

The earliest Italian-style mansion in Munich, with the city's only surviving High Baroque facade of its type.

As the grand town mansions along Kardinal-Faulhaber- and Prannerstrasse testify, this area was once the domain of the nobility.

Elector Karl Albrecht, devoted to gallantries – not only in art – was prodigal with palaces. He made a gift of this one to his mistress, who later became Countess Portia. In 1735 the Elector commissioned his architect, Cuvilliés, to remodel the original Baroque, *palazzo*-style structure by Zuccalli (1694) in accordance with Rococo taste, and engaged Zimmermann to complete the **facade** with suitably graceful stuccowork. Headquarters of a literary society during the nineteenth century, the building has belonged to the Bayerische Vereinsbank since 1934. The elegant Rococo interiors were destroyed during the Second World War. In the vestibule is a delightful Rococo sculpture, c. 1735, from the Archbishop's Palace [No. 30].

Portia Mansion (now Bayerische Vereinsbank).

Archbishop's Palace (formerly Holnstein Mansion).

30 Archbishop's Palace

Erzbischöfliches Palais

Kardinal-Faulhaber-Strasse 7

The only aristocratic mansion in Munich to have survived intact. One of Cuvilliés's finest works, its Rococo facade is certainly the most splendid in the city.

As soon as he had completed the remodelling of the Portia Mansion, Cuvilliés began work on this palace, intended by Elector Karl

Albrecht for his son, Count Holnstein, the issue of his liaison with a lady at court. Finished in 1737, the elegant building has a rhythmically articulated **facade★**, whose slightly projecting central bay contains the entrance portal, a balcony, and a triangular pediment. The stucco is by Zimmermann. Now the seat of the Archbishop of Munich and Freising, the palace's rooms are not open to the public, but they include perfectly preserved Rococo interiors, some of them with stucco and frescoes by Zimmermann.

31 Bayerische Hypotheken- and Wechselbank

Kardinal-Faulhaber-Strasse 10

An ambitious late nineteenth-century building whose proportions, though harmonious in themselves, jar with those of its neighbors.

Cuvilliés's two noble facades [Nos. 29, 30] are separated, not by a third *palazzo*, but by a palace of commerce which repeats their motifs on a rather more massive and pompous scale. Built in 1895-98 by Emil Schmidt, it is a characteristic example of a style rarely found in Munich, that of the *Gründerzeit*, the period of expansion following the unification of Germany in 1871.

Kardinal-Faulhaber-Strasse.

32 Neuhaus-Preysing Mansion
Palais Neuhaus-Preysing

Prannerstrasse 2

A noble Rococo facade designed by Cuvilliés.

Even where the great Cuvilliés himself did not lay hand on a project, his influence is often noticeable. For this second seat of the Counts of Preysing he apparently provided only the design, which was executed in 1737 by his assistant, Kögelsberger. The **facade** is rather more strait-laced than the similar one of the Archbishop's Palace [No. 30]. While it has survived intact, the rest of the building was restored in 1958.

Neuhaus-Preysing Mansion, Prannerstrasse.

Gise Mansion, Prannerstrasse.

33 Gise Mansion – *Palais Gise*
Prannerstrasse 9

A beautiful aristocratic town mansion of the late Rococo period.

Like the neighboring Seinsheim Mansion [No. 34], this building dates from the late Rococo period. Presumably a work of Royal Architect Lespilliez, built about 1765, it originally belonged to the Arco-Taufkirchen family. Although Cuvilliés's influence is obvious, the middle section seems rather lifeless, its pilasters apparently serving a purely decorative, rather than a functional, purpose – a sign of the Rococo style in decline.

Facing page: Archbishop's Palace, detail of the facade.

34 Seinsheim Mansion
Palais Seinsheim

Prannerstrasse 7

A dignified, sober facade marking the transition to Neoclassicism.

The facade of this mansion is now much longer than when it was built in 1764, having been extended to twelve bays during postwar reconstruction. It is a good specimen of late Rococo, the increased stringency of its decoration anticipating the Classical Revival.

Siemens Museum. Electronic stage-lighting system.

35 Siemens Museum
Prannerstrasse 10

A fascinating display of the 140-year history of electrotechnology.

The Siemens Museum, established in 1916 in Berlin, moved to Munich in 1954. Approximately 2,000 exhibits – historical equipment, demonstration systems and models, charts and photographs – provide an insight into the development of electrotechnology from the founding of the Siemens Company by Werner Siemens in 1847 to the present day and beyond, including many projects now in the research and planning stage. A library, including the company records and a pictorial archive, is open to the public.

36 Montgelas Mansion
Palais Montgelas

Promenadeplatz 2

An early Neoclassical town mansion with a French air, whose original interiors have partially survived.

When the former Salt Market became a tree-lined promenade in 1780, a number of fine residences began to be built there, above all

that of Minister Montgelas, designed in 1811 by the Portuguese architect, Herigoyen, and decorated by Métivier of France. Its cosmopolitan air is heightened by central bays divided by pilasters on the **facades** on Promenadeplatz and Kardinal-Faulhaber-Strasse and by **ceremonial rooms★** in the noble Empire style. As early as 1817 the building passed from private hands to the Ministry of the Royal House and External Affairs; since 1969 it has housed the Bayerischer Hof Hotel and has been extensively restored. The official reception rooms and the restaurant in the late medieval vaulted cellar are very much worth a visit.

37 Gunetzrhainer House
Promenadeplatz 15

A noble architect's residence with a graceful Rococo facade.

Very few of the distinguished facades on Promenadeplatz survived the Second World War. This one was reconstructed in 1960 to give posterity an idea of how well-to-do citizens of Munich lived during the early Rococo period. The first owner of the building was Johann Baptist Gunetzrhainer, Royal Architect, who designed it for himself about 1730. The slender Madonna protecting the house amidst stucco decor in the Regency style has been attributed to Ignaz Günther.

Gunetzrhainer House, detail of the facade.

Church of the Holy Trinity: View of the interior (above) and facade on Pacellistrasse (below).

38 Church of the Holy Trinity

Dreifaltigkeitskirche

Pacellistrasse 6

The first late Baroque church in Munich, with an impressive facade, a cupola fresco by Asam, and fine sculptures.

The founding of this church goes back to a vow made by Miss Lindmayr, daughter of a Munich valet, when she saw a horrific vision of the approaching war of the Spanish Succession. The citizenry of the town and the Provincial Estates supported her vow, and in 1716 the votive church – built by Zuccalli and Ettenhofer after designs by Viscardi – was completed.

Its soaring, vividly contoured **facade★** lends character to the entire street. The body of the building is a forcefully Bavarian version of Italian models, its groundplan combining circle and cross. Both the **interior** and the facade were of profound influence on Rococo architecture. In 1714-15 C. D. Asam, just twenty-eight years old at the time, cre-

Church of the Holy Trinity, detail of a fresco by C.D. Asam.

39 Wittelsbach Fountain
Wittelsbacher Brunnen

Lenbachplatz/Maximiliansplatz

One of the finest nineteenth-century fountains in Germany.

This most exuberant of all Munich fountains owes its existence to an important, if rather mundane, event – the completion, in 1895, of work on pipelines to supply all houses with water. The focus of the irregularly shaped Lenbachplatz, the fountain stands at the entrance to the gardens on Maximiliansplatz. A boy riding a fish-tailed horse and casting a stone, and a nymph on an aquatic steer holding out a bowl – symbols of the harmful and beneficial forces of water – flank a two-tiered basin that emerges from rugged artificial boulders: a latter-day interpretation of ancient mythology in the Baroque spirit by Adolf von Hildebrand.

ated frescoes in the vaults* that unite Italian tradition and his own virtuosity of composition. This first Baroque cupola fresco in Munich, *The Glorification of the Trinity* (with the artist's self-portrait at the upper right, next to the window), is flanked in the transepts by a Baptism and a Transfiguration of Christ. The event which led to the building of the church is recorded in the painting above the high altar, *The Trinity Over the Town of Munich,* by Wolff and Degler.

Wittelsbach Fountain and (above) one of its figures, an allegory of the beneficial powers of water.

Entrance to the Old Town: Karlsplatz (known as "Stachus"), with fountain and Karl's Gate.

40 Artists' Building – *Künstlerhaus*
Lenbachplatz 8

A characteristic Neo-Renaissance building erected during the Prince Regent's reign.

The Neo-Baroque of the Wittelsbach Fountain is echoed across the square by the Neo-Renaissance of the Artists' Building, both attesting to a period enamoured with historical pastiche. Designed for the Munich Artists' Association by Gabriel von Seidl and built from 1892 to 1900, the building's stepped gables recall the north German Renaissance style and its interiors, with opulent decor by Lenbach and others, that of the Italian Renaissance. Whatever the influences, the whole has an inimitable Munich flair. Some of the rooms are now used by a restaurant; many have survived intact or been painstakingly restored. Worth seeing is the original Venetian Room in the northeast corner of the ground floor.

The focus of Munich's bohemian life around the turn of the century, the building hosted many a masked ball and festive procession. Among the more prominent members of the Artists' Association at that time were the renowned portrait painter Lenbach, the architect Seidl, the sculptor Gedon, and the painter Rudolf von Seitz. Franz von Stuck, together with other progressive artists, had already left the group in 1892 to form the Munich Secession.

Artists' Building, Lenbachplatz.

41 Karl's Gate and Stachus
Karlstor, Stachus

Karlsplatz

The entrance to the Old Town and start of the pedestrian precinct.

Still irreverently known as "Stachus," after a popular innkeeper by the name of Eustachius Föderl, Karlsplatz takes its official name from Elector Karl Theodor, who in 1791 had the old town wall demolished and the square laid out. All that remained of the early four-

teenth-century fortifications were Karl's Gate and the two towers which Gabriel von Seidl later integrated into an impressive **crescent** (1899-1902).

Once the busiest traffic intersection in Europe, the Stachus has reverted to comparative tranquillity since it was made part of the pedestrian precinct in 1972. During the summer, the cooling vicinity of the **fountain** (by Winkler, 1972) is a favorite haunt of locals and tourists alike.

42   Brunnenbuberl
Neuhauser Strasse (in front of No. 46)

A delightfully arch piece of Art Nouveau sculpture.

An old satyr tenderly showering water on a nude boy who replies with a powerful jet – the Brunnenbuberl ("fountain lad") near Karl's Gate is a real eye-catcher. When Matthias Gasteiger created the Art Nouveau pair in 1895, Prince Regent Luitpold himself is said to have approached the artist with a request to give the boy a fig leaf. His petition was declined – which only goes to show that, in those days, the artist was truly king in Munich.

43   Civic Hall – *Bürgersaal*
Neuhauser Strasse 48

An interesting Baroque oratory with outstanding works of art, including Günther's Guardian Angel sculpture. The grave of Rupert Mayer is in the Lower Church.

The noble facade which, with its twinned pilasters, blends so unassumingly with the surrounding buildings, conceals a chapel

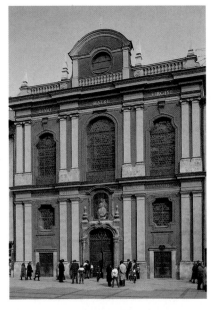

*"Brunnenbuberl" (above)
and Civic Hall (left).*

unique in kind and atmosphere. Not consecrated as a church until 1778, the building was initially designed as a meeting place for the Men's Marian Congregation of Germany (a Jesuit organization), as a place for religious services and exercises, and as a hall for the performance of sacred music. It was jointly constructed, in 1709-10, by Viscardi and Ettenhofer.

The **Lower Church,** formerly the congregational printing shop, now harbors a modern pilgrimage chapel which is always filled with worshippers. Pater Rupert Mayer, the "Brother Apostle" and resistance fighter against the Nazi regime who died in 1945 and was beatified in 1987, is buried here.

The spacious **Main Hall** on the first floor was once adorned by a huge ceiling fresco by Knoller. Although this painting was damaged beyond repair, the stuccowork by Appiani and Bader and the murals by

Gumpp – all three of them masters of the Baroque – have been restored. Also noteworthy are the seventeen oil paintings by F.J. Beich beneath the windows, depicting Bavarian places of pilgrimage (about 1710).

The altar bears a superb Annunciation relief★ (1710) that combines tenderness of expression with great force of design, a work by Faistenberger, the "patriarch of Munich sculptors." This central field is all that remains of the original altarpiece. Another outstanding work is Ignaz Günther's Guardian Angel sculpture★ of 1763, located underneath the gallery: a composition of Rococo brilliance, with the sublime and enigmatically smiling angel taking a chubby-cheeked boy under his great wing. Other surviving figures by Günther have been used to decorate the pulpit. The four fine silver busts★ on the altar were made after his models by the goldsmith Canzler in 1768.

Civic Hall: Interior (above) and Ignaz Günther's Guardian Angel sculpture of 1763 (right).

Gerhard's St. Michael Vanquishing Satan *on the facade of St. Michael's Church.*

44 Augustinerbräu Tavern
Neuhauser Strasse 16

A touch of Old Munich from the Prince Regent period.

For a taste of the cheer and comfort of turn-of-the-century Munich, the Augustinerbräu tavern is the place to go. Its **Shell Room**, with elaborate stuccowork and grottoes, hunting trophies and a dome of glass and iron, preserves the upper-middle-class style as personified by Franz von Lenbach [see No. 71], while its arcaded **courtyard** harbors one of the most pleasant beer gardens in town during the warm summer months. The oldest Munich brewery on record, it was established in 1328; the tavern, rebuilt by Emanuel von Seidl in 1896-97, was restored in 1982-83.

45 St. Michael's Church
Neuhauser Strasse 52

The largest Renaissance church in northern Europe and harbinger of the South German Baroque. An influential structure whose awesomely majestic interior has barrel vaulting second in size only to St. Peter's in Rome.

St. Michael's, the trumpet fanfare that introduced the Baroque to Germany, was an unprecedented achievement. Frankly intended as a demonstration of power, it was built by the equally pious and ostentatious Duke

The Shell Room, Augustinerbräu Tavern.

St. Michael's Church (left), architectural climax of Neuhauser Strasse in the pedestrian precinct. Next to it, the former Augustine Church, with the towers of the Cathedral behind it.

Wilhelm V as a monument to the Counter Reformation north of the Alps, to the fledgling Jesuit Order, and, not least, to himself. When a tower collapsed during construction (1583-97), this bad omen merely encouraged the duke to make his church even larger. The chief architect was his Supervisor for the Arts, Sustris, a Dutchman trained in Italy.

Adorning the steeply gabled, late Renaissance **facade**★ is a veritable gallery of the ancestors of Wilhelm V, statues of great rulers ranging from Charlemagne to the Habsburgs. The central niche contains a sculpture of *St. Michael Vanquishing Satan*★, a work by the incomparable Hubert Gerhard.

The real architectural innovation, however, was the **interior**★, with a barrel vault spanning a full sixty-five feet between massive engaged piers. Lateral vaults overarch the galleries above the side altars. Beyond the high transept is a deep, tall choir. These elements work together to create an effect of space which anticipated and introduced the Baroque concept of church design.

The duke employed artists from far and wide to carry out the iconographic program

75

The interior of St. Michael's, with barrel vaulting surpassed in size only by St. Peter's in Rome.

of the interior. The high altar painting of 1787, a tempestuous *Fall of the Angels* (**1**), is by a native of Munich, Schwarz, a brilliant but restless spirit. Reichle of Upper Bavaria modelled the dramatic *Mary Magdalene*★ at the feet of *Christ Crucified*★, a work of 1595 by his Flemish teacher, Giambologna, court artist to the Medicis in Florence (**8**). An artist from the Netherlands, Candid, created the youthfully exuberant *Annunciation* (1787), which is flanked, in moving contrast, by Straub's figures of St. Joachim and St. Anne (1770). The stucco in this chapel is especially elaborate (**4**). *The Martyrdom of St. Ursula* is

another work by Candid (**5**), while a countryman of his, Gerhard, sculpted the classical angel on the font★ (**6**) and designed the surrounding hosts of stucco angels. Also worthy of note are the exquisite *Cosmas and Damian Shrine*, c. 1400 (**7**), and the tomb of Eugène Beauharnais★, executed by Thorwaldsen (1830) to a design by Klenze (**3**). The **Royal Sepulcher** beneath the choir contains the sarcophagi of many Bavarian rulers, including Duke Wilhelm V, Elector Maximilian I, and King Ludwig II (entrance at **2**).

The **Jesuit College** adjoining the church to the west, designed by Sustris in 1585-87,

Plan of St. Michael's, with numbers indicating the key points of interest mentioned in the text.

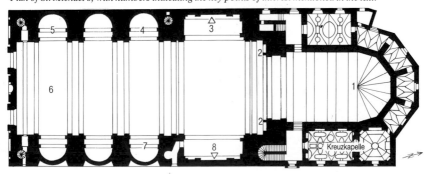

Cathedral: the twin-tower Gothic facade of 1488 topped by "Italian caps" added in 1525.

served the Order until its abolition in 1773. Occupied from then on by the Bavarian Academy of Sciences, the university, and the Art Academy, the building is now known as the Old Academy.

German Museum of Hunting and Fishing.

46 Former Augustine Church – German Museum of Hunting and Fishing

Ehem. Augustinerkirche – Deutsches Jagd- und Fischereimuseum

Neuhauser Strasse 53

An important ecclesiastical building in the Gothic style and a characteristic Munich landmark. Houses one of the finest museums of its kind.

The shops lining the ground floor indicate clearly enough that this great church now serves worldly ends. Yet it is equally evident that the building, standing at right-angles to St. Michael's, is among the oldest and most important churches in Munich. Erected at the end of the thirteenth century by Augustine anchorites, it was expanded and renovated again and again until being converted into a customs house after secularization in 1803. In 1911, a stairway and concert hall, known as the White Hall, were built into the interior by Theodor Fischer, leaving the early Baroque vaulting and stuccowork unaltered. Renovated after the war by Schleich, the building has housed the **German Museum of Hunting and Fishing** since 1966.

The core of this very popular museum was formed in 1934, when Count Maximilian of Arco-Zinneberg donated his famous collection of antlers to the city. There is a fine department of hunting arms from the royal houses of Europe, Bavaria being well represented by pieces from the Renaissance and Baroque periods. Fascinating views of the natural habitats of wild animals are provided by the many dioramas, based on eighteenth-century drawings by the painter and engraver Ridinger, a renowned chronicler of the hunt. An abundance of paintings and drawings illustrating the hunting life and customs of earlier epochs rounds off the collection. In 1982 a department devoted to the history and development of fishery was added.

47 Cathedral Church of Our Lady

Domkirche zu Unserer Lieben Frau

Frauenplatz 1

Dominating the city's skyline, this Late Gothic building (usually referred to as the Frauenkirche) is one of the largest hall churches in southern Germany. Its towers are the oldest and best-known landmarks of Munich.

Munich's symbols are many, but only the bulbous domes atop the towers of its Cathedral have the fascination of a magic charm. Yet there is nothing ingratiating about this brick building; its dignity arises solely from the austerity of its design.

Facing page: Cathedral, view of nave with Crucifix of 1953 by Josef Henselmann.

Shrine of St. Benno, 1601, in St. Benno Chapel.

The Lamb of God, *stained glass window, c. 1430.*

The history of the church's construction is equally straightforward. In 1468 Duke Sigismund laid the foundation stone, naming Jörg von Halsbach of Polling (later erroneously called Ganghofer) as its architect. The towers

were completed in 1488. Master Jörg died a short time later, and was succeeded by Rottaler from Lower Bavaria. The domes – or "Italian caps," as these harbingers of the Renaissance were called at the time – were added to the towers in 1525.

Although the **interior** was planned for a congregation of 20,000 – Munich's population numbered only 13,000 at the time – its dimensions by no means appear overwhelming. The nave has been skillfully divided by eleven pairs of slender columns that form a translucent curtain between nave and aisles, all spanned by seemingly weightless star-ribbed vaulting. Modernization work was finished in 1970.

Of the rich **furnishings,** only a few can be singled out for special mention. In the choir, expressive figures of prophets and the apostles, and small statues of saints, by Grasser and his workshop, 1502 (**1**). Delightful *Life of the Virgin* reliefs by Günther, 1774, and a painting by Polack, *Mary in a Gown of Sheaves*, 1495 (**3**). Three masterful, early sixteenth-century sculptures from the school of Leinberger: *St. George*★, *St. Maurice*, and *The Virgin and Child with St. Anne* (**4**). A large composition by Candid, *The Assumption of the Virgin*, 1620, formerly part of the high altar (**5**). A St. Christopher★ struggling against the wind, a superb, vivid sculpture from the school of Leinberger, c. 1520 (**6**). The ornate tomb of Emperor Ludwig the Bavarian★ (actually a memorial), with Late Gothic tombstone by Marx and Matthäus Haldner (or by Kriechbaum, according to some experts) showing the Emperor enthroned and the reconciliation of Duke Albrecht III with his father, Ernst, is enclosed in a structure of black marble with bronze figures of Duke Wilhelm V and Albrecht V by Krumper and standard-bearers by Gerhard and Pallago (**7**). On the wall, the gravestone of the Master Builder of the Cathedral, Jörg von Halsbach (**8**). A moving *Pietà*, Bohemian, c. 1400 (**9**). The *St. Benno Shrine*★, a piece in gilded silver made to the design of Krumper, 1601 (**11**). The large *Munich Cathedral Crucifixion*, c. 1455 (the wings of which are copies; **14**).

Plan of the Cathedral.

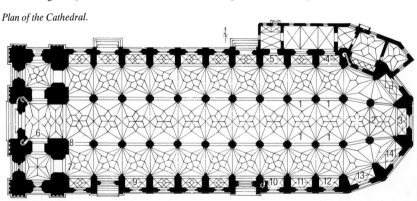

Cathedral: Tomb of Emperor Ludwig the Bavarian (above) and detail of St. Benno Portal (below).

Stained-glass windows of the fifteenth and sixteenth centuries may be seen particularly in chapels 3 and 10 to 13; chapel 10 has a window with the *Münchner Kindl* [see No. 2], 1573. The **Royal Sepulcher** (entrance at **2**), the largest burial place of the Wittelsbach dynasty in Munich, houses the remains of Emperor Ludwig the Bavarian and of all Bavarian dukes from Ludwig V to Albrecht V. The cathedral **portals★** were designed by Ignaz Günther.

48 Convent Church of St. Anne and former Convent

Damenstiftskirche St. Anna, ehemaliges Damenstift

Damenstiftstrasse 1 and 3

A beautiful late Baroque church with restored interior decoration by Asam.

One might almost hesitate to enter the presbytery because of the crowd of people on the left – but, on second glance, it turns out to be a group of gesticulating apostles from a vividly realistic depiction of the Last Supper. This sculpture from the early eighteenth century complements the emphatic altar paintings, replicas of the originals by Ruffini (*The Virgin and Child with St. Anne*, main altar), Albrecht (*The Glorification of St. Francis of Sales*, right), and Desmarées (*The Visitation*, left). The solidly Bavarian **interior** is a work of the Gunetzrhainer brothers, 1732-35. Destroyed during the Second World War, the interior was reconstructed to original plans and the ceiling frescoes by C.D. Asam

restored – using sepia instead of full color, because the only existing photographs were black and white (center: *St. Anne and the Virgin in Glory*; front: *Adoration of the Angels*; back: *Choir of Angels*).

The superb stucco ornament by E.Q. Asam belongs to the Regency, a transitional style between Baroque and Rococo. The **facade** is also typical of the Regency style, with classical nuances very much Gunetzrhainers' own.

Like the church itself, the adjacent long building, the former **convent**, once belonged to the order of Visitation Nuns, who settled in Munich in 1667 and moved into the building designed by I.A. Gunetzrhainer in 1739.

49 Lerchenfeld Mansion
Department of Municipal Cemeteries

Palais Lerchenfeld – Städtisches Bestattungsamt

Damenstiftstrasse 8

An elegant mansion of the early Rococo period.

This former town house, with flanking noblemen's quarters, has a facade of classical poise heightened by brilliant Regency stuccowork. While the **building** itself is probably the work of I. A. Gunetzrhainer (after 1726), the **facade** was presumably designed by Stuber. The mansion is now occupied by the Department of Municipal Cemeteries.

Convent Church of St. Anne: interior (above) and Last Supper group (below).

In 1784 it became a religious foundation for aristocratic ladies ("Damenstift"), and is now a school. The building's facade is a stately example of early Neoclassicism, with portal decoration by Feichtmayer the Younger.

Lerchenfeld Mansion on Damenstiftstrasse, probably by I. A. Gunetzrhainer.

All Saints Church at the Crossing: Exterior (above) and tabernacle by J. B. Straub (below).

50 All Saints Church at the Crossing
Allerheiligenkirche am Kreuz

Kreuzstrasse 10

A distinctive building by the Master Builder of Munich Cathedral.

Staunchly straightforward with its exposed brickwork, stepped buttresses, and high tower capped by a sharply tapered hexagonal spire, this church, built as a cemetery chapel for St. Peter's parish after 1478, has traditionally been attributed to Jörg von Halsbach. The only reminders of the original building in the largely Baroque **interior** are the net vaulting and a fresco fragment depicting Christ in His Glory, above the walled-in east portal (the church faces south). The furnishings include such outstanding works as Krumper's Renaissance epitaph for the banker Philipp Goetz (1627), let into the choir wall, and a wooden Crucifix of the Leinberger School (c. 1520) on the west wall. The high altar painting of The Vision of St. Augustine (1614) is by Rottenhammer, the fine Rococo tabernacle★ with adoring angels (1741-43) by Straub.

51 Asam Church – St. John of Nepomuk
Asamkirche – St. Johannes Nepomuk

Sendlinger Strasse 62

The brilliant legacy of the Asam brothers, a masterpiece of sumptuous Rococo interior design and decoration.

Everything is unusual about this church, even the fact that it is popularly known, not by the name of its patron saint, but by that of its donor. Egid Quirin Asam, respected architect, sculptor, and stuccoworker, bought a house on Sendlinger Gasse in 1729. That same year, the martyr John of Nepomuk was canonized, just when the residents of this neighborhood were petitioning for their own church. The artist decided to build one at his own expense, next to his house. Construction, decoration, and iconographical program (1733-46) were all in the hands of Asam and his brother, the painter and architect Cosmas Damian. The result was a brilliant climax to the body of work that the brothers had executed throughout southern Germany.

From a foundation of rough boulders, the delicately tinted **facade**★ projects in a gentle curve into the street. Above the portal is a sculpture representing St. John of Nepomuk ascending to heaven, borne aloft by angels. Passing through the vestibule, the visitor is confronted by an **interior**★ that seems a cross between lavish theater auditorium and mystic grotto. High and narrow, with a gallery running round it on all sides, the nave opens onto a two-tiered high altar at front and, above, onto a ceiling fresco seen through a

Asam Church: Detail of choir.

framing of silver cavetto moulding. Architecture, painting, and sculpture combine to produce an effect of hovering motion, a shimmering atmosphere of color and light, an ecstasy of angels and cherubim. Weightlessly unreal, yet the focus of the whole church, is Egid Quirin's vivid *Throne of Mercy*★, the crucified Christ held in the arms of God. Beneath the radiating gloriole on the high altar is a sarcophagus containing relics of St. John of Nepomuk, while in the gallery altar, above two adoring angels by Günther, the saint kneels at the feet of the Virgin. This sculpture, and the amber window behind, are much-debated free reconstructions of the lost originals, made in the course of interior restoration by Schleich in 1982.

Above: Exterior of Asam Church, with Asam House (left) and Priest's House (right).
Facing page: View of the interior of Egid Quirin Asam's private chapel.

The ceiling fresco by C.D. Asam narrates events from the life of St. John of Nepomuk, supplemented by the stucco reliefs in the cavetto moulding, by E.Q. Asam. Since St. John of Nepomuk was a father confessor, special emphasis was placed on the confessionals in the nave and vestibule. The life-size figures adorning them respresent Death, the Last Judgment, Hell, and Heaven. Günther's epitaph for Count Zech★ (1758) in the vestibule is considered a crowning accomplishment of Rococo funerary art.

52 Asam House
Sendlinger Strasse 61

A well-proportioned facade with swirling stucco ornament, attesting to a Rococo master's self-assured skill.

The situation was unique – an architect built "his" church next to his private house, designed complementary facades, one dedicated to a Christian saint and the other to Apollo, and provided a window in the

Sendling Gate, looking north.

Marionette Theater on Blumenstrasse.

house's interior through which he could see the high altar. Egid Quirin Asam converted an existing building in 1733, giving it a graceful **facade**★ that is rich in philosophical allusion. Above the porch are personifications of poetry, sculpture, painting, architecture, and music; above the ground-floor windows, Pallas Athene leading an innocent babe on the path of wisdom; figures representing the Arts and Sciences; Pegasus and, above him, the classical pantheon with Apollo. To the right, on the projecting bay, the Christian heaven is symbolized and, at the far left, the temporal world, with Cupid, a satyr, and fauns.

53 Sendling Gate
Sendlinger Tor

One of the three surviving gateways of the old town wall, otherwise largely destroyed.

Like Karl's Gate and Isar Gate, the Sendling Gate belonged to the second fortification of Munich, carried out in about 1318 under Emperor Ludwig the Bavarian. The gate was once the main entrance for north-south traffic. Although the dominant middle tower was demolished in 1808, the two hexagonal flanking towers and the lateral walls of the bailey remained standing, and were restored in 1860 and again in 1978-82. In 1906 a single large arch replaced the original three.

54 School of Fashion Design
Meisterschule für Mode

Rossmarkt 15

The last Munich building in the Baroque spirit.

Commissioned to design a new House of Representatives for the Bavarian Provincial Estates, Cuvilliés the Younger built this palace in 1774-75. Its Italian Baroque design turns away from the Rococo style and shows the influence of an earlier architect, Zuccalli, while also possessing a stringency that anticipates the Classical Revival. After the Provincial Estates were dissolved in 1808, the building served various purposes until 1931, when the School of Fashion Design moved in.

55 Munich Firefighting Museum
Münchner Feuerwehrmuseum

Blumenstrasse 34

The largest museum of its kind in Germany.

The first turntable ladder, made in 1802, with an extended length of fifty-nine feet; the "pyroscope" used during the last century by the watchman on the tower of St. Peter's to locate fires by night; a complete air-raid shelter from the Second World War; firefighting equipment old and new – these are only some of the fascinating exhibits illustrating the history of firefighting up to the present day. Munich's official fire department was established in 1879; its centenary was marked by the inauguration of the museum in the headquarters building. So many interesting items came from public and private sources that this youngest of the country's museums of firefighting was soon its largest as well.

Firefighting Museum: Fire-control office in a Second World War air-raid shelter.

Munich City Museum, Jakobsplatz, with former armory from the medieval period (left).

56 Munich Marionette Theater
Münchner Marionettentheater

Blumenstrasse 29 a

The first marionette theater building in Europe.

This chubby little children's temple of the muses came from the drawing board of the architect Fischer in 1900. The puppet theater itself had been in existence since 1858, a joint enterprise of Joseph Schmid, an actuary who was popularly known as "Papa Schmid," and Count Pocci, the author of many comedies starring Kasperl Larifari, the Bavarian Punch. Marionettes continue to work their magic on the young – and on the young at heart. For opera fans the Marionette Theater offers an evening program of Mozart, Orff, and Egk.

57 Municipal Multistorey
Städtisches Hochhaus

Blumenstrasse 28 a/b

The only tall building from the early modern period in Munich.

Giant confronts dwarf on Blumenstrasse – an eleven-storey building across from the Marionette Theater, designed by Leitenstorfer and built in 1927-29. This reinforced concrete structure is the city's sole example of early skyscraper architecture. The raw brick purposely alludes to the Cathedral, a reference still made today by many Munich architects. The building now houses various departments of the municipal administration.

58 Munich City Museum
Münchner Stadtmuseum

Sankt-Jakobs-Platz 1

Munich's most varied and popular museum of cultural history, with an unsurpassed collection on the development of the city, featuring historical interiors, internationally oriented special collections, imaginatively presented changing exhibitions, lectures, films, and other events.

City Museum: Morris Dancer by Grasser.

Sankt-Jakobs-Platz was once the town green, where great fairs were held on church holidays. In 1410, a storehouse for grain, arms, and wagons was built on the northeast side; later called the **Marstall** (stables), it has now been rebuilt. The **Armory,** erected to the northwest in 1431, became a focus of civic pride after its expansion in 1491-93. Centuries passed, and the weapons it contained mouldered into antiques – as the citizens realized with chagrin in 1848 when they attempted to use them in their uprising against the monarchy. The Armory was duly converted into a museum in 1888. Four tracts have since been added to Armory and Marstall, making a great enclosed square.

The **Museum★** records all facets of cultural history in Munich and Bavaria. Armor and weaponry, including many rare fifteenth-century pieces, are on view in the Late Gothic

Munich City Museum: Cannon Room (above) and Makart Room (below; currently closed).

Cannon Room of the old Armory. Another imposing room is given over to the ten original *Morris Dancers*★ by Erasmus Grasser, performing their round-dance of courtship. The town council silver, guild presents, goldsmiths' work, glass painting, votive offerings, wax tapers, toys, traditional folk costumes, and everyday apparel provide a mosaic of life in Bavaria through the centuries. The present day is represented by haute-couture models designed by students of the Munich School of Fashion Design. Changing taste in interior design is recorded in typical examples from the seventeenth to the twentieth century. Art Nouveau furnishings★ are particularly well represented. Many of the items can be shown only on special occasions – the museum's collection includes 2,000 paintings, 110,000 specimens of graphic art, and 25,000 posters.

Some of the departments have developed from humble beginnings to become veritable museums within the museum. A world-

City Museum: Art Nouveau vase from Nancy, France, c. 1900 (above), and poster of about 1918 (below).

Silver centerpiece by Ignatius Taschner (above), and stills from Fritz Lang's The Nibelungs *(below left) and Karl Valentin's* In the Apothecary *(below right).*

renowned **Puppet Theater Museum,** with puppets and stages from Europe, Asia, and Africa, presents frequent live performances. The **Film Museum** puts on a daily bill that is a must for Munich movie buffs. Then there is the **Museum of Photography,** one of whose main attractions is the Emperor's Panorama with its stereoscopic slides. The **Museum of Musical Instruments** includes a major collection of pieces from Africa and South America, while in the **German Brewery Museum** the visitor may be amazed to find that the ancient Egyptians had already contributed significantly to the the brewer's art.

Kasperl, from the City Museum's Puppet Theater Collection.

59 Ignaz Günther House
Sankt-Jakobs-Platz 15 / Oberanger 11

A lovingly restored, unpretentious house typical of Old Munich, where the greatest Rococo sculptor in Europe lived and worked.

Ignaz Günther, court sculptor of the Bavarian elector, took up residence with his family in this house in 1761, at the age of thirty-six; he died here in 1775, just fifty years old, having brought European Rococo to perfection. A large part of his oeuvre may be seen in Munich churches and in the Bavarian National Museum. The house, restored as a monument to the artist and as a historical example of a combined residence and workshop, is a duplex of Gothic origin, with two facades. It is now used for exhibitions, and contains the offices of the administration of the Munich

City Museum [No. 58]. There is a replica of Günther's **House Madonna** on the Oberanger street facade (the original is in the Bavarian National Museum).

60 Viktualienmarkt
Where Munich is most itself.

Wooden kegs full of pickles and sauerkraut next to fine French wines and cheese, cabbages and mushrooms alongside papayas and maracuyas, great hams consorting with lobsters, marketwomen bantering and bargaining with their smart-set clientele, a whiff of fish, then perfume – Viktualienmarkt (Farmers' Market) is a world in microcosm.

The dance of the marketwomen on Shrove Tuesday, the giant maypole, chestnut trees shading the beer garden in summer, and the odor of pines permeating the square in winter – all pass with the changing seasons, but what never changes is the talk and gossip among the stalls, the perennially wry and biting wit of Munich. It is immortalized in fountain sculptures of the famous comedians Karl Valentin, Weiss Ferdl, Liesl Karlstadt, Elise Aulinger, Roider Jackl, and Ida Schumacher.

First held in 1807 on the former site of the Holy Ghost Infirmary, the market burgeoned

Ignaz Günther House, home and studio of Munich's greatest Rococo sculptor.

Facing page: Viktualienmarkt.

Karl Valentin Fountain, Viktualienmarkt.

until it reached its present size just one hundred years ago. Little remains of the large market hall, built in emulation of the Paris Halles in 1851, but Butchers' Row (1881) beneath St. Peter's has survived. The market affords a picturesque view of the various Gothic and Baroque towers to the north. St. Peter's [No. 6] watches over the bustle and abundance below like a stately matron, the Church of the Holy Ghost [No. 5] like an aloof lady.

Liesl Karlstadt Fountain, Viktualienmarkt.

61 Isar Gate – *Isartor*

Tal 43

An imposing medieval gateway, the only one in Munich to have survived largely intact.

The former eastern gate of the town fortifications, built under Emperor Ludwig the Bavarian and recently restored, is unique in presenting very much its original appearance of 1337 and 1499 – a tall main tower, two front towers, and a bailey. Also restored was the fresco by Neher, done for King Ludwig I in 1835, which represents the triumphal entry into the city of Emperor Ludwig after his victory over Frederick the Handsome of Habsburg in the Battle of Ampfing in 1332. The last remnants of the town wall may be seen north of the gate (below ground) and in Jungfernturmstrasse (above ground).

62 Karl Valentin Museum, Isar Gate

Valentin-Musäum, Isartor

Tal 43

A paradise for fans of the Munich humorist, Karl Valentin, and anybody with a sense for the sublimely obvious and the profoundly absurd.

This eccentric **"Musaeum"** is dedicated to a spindly man who was all angles except for his round black hat – Karl Valentin (1882-1948), the great Munich original beloved of all Germans. Assembled in the spirit of his crazy world, it was opened in 1959 by the painter and collector Hannes König, in the southern tower of Isar Gate. The museum opens at 10.01 or 11.01 a.m. and admission costs 1.99

Beer garden in the Viktualienmarkt.

Isar Gate with towers of the Old Town: St. Peter's, Holy Ghost, Old and New City Hall, Cathedral.

DM. Like all good humour, Valentin's is both universal and well-nigh untranslatable.

While many of this master's extraordinary visual creations, like "Chimney-Sweep by Night" and "Rupture," elude art historical classification, "Reclining Stand-Up Collar" and "Leather Breeches Braces on the Blink" astonishingly anticipate modern art's cult of the object, and such pieces as "The Rock Where Little Mary Sat," the cryptic "Winter Toothpick," and "Bookbinder Wanninger's Telephone" can only be called the finds of an archaeologist of contemporary life.

Since 1973 the north tower has harbored a charming **Folk Singers Museum.** Complementing it in the south tower is a **Folk Singers Tavern,** a comfortable place to have a chat and relax over coffee or beer, and gird oneself for re-entry into the real world.

Folk Singers Tavern in the Valentin Museum, south tower of Isar Gate.

93

63 Theater on Gärtnerplatz
Gärtnerplatz 3

A late Neoclassical building, a noble setting for a popular theater.

The roundabout of Gärtnerplatz, center of the Isarvorstadt district, still gives a feeling of sheltered calm, despite the fact that its original enclosed form of the late nineteenth century was lost in postwar rebuilding. Its mood is set by the delicately serene facade of the **theater,** whose stage has been expanded to the rear by a modern addition. The interior was restored in 1968-69, and the exterior in 1976-78, recreating Reifenstuel's original design of 1865, a miniature replica of the National Theater with festive royal boxes and a domed ceiling by Neureuther – truly "a popular theater fit for a king," as Ludwig II said. In addition to ballet, the theater puts on German-sung performances of opera, operetta, and musical comedy.

Theater on Gärtnerplatz: Exterior (above) and auditorium with view of ceiling (below).

Maxvorstadt, the Pinakotheks, Ludwigstrasse

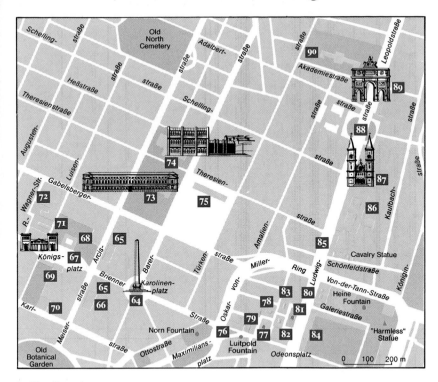

Karolinenplatz with obelisk.

64 Karolinenplatz

A notable Neoclassical square.

Karl von Fischer's plans for this area concentrated on Brienner Strasse, the former royal road from the Residence to Nymphenburg Palace, which was widened into a great thoroughfare and became the central axis of a new suburb, Maxvorstadt. Although his original conception, limited to villas and mansions, was only partially realized, Fischer's roundabout gave street and neighborhood a delightful point of focus. For its centerpiece, Klenze created an **obelisk** in 1833, a memorial to the 30,000 Bavarian soldiers who died in Napoleon's Russian campaign in 1812. Its iron plates were cast from cannons from Turkish and Egyptian warships sunk in the Battle of Navarino (1827).

65 College of Music and Cultural Institutes Building

Musikhochschule, Haus der Kultur-institute

Arcisstrasse 12 and Meiserstrasse 10

Pilot projects for Nazi architecture in Munich, built in conjunction with a redesigning of Königsplatz. Harbingers of Hitler's megalomaniac plans to expand Munich into "the Capital of the Nazi Movement."

These two buildings at the eastern end of Königsplatz were erected by Ludwig Troost in 1933-35. To the north is the erstwhile "Führer Building," where the Munich

Collection of Graphic Art: Sustris's design for the Perseus Fountain in the Residence (above) and a Rembrandt drawing (right).

Agreement was signed in 1938 – now the **College of Music** – and to the south, the former National Socialist Headquarters, now the offices of several scholarly institutes and home of the State Collection of Graphic Art [No. 66]. Located between the two structures were two so-called Temples of Honor, which were demolished in 1947.

66 State Collection of Graphic Art

Staatliche Graphische Sammlung

Meiserstrasse 10

The most significant collection of prints and drawings in the Federal Republic outside Berlin.

Regular special exhibitions at the Neue Pinakothek point up the quality and scope of this collection, whose stock of prints and drawings has now passed the 300,000 mark. Emphases of the collection are early German single-sheet woodcuts and engravings of the fifteenth century; prints of the Dürer and Rembrandt periods (including a rare Dürer *Apocalypse* in the first edition of 1498, and Rembrandt's *Hundred Gulden* etching); southern German drawings of the sixteenth to the eighteenth century and German drawings of the nineteenth century; and, finally, German Expressionist prints and international contemporary graphic art.

The foundation of the collection was laid when Elector Karl Theodor's Drawing Cabinet, containing superb specimens of the Italian masters, was brought from Mannheim to Munich in 1794. This core was zealously expanded by Max I Joseph and Ludwig I, who even managed to acquire three rare drawings by Leonardo. Bequests from Ludwig, with drawings by the contemporary artists he supported, and from Klenze, together with a gift from the Augsburg art dealer, Felix Halm, of 2,500 drawings mostly by Bavarian artists, expanded the southern German department. In the 1930s and 1940s, the Nazis' campaign against "degenerate art" and war bombing decimated the holdings by one-third. Yet after the war most of the gaps were filled, and the collection was augmented by examples of modern printmaking and drawing from the early European avant-garde to the most recent work of American artists.

Propylaeum with Glyptothek (left) and Collection of Antiquities (right).

67 Königsplatz

*A superb Neoclassical ensemble and one of the
major works in Ludwig I's "Athens on the Isar."*

Truly a "Kingly Place," this square was conceived by Ludwig I in collaboration with his
architect, Klenze, to provide a sanctuary for
the arts. Instead of imitating the forms and
orders of classical antiquity, Klenze recreated
them in the spirit of the new age: Ionian in
the Glyptothek [No. 68], Corinthian in the
Exhibition Building [No. 69], and Doric in
the **Propylaeum.**

The gateway (called Propylaeum, the
Greek word for the entrance to a temple)
terminating the main traffic artery of Brienner Strasse commemorates the Greek wars of
independence and the Wittelsbach monarch,
Otto of Greece. These are the subject of
Ludwig Schwanthaler's sculptures on the two
tympana, which reflect both the aesthetic and
the political enthusiasm that Greece inspired
at that time. The Greek gateway is set off by
Egyptian elements that heighten the noble
pathos of the whole. Designed in 1817,
Klenze did not complete it until 1862.

The austere and rather martial stone paving, an addition of the Third Reich, will soon
be replaced by the lawns that were a part of
the original conception of the square.

68 Glyptothek
Königsplatz 3

*A nobly proportioned, Greek Revival building,
the first museum of sculpture in Germany and
today housing one of the world's finest collections
of antique sculpture.*

Working for Crown Prince Ludwig in Rome,
art agent Martin von Wagner secured the
breathtaking *Barberini Faun*★, and in Greece
the *Aeginetes*★, a famous group of sculptures
which had been excavated in 1811. Klenze, in
Paris, successfully bid for a series of antiquities including the goddess of peace,

Glyptothek: Athena, *from the western
pediment of the Temple of Aegina, c. 500 B.C.*

Glyptothek. Exterior view of Klenze's finest building (above) and masterpieces from the collection:
Mnesarete Tomb Relief, *c. 380 B.C. (left), and the* Barberini Faun, *c. 220 B.C. (below).*

Glyptothek: The Aeginetes, *Archaic sculptures from the Temple of Aphaia in Aegina, c. 490 B.C.* (above), and view of Room XI, with 62 Roman busts of the first century B.C. (below).

Eirene, and the *Diomedes Torso*. And in Vienna, Ludwig himself acquired the *Ilioneus*.★ To house these treasures, 150 all told, and his collection of contemporary sculpture, the Crown Prince had Klenze build a special museum in 1816-30 which, from the outset, was to be open to the public. Its four wings are grouped around a square court; its Neoclassical facade, a temple front in the Ionian mode, is flanked by side-pieces with deeply indented niches. The pediment sculptures (Athena surrounded by artists) and the statues in the niches are by various artists of Ludwig's time and represent Hephaestus, Prometheus, Daedalus, Phidias, Pericles, and Hadrian (facade); sculptors of the Renaissance (west wing); and contemporary sculptors (east wing). The interior was originally decorated in opulent style, with imitation marble, stucco reliefs, and monumental frescoes by Cornelius on historical subjects.

Shorn of their decoration by the Second World War, the rooms have been restored without it. The arrangement of the now exclusively Greek and Roman collection is highly effective, and illustrates the development of classical sculpture chronologically from the Archaic figures of youths of the sixth century B.C. to the realistic portrait busts of the first century A.D. – an extraordinary collection in terms of both quality and scope.

69 State Collection of Antiquities
Staatliche Antikensammlungen

Königsplatz 1

The richest collection of antiquities in the Federal Republic, including pieces of the highest quality and an important collection of vases.

Not Court Architect Klenze, who had just fallen out of favor, but an architect named

State Collection of Antiquities: Golden garland from Armento, 4th century A.D. (detail).

Ziebland was commissioned by King Ludwig I in 1838 to design the "Exhibition Building for Art and Industry" across from the Glyptothek. With its middle section in the style of a Corinthian temple (the pediment adorned by Ludwig Schwanthaler's group of figures surrounding Bavaria as Patroness of Arts) and with its rather steep flight of steps, Ziebland's **building** could not quite match the noble proportions of Klenze's Glyptothek.

Rebuilt in 1967, the museum now contains all of the Munich **collections** of antique craftsmanship. The vase collection★ is second

State Collection of Antiquities: Corinthian pitcher, c. 630 B.C. (above), and Attic plate with Gorgon head, 560-550 B.C. (below).

Portico, State Collection of Antiquities.

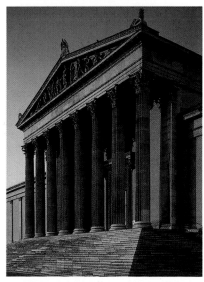

only to those of the British Museum and the Louvre. It ranges from Mycenaean vessels of the fourteenth to Greek vessels of the second century B.C. and includes an exquisite group of Attic vases. Small sculptures, idols, statuettes, and animals in bronze and terracotta; Etruscan bronzes of the sixth century B.C. excavated near Perugia; Etruscan, Mycenaean , and Greek gold jewellery; antique glassware and silver vessels; all this provides a superb – and superbly presented – overview with first-rate individual pieces.

St. Boniface: Sarcophagus of Ludwig I in right aisle (above) and capital from the portico on Karlstrasse (below).

Determined to reconcile art and religion, King Ludwig I wanted to complement the "heathen temple" of the Glyptothek with a church building. However, the Catholic authorities objected to the site, so Ziebland built the Church and Benedictine Monastery of St. Boniface on Karlstrasse, with its back to Königsplatz [No. 67]. The **basilica,** based on early Christian models which the architect had studied in Rome and Ravenna, was erected from 1835 to 1845. The original church had a nave and four aisles; only half of the nave and the Corinthian portico were restored after severe war damage, giving little idea of the dignified beauty of the former interior and its rich and colorful decoration. The northern section, which houses the parish administration, is a modern addition.

The king was interred in "his" basilica in a plain stone sarcophagus (located in the east aisle). His wife Therese is buried in the crypt.

71 Municipal Gallery in Lenbach House
Städtische Galerie im Lenbachhaus

Luisenstrasse 33

Palatial residence of one of the most successful artists of the fin de siècle, *now a museum of Munich art with a unique collection of early modern paintings and a full program of changing exhibitions. Its Blue Rider collection is a mecca for art lovers from around the world.*

This museum had already achieved European fame a hundred years ago, when it was still

Central tract of Lenbach House.

70 St. Boniface – *St. Bonifaz*
Karlstrasse 34

The fragment of a much-admired church, conceived by Ludwig I and the site of his tomb.

Municipal Gallery, Lenbach House: Self-Portrait with Skeleton *by Lovis Corinth, 1898.*

the **villa** of the immensely successful painter, Franz von Lenbach, for whom the Pope, Kaiser Wilhelm, Bismarck, and Eleonora Duse sat for their portraits. Built in 1887-91 by Gabriel von Seidl, this country *palazzo* with studio might have been spirited straight from Italy, garden, arcades, Palladian windows, columns, and all. How Lenbach lived

among his red velvet covered walls and gilded carvings can only be surmised from the restored salons.

Yet the hallowed mood is immediately put to flight by an artistic revolution, the one started in Munich by the Blue Rider ("Blauer Reiter") group in 1911, which paved the way for a new art – expressionist and abstract. Its

Lenbach, Self-Portrait with Family *(detail).*

Salon in Lenbach House.

August Macke, Farmboy of Tegernsee, *1910.*

protagonists are brilliantly represented in ten rooms of the museum, with ninety-four oils and three hundred watercolors, drawings, and prints by Kandinsky alone, about sixty works by Klee, and dozens by Marc, Macke, Jawlensky, and Gabriele Münter (who herself donated large parts of the collection in 1957). It was later supplemented by a Kubin Archive with 600 works by this eccentric artist.

The **Municipal Gallery★**, established in 1925 after the purchase of the house from Lenbach's widow, traces the history of art in Munich back to the Late Gothic period. Well represented are the Munich School of the nineteenth century, Realism, Impressionism, and Art Nouveau, with famous paitings by Rottmann, Kobell, Leibl, Corinth (*Self-Por-*

Karl Spitzweg, Customs Inspection, *c. 1860.*

trait with Skeleton), Stuck (*Salome*), Riemerschmid, and many more.

But beyond all this, what makes the museum particularly interesting is its commitment to contemporary art. Displayed on two floors are acquisitions of consistently high quality from many and diverse artists, including Joseph Beuys, Pichler, and Rainer. The permanent collection is supplemented by frequent exhibitions on certain themes or individual artists, keeping Munich up to date on the current international art scene. The openings at the Municipal Gallery might be called the whirlwinds of the city's artistic climate.

72 Bavarian State Paleontological Collection
Bayerische Staatssammlung für Paläontologie

Richard-Wagner-Strasse 10

A fascinating look into the world of fossils, plant and animal, from the prehistoric period in Bavaria and around the globe. After Frankfurt and Stuttgart, the finest collection of its kind in West Germany.

Interior court, Paleontological Collection.

This large **building** in the Neo-Renaissance style was erected around the turn of the century to serve as a school of arts and crafts for young ladies. Since 1950 it has housed a fossil zoo and botanical garden. The most sensational item in the **collection,** which runs the gamut from dinosaur to Ice Age mouse and from mammoth tree to blue algae, is the skeleton of a giant mastadon, discovered in 1971 in the River Inn. It measures ten-and-a-half feet in height and weighs almost one-and-a-half tons. Owing to lack of space, the museum can show only about 400 of its one million objects at any one time. It will soon move into new premises at the planned Natural Science Education Center.

Facing page: Kandinsky's Mural for Campbell, *Municipal Gallery.*

Alte Pinakothek: Entrance (above) and Altdorfer's Susanna in her Bath *(detail, right).*

73 Alte Pinakothek

Barer Strasse 27

A picture gallery of world renown, whose immense collection of Old Masters attracts thousands of visitors every year.

This unusually elongated **building** of exposed brick was built by Klenze in 1826-36, his first work to be based, not on classical, but on Italian Renaissance models. Heavily damaged during the Second World War, it was rebuilt in 1957 by Döllgast who, besides other necessary changes, replaced the old staircase arrangement and the loggias to the south by an impressively theatrical double staircase. The **collection★**, whose removal to safety began on the second day of the war, survived

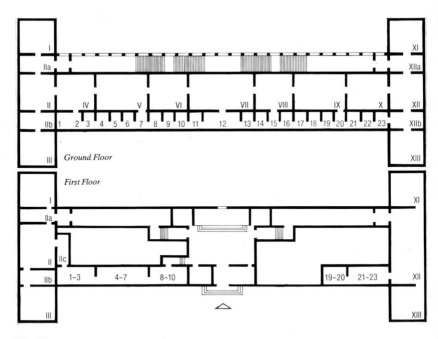

First Floor

Early Netherlandish Painting   I-II a
Early German Painting   II-III
Italian Painting   IV, V, X, XIIb, 1-6, 23
German Painting, 16th-17th C.   II
Flemish Painting   VI-VIII, 7-10, 12
Dutch Painting   IX, 13-22

French Painting   XI-XII a
Spanish Painting   XIII

Ground Floor

Early German Painting   I-III, 1-10
Painting of the 16th-17th C.   XII-XIII, 19-23

(Roman numerals indicate large rooms, arabic numerals small rooms.)

Alte Pinakothek: Dürer, Self-Portrait, *1500.*

Raphael, Tempi Madonna, *before 1508.*

completely unscathed – a treasure to which Munich owes its fame as a major art center.

It all began with the avid collectors of the House of Wittelsbach. Wilhelm IV commissioned a number of history paintings, including Altdorfer's *Battle of Alexander*★ which later hung for a time in Napoleon's bathroom as French booty. Maximilian I, a great admirer of Dürer, let himself be "bribed" into making political concessions to Nuremberg in exchange for *The Four Apostles.*★ Max Emanuel acquired Flemish and Dutch paintings, including Rubens's estate. Karl

Theodor arranged to have the Mannheim collection, and Max I Joseph the collections in Zweibrücken and Düsseldorf, brought to Munich, with their fine examples of the French School, van Dyck, Rembrandt, and Rubens. Ludwig I, besides buying Italian art, made a great haul of Early Netherlandish and Early German paintings when he acquired the Boisserée and Oettingen-Wallerstein collections.

Just a few of the most important works will be listed here. On the **ground floor,** fifteenth- and sixteenth-century art, including Pacher's

Alte Pinakothek: Pieter Brueghel the Elder, Land of Cockaigne, *1567.*

Alte Pinakothek: Claude Lorraine, Sea Harbor, *1674.*

Rubens, Fall of the Angels, *1622.*

Altarpiece of the Church Fathers (Room II), Lochner's *Virgin and Child* (IIc), Brueghel's *Land of Cockaigne* (Cab. 23). On the **first floor,** Rogier van der Weyden's *Columba Altarpiece* (I), Dürer's *The Four Apostles* (II) and Christ-like *Self-Portrait* (IIb), Altdorfer's *Battle of Alexander* (III) and *Danube Landscape* (the first depiction of pure landscape in German art; IIb), Grünewald's *Mocking of Christ,* and Cranach's *Crucifixion* (both II).

The Florentine and Venetian paintings of the fifteenth and sixteenth centuries include Raphael's *The Tempi Madonna* (IV), Tintoretto's *Mars and Venus Surprised by Vulcan* (V), Titian's *Emperor Charles V* (V), and Leonardo's *Virgin and Child* (Cab. 3). Rubens is seen at his best in *Hélène Fourment in her Wedding Dress, The Rape of the Daughters of Leucippus* (VII), *Susanna and the Elders* (Cab. 9), and *The Fall of the Damned* (Cab. 12). Highlights of Dutch seventeenth-century painting are Rembrandt's *Man in Oriental Costume* (IX) and

Boucher, Madame Pompadour, *1756.*

Neue Pinakothek: View of cafeteria and main entrance from corner of Barer- and Theresienstrasse.

Passion Cycle (Cab. 16), and Hals's *Portrait of Willem van Heythuysen.*

Italian Baroque triumphs in Tiepolo's *Adoration of the Magi* (X), the French Rococo in Boucher's *Madame Pompadour* (XII) and in his and Fragonard's portraits of girls (XIIa), and seventeenth-century Spanish painting in Velazquez's *Young Spanish Nobleman* (XIII).

74 Neue Pinakothek
Barer Strasse 29

Extraordinary survey of nineteenth-century European painting, installed in a new and quite effective post-modern building.

This controversial new museum and administration **building** (1975-81) by Alexander von Branca, a monumental yet sensitively articulated structure in granite and concrete faced with sandstone, follows accepted post-modern practice by quoting the escape stairs of medieval castles and the rows of round-arched windows from Klenze's Alte Pinakothek. On display in its well-proportioned and illuminated rooms – twenty-two large rooms and ten small "cabinets" on various levels – are about 550 paintings and 50 sculptures, approximately one-tenth of the total collection.

Founder of the **collection**★ and of the original Neue Pinakothek building, which was so severely damaged in the Second World War

Waldmüller, Young Peasant Woman, *1840.*

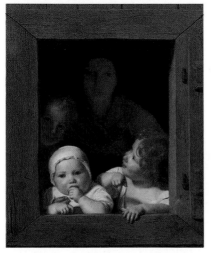

David, Marquise de Sorcy de Thélusson, *1790.*

Neue Pinakothek: Room 13 with paintings by H. Vernet and C. von Piloty.

Neue Pinakothek, Plan

A, B	Changing exhibitions of graphic art	13, 13a	History and Society Painting
1, 2, 2a	International Art around 1800	14, 14a	Painting of the *Gründerzeit*
3, 3a	Early Romantic Art	15	Hans von Marées
4, 4a	Court Art in the Reign of Ludwig I	16	Böcklin, Feuerbach, Thoma
5, 5a	German Neoclassical Art in Rome	17	Leibl and his Circle
6	Georg Schäfer Collection	18	French Impressionism
7	The Nazarenes	19	Cézanne, Gauguin, van Gogh
8, 9	Biedermeier	20	Social Realism
10, 10a	French Late Romantics and Realists	21	German Impressionism
11, 11a	German Late Romantics and Realists	21a	Art of the Secession
12	Designs by Kaulbach	22, 22a	Symbolism and Art Nouveau
		R	Restaurant, café (basement)

Neue Pinakothek: Vincent van Gogh, Vase with Sunflowers, *1888 (above); Adolph Menzel,* Living Room with Menzel's Sister, *1847 (detail, below); Wilhelm Leibl,* My Niece, Lina Kirchdorffer, *1871 (detail, right).*

that it had to be razed in 1949, was Ludwig I. His private collection of contemporary art ranged from history paintings by members of the Munich Academy to landscapes by the leaders of the avant-garde of the time. Superb additions were made after the turn of the century in the fields of French and German Impressionism and Symbolism. To emphasize the continuity of nineteenth-century painting, the collection has been rearranged to include the late eighteenth century, and now extends from Goya to Cézanne.

After an elegant introduction by Gainsborough, David, and Goya (Rooms 1, 2), the early Romantic period in Germany follows with Friedrich, Blechen, Rottmann, Dillis, and Kobell (3). Art at the court of Ludwig I is represented by such canvases as Stieler's *Portrait of Goethe* and Hess's *King Otto Marching into Greece* (4). The programmatic

Italia and Germania by Overbeck is the focus of the Nazarene Room (7). After art of the German Biedermeier period, from Schwind to Waldmüller (8, 9), come French and German late Romantics and Realists: Delacroix, Millet, Daumier, Corot, Menzel, Schleich, and Spitzweg, with his famous *Poor Poet* (10, 10a, 11, 11a). The Marées Room sadly illustrates how paintings can deteriorate despite all the skill of the restorer's art (15). Feuerbach's *Medea* and Böcklin's *Pan in the Reeds* (16) provide a fascinating contrast to Leibl's

Neue Pinakothek: Böcklin, Play of the Waves, *1883.*

My Niece, Lina and Schuch's *Still Life with Asparagus* (17). Highlights of the collection of French Impressionism and Post-Impressionism are Manet's *Breakfast in the Studio* (18), Cézanne's *Railway Cutting* and *Still Life with Apples,* Gauguin's *Birth of Christ,* and van Gogh's *View of Arles* (19). Liebermann, Slevogt, and Corinth are particularly well represented in the department of German Realism and Impressionism (20, 21), and Stuck (*Sin*), Klinger, Hodler, Klimt, and Schiele in that of Symbolism and Art Nouveau.

Neue Pinakothek: Manet, Breakfast in the Studio, *1868.*

Mineralogical Collection: A rhodochrosite.

75 State Mineralogical Collection
Mineralogische Staatssammlung

Theresienstrasse 41

A small but fine collection, a pleasure both for the inquiring mind and the discerning eye.

The early history of this famous collection was largely shaped by the gifted chemist and minerologist, Johann Nepomuk Fuchs, and Franz von Kobell, who was both a minerologist and a poet. During the last century, these two men were the curators who raised the collection to international rank by incorporating the superb collection of the dukes of Leuchtenberg. Sadly, fully eighty percent of the original holdings were lost in the Second World War; they now comprise 20,000 items. A permanent exhibition titled *The World of Crystals,* with 700 specimens, illustrates the genesis of minerals, their configurations and properties, rich color variations, and geological sites.

76 Almeida Mansion
Palais Almeida

Brienner Strasse 14

A noble Neoclassical mansion with Parisian flair.

This most aristocratic of all the great houses that once graced Brienner Strasse was built in 1824 by Métivier, who combined local Neoclassicism with Parisian grandeur in the exterior and created interiors that were famed far and wide before their destruction in the Second World War. Originally the residence of Baroness Sophie Bayrstorff, the mistress of Prince Carl who was raised to the peerage after becoming his wife, the mansion passed by way of her daughter to Count Almeida.

77 Wittelsbacher Platz

One of the city's loveliest squares, lined by decorous palatial architecture that lends it harmony and unity; site of the finest equestrian monument in Munich, a masterpiece of Neoclassicism.

The **commander** pointing his troops the way with an inimitable combination of aplomb and conviction is Elector Maximilian I, commemorated by the grand master of the Neoclassical style, Thorwaldsen, and cast by Stiglmaier in 1839. From the Brienner Strasse end of the **square** the statue is surrounded on three sides by palatial frontages designed by Klenze. Partly erected for speculators of the period, these buildings soon became the residences of aristocratic Munich families, and today they house commercial premises and administration offices.

78 Ludwig Ferdinand Mansion
Palais Ludwig Ferdinand

Wittelsbacher Platz 4 and Fürstenstrasse 1

A dignified Neoclassical building, originally the home of the famous architect Leo von Klenze.

From his house on the northern side of the square, Klenze had a view of many of his own architectural creations: the Odeon, Leuchtenberg Mansion, Ludwigstrasse, and Wittelsbacher Platz. This classically inspired palace, with its graceful round-arched windows – the facade was Klenze's own design – was built in 1825, and from 1878 belonged to the princes Alfons and Ludwig Ferdinand, grandsons of King Ludwig I and sons of Prince Adalbert Georg, who chose to live here rather than in the Residence. It is now the headquarters of the Siemens Company.

79 Arco-Zinneberg Mansion
Palais Arco-Zinneberg

Wittelsbacher Platz 1

A finely proportioned Neoclassical building, one of Klenze's mature works.

Almeida Mansion.

Wittelsbacher Platz: Monument to Elector Maximilian, Ludwig Ferdinand Mansion, and Odeon.

The column-flanked portal and Palladian windows of the kind often seen in Venice lend charm to this rather austere and elongated *palazzo* on the western side of the square. Built in 1820 and authentically restored in 1960, the former palace of the Counts of Arco-Zinneberg is now a commercial establishment.

80 Odeonsplatz and Ludwigstrasse

A monumentally proportioned Neoclassical avenue, built to embody the power and prestige of the Bavarian monarchy under Ludwig I. One of the most ambitious projects of its kind undertaken in the nineteenth century.

Around 1800, the area just north of the Theatine Church and the Residence was a picturesque jumble of Schwabing Gate, town wall, riding establishment, inn, and dirt road. Crown Prince Ludwig decided to lay out a square here, complete with a new royal road leading north along the axes of Schwabing–Schleissheim Palace and Freisinger Strasse. In 1816 Leo von Klenze took charge of the project and conceived a long avenue lined by palaces, without trees, gardens, or driveways, in the grandly austere spirit of the Italian Renaissance. Though sponsors were sought among the prosperous citizenry, not enough were found, and Ludwig decided to erect public buildings instead. After a quarrel with Klenze in 1827, the king appointed Gärtner architect of the project.

At this point Klenze had already finished the section between Odeonsplatz and the War Ministry [No. 85] in a dignified Neo-

Renaissance style. Gärtner then went on to complete the avenue from the State Library [No. 86] to the Triumphal Arch [No. 89] in equally successful adaptations of Romanesque and Byzantine architecture, finishing the whole in 1847.

The architectural unity and uniqueness of Ludwigstrasse have been just as widely praised as its forbiddingness and monotony have been damned. Of course, it was never intended to be a lively boulevard but, rather, a royal *via triumphalis* and a monument to the art of town planning. Ironically, it was also the scene of Ludwig's demise when, in

Monument to King Ludwig I by Max Widnmann, on Odeonsplatz.

Ludwigstrasse: View of Field Marshals' Hall, Theatine Church, and Cathedral from St. Ludwig's.

1848, an outraged populace gathered in front of St. Ludwig's church to demand his abdication. What remained, and continued to grow, was the fame of the scholarly institutions which the king had located along his avenue.

81 Equestrian Monument to King Ludwig I
Reiterdenkmal für König Ludwig I.

Odeonsplatz

A homage to the founder of Ludwigstrasse.

The royal patron of the arts has his memorial at the point where the avenue of his dreams begins. Mounted on a stallion and flanked by two pageboys, Ludwig I is celebrated in allegory on the pedestal as the protector of religion and art, poetry and industry. The monument, which represents Klenze's revision of a design by Ludwig Schwanthaler, was executed by Max Widnmann in 1862.

82 Odeon
Ministry of the Interior
Odeon – Innenministerium
Odeonsplatz 3

An impressive specimen of Klenze's style, although only the exterior was rebuilt after the war and not the famous concert hall inside.

Against considerable popular resistance, Ludwig I financed the building of the Odeon Concert Hall with funds earmarked for the defense of the realm. He entrusted Klenze with the project, who in 1828 erected a hall with colonnades and a semicircular apse for the orchestra, an interior of great elegance renowned for its acoustics. The **facade** of the building, which also housed a great ballroom, was based on that of Leuchtenberg Mansion [No. 83]. In the course of rebuilding in 1954 to accommodate the Ministry of the Interior, the former concert hall was left unroofed to form a **court.** The Odeon is associated with a century and a half of musical history in Munich.

83 Leuchtenberg Mansion
Ministry of Finance
Leuchtenberg-Palais – Finanz-ministerium

Odeonsplatz 4

The largest aristocratic mansion in Munich and one of Klenze's finest works.

The first nobleman to settle in this newly developed area of town was Eugène Beauharnais, the stepson of Napoleon and son-in-law of Max I Joseph, who raised him to the rank of Duke of Leuchtenberg. Later, Prince Regent Luitpold and Crown Prince Rupprecht lived in this opulent palace, built by Klenze in 1816-21 along the lines of the Palazzo Farnese in Rome – a Renaissance Revival that set the tone of the entire Ludwigstrasse. The great complex, with interior court and three identical facades, was designed in such a way that it could be divided into private apartments if necessary. It now houses the Bavarian Ministry of Finance.

84 Bazaar Building – *Bazargebäude*
Odeonsplatz 6-18

Bazaar Building on Odeonsplatz.

An early example of commercial building in the Neoclassical style.

The oriental name for a series of shops under one roof came to Munich by way of Paris. However, with its elegant sequence of central building, extended wings, corner pavilions (originally lower), and arcades leading to the Court Garden, this "bazaar" bears more resemblance to a country pleasure-seat. It was built by Klenze in 1825-26, on the site of a riding and tournament hall and a legendary café of the Biedermeier period, Tambosi's. The café tradition has continued without a break to this day.

War Ministry: Forecourt on Schönfeldstrasse.

85 War Ministry
Central State Archives
Kriegsministerium – Hauptstaatsarchiv

Ludwigstrasse 14 – Schönfeldstrasse 3 and 5

A very personal, boldly articulated design by the prolific Klenze.

This edifice is as impressive as its function was secondary, for Ludwig I hated to spend money on military matters. Klenze gave the Ministry of War a palace à la Florentine Renaissance. The only features that allude to its purpose are trophy reliefs in the spandrels above the arcades (1824-30), and even these are more graceful than belligerent. The great complex on Ludwigstrasse and Schönfeldstrasse (where its lovely forecourt is located) is now occupied by the Central State Archives, the largest collection of documents in Europe.

Ludwigstrasse: War Ministry, State Library, St. Ludwig's Church, and Triumphal Arch.

Bavarian State Library: Repository for the Uta Gospels, *Regensburg, 11th century (top), and* St. Luke, *from the* Gospels of Otto III, *Reichenau, late 10th century.*

Entrance, Bavarian State Library.

86 Bavarian State Library
Bayerische Staatsbibliothek

Ludwigstrasse 16

The largest general library in Germany, housed in a Neoclassical palatial building of stark monumentality.

The Bavarian State Library is a **collection** of superlatives – five million volumes, including 58,000 manuscripts, many of them of immeasurable value; the most comprehensive Oriental collection in Europe, with approximately half a million volumes; 30,000 periodicals on subscription; a Bavarian central catalogue with over fifteen million items ... the list could be extended almost indefinitely.

The emphasis of the library has always been on the humanities – ever since the sixteenth century, when it emerged from the humanistic book collections of dukes Albrecht V and Wilhelm V. Its most significant additions came when the monastic libraries were dispersed during the secularization period. Since the seventeenth century, the library has received a compulsory copy of everything printed in Bavaria.

This palace of books, built in 1832-43, was Gärtner's first, very self-confident contribution to the architecture of Ludwigstrasse. He employed elements from the Italian *palazzo* style to articulate the enormous, 500-foot-long brick structure above a high ground floor of rusticated stone. Seated on the balustrade of the steps leading to the entrance are figures that, in Munich, go by the nickname of "The Four Magi" – Thucydides, Homer, Aristotle, and Hippocrates, replicas of the original statues by Ludwig Schwanthaler. The *tour de force* of the interior, a monumental main stairway, was modelled on the Scala dei Giganti in the Doges' Palace in Venice; it was entirely reconstructed after the Second World War, with the exception of the original ceiling frescoes. Waiting on the landing to receive their visitors are the masters of the house, Albrecht V and Ludwig I, carved in marble by Ludwig Schwanthaler.

87 St. Ludwig's Church
Ludwigstrasse 20

A highly individual combination of Byzantine and Romanesque elements, containing a monumental wall-painting by Cornelius.

It was an ingenious idea of Gärtner's to follow the long, low mass of the State Library with the verticals of the Parish and University Church of St. Ludwig. Its twin-towered **facade** (1829-44), flight of steps, colonnade, and vestibule produce a lively effect that is equally fine when seen full-face from Schellingstrasse or diagonally against the spires of the Theatine Church [No. 27]. The mood of the **interior** is both grave and strangely

St. Ludwig's Church (built 1829-44): Interior by Friedrich Gärtner.

Ludwig-Maximilian University: Spacious interior court by German Bestelmeyer.

romantic, especially when the sun is streaming in from outside. Its **frescoes** are the work of Cornelius, a member of the Nazarene group who had advanced to become Munich's leading art authority and was renowned for his "Raphaelesque line." His painting in the choir, *The Last Judgment* (1836-40), is the largest mural in the history of art after Michelangelo's *Last Judgment* in the Sistine Chapel. The sermons given in St. Ludwig's after the last war by the theologian Romano Guardini were an unforgettable experience for all who heard them.

88 Ludwig-Maximilian University
Geschwister-Scholl-Platz/Professor-Huber-Platz

An expansive urban complex in the Neoclassical style and a center of German intellectual life.

In front of the university, Ludwigstrasse widens into a **forum** with two graceful fountains that lend it a Mediterranean air. The tripartite main building to the west has a round-arched arcade and windows whose regular rhythms reveal the influence of Romanesque architecture. Its counterparts across the way, more stringent and reserved, are the former seminary for priests, the **Georgianum** (to the south), and the **Max Joseph Foundation,** earlier a boarding school for young ladies of rank (to the north). All of these buildings, now part of the university, were designed by Gärtner and erected in 1835-40. Extensions were added on Amalienstrasse in 1909, and on Adalbertstrasse in 1960. Many institutes and departments of the university, which, with a student body of 55,000, is the largest in West Germany, are located in various other parts of town.

Founded in Ingolstadt in 1472 and later relocated in Landshut, the university was brought to Munich by Ludwig I in 1826. Among the great scholars to whom it owes its fame are Fraunhofer and Roentgen in physics, Pettenkofer in public health, Ringseis and Sauerbruch in medicine, Liebig and Wieland in chemistry, Martius in botany, Kobell in mineralogy, Feuerbach in law, Schelling, Riehl, and Görres in philosophy and cultural history, Max Weber in sociology, Bodenstedt in oriental studies, and, in art history, Wölfflin, Pinder, and Jantzen.

The spacious Neoclassical **interior court** of the university building, inspired by ancient Roman baths, was designed by an architect of the Munich Secession, Bestelmeyer, and built in 1906-09. It was the site of a courageous leaflet action by the White Rose, a resistance group in the Third Reich organized by two medical students, Hans and Sophie Scholl, and Kurt Huber, a musicologist; they were put to death in 1943.

Forum on Ludwigstrasse: View of university (below) and St. Ludwig's (facing page).

Imposing entrance to downtown Munich: Gärtner's Triumphal Arch.

89 Triumphal Arch – *Siegestor*

*An imposing gateway from the north into Neo-
classical Munich (incidentally providing a perfectly framed view of St. Ludwig and the Theatine
Church). From the south, the focal point of Ludwigstrasse and the architectural culmination of
the university forum.*

Munich's *via triumphalis* begins and ends
with the great arches of Field Marshals' Hall
and the Triumphal Arch. Neither monument, however, was conceived in a spirit of
belligerence, but was intended to evoke "a
timeless ideal in the forms of classical antiquity" and to shape the city through the
urban planner's art. This triple arch, based
on the Arch of Constantine in Rome, is dedicated to the Bavarian army and crowned by a
statue of Bavaria accompanied by a quadriga
of lions striding out to meet the returning soldiers. The reliefs show battle scenes, the
medallions allegorical depictions of the Bavarian provinces. Begun in 1843 by Gärtner,
the arch was completed by his pupil, Metz-

Academy terrace: Castor and Pollux.

ger, in 1850; the sculptures were designed by
Martin von Wagner. The inscription on the
south side, composed after the Second World
War by Hanns Braun, professor at Munich
University, reads "Dedicated to victory, des-
troyed in war, exhorting to peace."

90 Academy of Visual Arts
Akademie der Bildenden Künste

Akademiestrasse 2

*An art school with a long and illustrious tradi-
tion, housed in a palatial building typical of late
nineteenth-century Germany.*

This rather pompous, three-winged **building,**
with its broad flight of steps, colonnaded balcony, and equestrian sculptures (Castor and
Pollux), was obviously designed to create an
imposing effect. It was built by Neureuther
from 1876 to 1885. The Academy had had no
permanent home since its founding in 1808.
The activities of the new institution were
based on the precepts of Schelling, the great
philosopher who served as its first Secretary
General. Many of the most famous names in
German art have participated in the **history**
of the Academy as teachers or students. At
the turn of the century, the avant-garde mar-
shalled its forces here to do battle with tradition: Klee, Kandinsky, Marc, Jawlensky,
Kanoldt, and de Chirico were students here.
After the Nazi dictatorship and the monopoly
on art held by the teachers Ziegler and
Thorak, a new beginning was made by such
artists as Henselmann, Caspar, Preetorius,
and Geiger, all of them professors here. They
were succeeded during the campus rebellion
of the 1960s and 1970s by teachers like Nest-
ler, Dahmen, Zimmermann, and Fruhtrunk.

English Garden, Schwabing

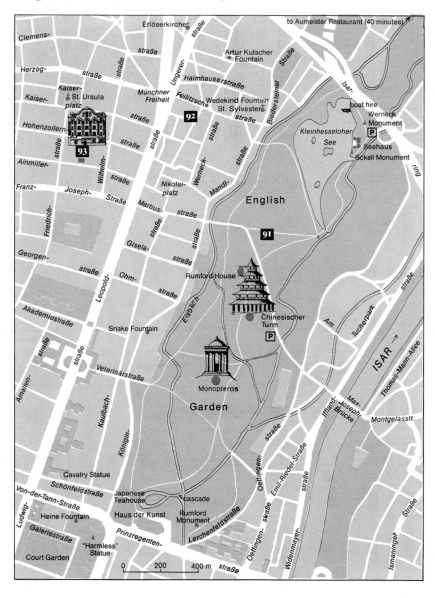

Map labels:

Clemens-straße
Erlöserkirche straße
to Aumeister Restaurant (40 minutes)
Herzog-straße
straße
Artur Kutscher Fountain
Kaiser-platz
St. Ursula
Isar
Kaiser-
Münchner Freiheit
Haimhauserstraße
Ungerer
Biedersteiner
boat hire
Werneck Monument
Hohenzollern
Feilitzsch
Wedekind Fountain
St. Sylvester
92
straße
Kleinhesseloher See
P
Seehaus
Sckell Monument
Ainmiller-
straße
Werneck
Mandl-
straße
ring
93
Nikolai-platz
Franz-
Joseph-
Straße
Martius-
English
Wilhelm-
straße
Friedrich-
Gisela-
straße
91
Georgen-
straße
Leopold-
Ohm-
straße
Rumford House
straße
Akademiestraße
Snake Fountain
Eisbach
Chinesischer Turm
P
Am
Tucherpark
straße
Amalien-
straße
Veterinärstraße
Monopteros
ISAR
Thomas-Mann-Allee
Kaulbach-
Garden
Königin-
Max-Joseph-Brücke
Iffland-straße
Montgelasstr.
Cavalry Statue
Schönfeldstraße
Japanese Teahouse
cascade
Oettingen-straße
Emil-Riedel-Straße
straße
Von-der-Tann-Straße
Heine Fountain
Haus der Kunst
Rumford Monument
Ludwig-
Galeriestraße
Prinzregenten-
Lerchenfeldstraße
Widenmayer
Ismaninger
straße
"Harmless" Statue
Court Garden
0   200   400 m
straße

Horsedrawn taxi in the English Garden.

91 English Garden
Englischer Garten

Munich's popular central park, one of the
earliest landscape gardens on the continent and
still the largest green area in any big city in
Europe.

Munich owes its "English Garden" (the German term for landscape garden) to an American: Benjamin Thompson, alias Count Rumford (1753-1814), a farmer's son, physicist, social reformer, and Bavarian Minister of War. In the course of transforming the northern section of the Isar marshlands into a park for the militia, he persuaded Elector Karl Theodor to establish a public park into the bargain. The year, not incidentally, was 1789. Designed by the great landscape architect Sckell, the **park** was completed in 1808; in keeping with Enlightenment philosophy, it was to serve not only recreation but a mingling of all the social classes. Agricultural use and educational aims were fostered by model farms, a tree nursery, a veterinary school, and other facilities.

With a present area of about 900 acres, the English Garden extends from Prinzregentenstrasse in the south to the Freimann district in the north. Bounded by the River Isar on the east, it is criss-crossed by waterways and has vistas accentuated in the English style by monuments and pavilions. At its heart is the Kleinhesseloher See, a lake with three islands that is the perfect place for relaxing.

English Garden: Chinese Tower with Munich's most popular beer garden (facing page), the Monopteros (above), and the lovely view of the city's skyline from it (below).

Art Nouveau facade at No. 22 Ainmillerstrasse, by Helbig and Haiger, 1899-1900 (above), and detail of facade at No. 20.

Meter Museum: Edison's electrolyte meter, 1881.

The park's **buildings and monuments** include a Japanese Teahouse where authentic tea ceremonies are held (architect Mitsuo Nomura, 1972); the Rumford Monument (by Franz Jakob Schwanthaler, 1796); the Monopteros, a Neoclassical circular temple with a wonderful view of the city (by Klenze, 1838); the Chinese Tower (Chinesischer Turm), with its lively beer garden, modelled on the outlook pagoda in Kew Gardens, London (by Frey, 1760; reconstructed 1952); Rumford House, an officers' casino in the English colonial style (Lechner, 1791); the Sckell Monument (designed by Klenze and executed by Bandel, 1824); Lake House (Seehaus), a restaurant and beer garden (Hürlimann and Wiedemann, 1984); and the Werneck Monument dedicated to Rumford's successor as Chief Park Superintendent (designed by Klenze, 1838).

Located at the north end, beyond the Isar Ring Road, is the Aumeister Restaurant with its large beer garden, named for the master of the chase who earlier had charge of hunting in the Isar Meadows ("Auen") and designed by Deiglmayr in 1811.

92 Meter Museum – *Zählermuseum*
Franzstrasse 9

A specialized museum with a more than specialist interest.

Edison's 1882 invention, an "electrolyte meter" as simple as its name, has since given birth to such complicated apparatuses as multiple rate meters, surplus consumption meters, and even apparent consumption meters. Munich's smallest museum is the only one of its kind, illustrating the hundred-year history of the electric meter with 700 fascinatingly diverse specimens from around the world and including an archive and library.

93 Art Nouveau Apartment House
Jugendstil-Wohnhaus

Ainmillerstrasse 22

An attractive and colorful Art Nouveau facade.

A facade should be "like a precious jewel on a lady's gown," said the architects Helbig and Haiger, obviously with something rather striking in mind. Their design is richly articulated by pilasters and arches, burgeoning floral and figurative ornament, and bright color (built 1899-1900, restored several times, then returned to its original color scheme in 1982). Equally noble are the Art Nouveau facades of Nos. 20, 33, 34 (where Rilke lived), 35, and 37. Neo-Baroque facades may be seen at Nos. 7, 9, 13, and 17. Other noteworthy nineteenth-century apartment buildings in Schwabing are located along Martius-, Franz-Joseph-, and Elisabethstrasse and their side streets.

Prinzregentenstrasse, Lehel, Bogenhausen

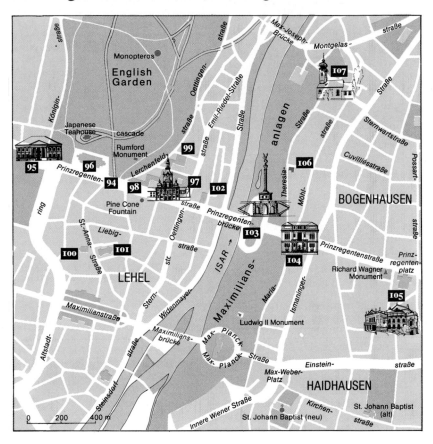

94 Prinzregentenstrasse

The last Munich avenue built under the Wittelsbach monarchs. Unlike the other great royal avenues, it was planned as an informal road in natural surroundings, but this conception was only partially realized.

Thomas Mann's ironic quip about "Munich resplendent" was inspired by the reign of Prince Regent Luitpold at the turn of the century. Among the projects of this honest ruler and tasteful gentleman was an avenue up to the high left bank of the Isar, leading from Prince Carl Mansion [No. 95] to Prince Regent Theater [No. 105] and finding its

serene climax in a landscaped terrace at the riverside surmounted by the Angel of Peace [No. 103]. In keeping with the patriotic spirit of the time, the Bavarian National Museum [No. 97] resembles an outsized medieval German castle dominating the avenue before the bridge. The less naive patriotism of the Nazi period disfigured the park end of the boulevard with a pompous House of German Art [No. 96] and isolated the Prince Carl Mansion by cutting a huge traffic swath at right angles to it and digging a gaping tunnel. Nevertheless, the "Museum Mile" is still a picturesque part of Munich in more than one sense of the word.

Prince Carl Mansion, Prinzregentenstrasse.

95 Prince Carl Mansion
Prinz Carl Palais

Königinstrasse 1

Munich's finest building in the local Neoclassical style and the only work of Karl von Fischer, a brilliantly precocious architect, to have survived in almost its original state.

This building, with its prominent colonnaded portico and triangular pediment on the **main elevation,** is the western focus of Prinzregentenstrasse. A masterpiece of the Classical Revival, it was Karl von Fischer's first project for Munich, built in 1804-06. Modern traffic planning has sadly deprived it of its original character of a Palladian villa set in a garden. The superb **interior decoration** is by Méti-vier. The palace initially belonged to Minister Pierre de Salabert, then to Prince Carl, brother of Ludwig I. Since 1924 it has been the official residence of the Minister-President of Bavaria.

96 Haus der Kunst
Prinzregentenstrasse 1

Dedicated to the cult of Nazi art and now the scene of important international exhibitions, this museum houses the State Gallery of Modern Art, a great collection of contemporary art from around the world.

The fine exhibitions of international art now presented in this building might have banished the diabolic spirit that presided over its opening, if the architecture itself did not continually remind us of it. Paul L. Troost designed the **building** as early as 1932, to replace the Crystal Palace, which had been destroyed by fire, and supervised its construction for the Nazis. Not long after its inauguration in 1937, the sprawling temple received the nickname "white sausage alley," which perfectly characterizes its desolate row of columns and explodes the claim of its creators to have carried on the great tradition of Munich Neoclassicism. It was an ominous sign indeed when, as Hitler laid the cornerstone, the shaft of his hammer broke after the first blow.

The middle section and east wing of the museum now host special exhibitions and regular showings of work by Munich artists and groups, including the annual Munich Comprehensive Exhibition. The west wing contains the treasures of the State Gallery.

State Gallery of Modern Art. The excellent collection of the Staatsgalerie moderner Kunst has been restricted to international art of the twentieth century since 1980. Its major emphasis lies on the Early Modern period, represented on the ground floor in all its variety from Expressionism to New Objectivity. Great artists like Beckmann, Kirchner, Klee, Marc, Munch, Moore, and Picasso have entire rooms to themselves.

Developments during the second half of the twentieth century are seen on the top floor, with an emphasis on American, Italian, and German art. There are outstanding examples of American Abstract Expressionism by Kline, de Kooning, and Francis; of Pop Art by Warhol, Rauschenberg, and Segal; and of Minimal Art by Morris, Andre, and Flavin. The protagonists of contemporary Italian art include Fontana, Vedova, Paolini, Pomodoro, and Dorazio. German

Haus der Kunst, Prinzregentenstrasse.

art is covered from the Zero Group to the Neo-Expressionists and Photorealists, with noteworthy examples from the oeuvres of Beuys, Antes, Klapheck, Rückriem, Lechner, Baselitz, Penck, and Heizer.

Haus der Kunst, State Gallery of Modern Art: View of interior (above) and Landscape with Yellow Church Spire *by Paul Klee, 1920 (below).*

Prinzregentenstrasse, Lehel, Bogenhausen: *map on page 127*

Bavarian National Museum,
Floor Plans

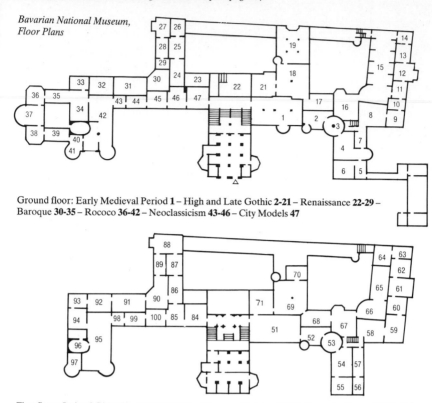

Ground floor: Early Medieval Period **1** – High and Late Gothic **2-21** – Renaissance **22-29** – Baroque **30-35** – Rococo **36-42** – Neoclassicism **43-46** – City Models **47**

First floor: Stained Glass **51** – Miniatures **52** – Baroque Sketches **53/54** – Ivory Sculpture **55/56** – Inlay Work **57** – Clocks **58/59** – Porcelain **84-97, 98-100** – Precious Metals **88** – Plaques **89** – Ceramics **90** – Stoneware **91** – Majolica **92** – Faience **93-95, 97**

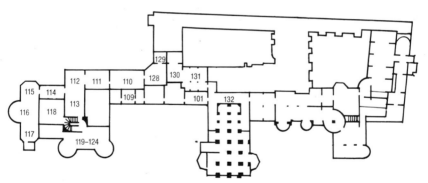

Basement: Cottage Interiors **101-109** – Religious Artifacts **110-117** – Household Utensils **119-124** – Folk Art, Costumes **128-131** – Toys **132**

Bavarian National Museum: Detail of "February" from a tapestry depicting the months, by Hans van der Biest (1613).

130

Bavarian National Museum, Prinzregentenstrasse: Forecourt and Monument to the Prince Regent.

97 Bavarian National Museum

Bayerisches Nationalmuseum

Prinzregentenstrasse 3

A renowned museum of art and cultural history, with first-rate collections and priceless individual objects of Bavarian, South German, and international provenance. Its unique Nativity Groups and extensive Department of Folk Art are extremely popular. The building itself is a remarkable example of nineteenth-century museum architecture, a Historical Revival creation of great originality.

The "total work of art" was a characteristic idea of the nineteenth century, and it was seldom realized so fully as in this museum. Designed by Gabriel von Seidl and built in 1894-99, its **architecture** is based on German models of the Romanesque, Gothic, Renaissance, and Baroque periods. For all the diversity of sources, the result is surprisingly unified. In the interior Seitz adapted each room stylistically to the objects on exhibit. Entire vaulted ceilings were taken from historic buildings or copied with irrepressible bravura. Although additions and conversions have since reduced Seitz's designs to their bare bones, his inimitable style can still be sensed behind the modern installations.

Established in 1855 by Max II, the **Bavarian National Museum★** originally occupied the premises of today's Museum of Ethnology [No. 112], which soon proved too small to house the collection. Works in the possession of the Wittelsbach family formed the basis of the museum's holdings, which were enriched by many donations, bequests, and

acquisitions. Today, the collection comprises some 18,000 items, many of them exquisite and unique, adding up to an illuminating record of developments in fine and applied art over nine centuries.

The **Fine Art Collection**★ presents art from late antiquity to the nineteenth century in Rooms 1-47. The emphasis lies on sculpture, including such outstanding pieces as the intimate *Seeon Madonna*★ (c. 1430); the unusual

Bavarian National Museum: St. Sebastian, *ivory, c. 1630, by Georg Petel (above);* Judith, *alabaster, 1512-14, by Konrad Meit (right); detail of a Franconian tapestry depicting the capture of a unicorn, c. 1450-60 (below).*

Bavarian National Museum: Weapons Room with elaborate armor, helmets, and battle regalia.

group of the *Christ Child with Angels helping Him to take His first steps* (c. 1480); Grasser's expressive, Riemenschneider's soulful, and Leinberger's vivacious Late Gothic figures; Hubert Gerhard's powerful *Mars and Venus;* Günther's elegant Rococo sculptures; and Bustelli's charming porcelain figurines of Commedia dell'arte players.

Complementing the paintings and sculptures are fine examples of **Applied Art★**, including the densely painted wooden vaulting from a fifteenth-century Augsburg guild hall; Brussels tapestries of the sixteenth century, acquired by Duke Wilhelm V; a cabinet from a Cuvilliés palace, with paintings on silk taffeta; and a Neoclassical interior, with furnishings that date from the reign of Elector Karl Theodor.

The **Special Collections★** on the top floor cover applied art of the sixteenth to the nineteenth century, with porcelain, silver- and goldsmiths' work, faience, clocks, and scientific instruments from throughout Europe. Of particular note are the examples

Tilman Riemenschneider: Christ in the House of Simon, *1490-92 (left), and* St. Barbara, *c. 1510.*

Ignaz Günther, Minerva *(detail), c. 1772.*

Glass tumbler, Syrian, 1250/1300.

of stained glass from the thirteenth to the nineteenth century.

The special collections on the ground floor present folk art, both religious and secular, in all its facets, from farmhouse interiors, pottery, and toys to devotional images, votive offerings, and cult objects. The collection of **Nativity Groups★** from all over Europe, exhibited in sixty showcases, is exceptional.

The **equestrian monument** to Prince Regent Luitpold in front of the museum is by Hildebrand and dates from 1913.

Bavarian National Museum: Julia, *porcelain figurine by Bustelli, Nymphenburg, c. 1760 (facing page); the* Three Magi and Retinue, *from a Tyrolean Nativity scene, c. 1750 (below).*

The New Collection: Meissen tableware designed by Henry van de Velde, 1903.

98 The New Collection
Die Neue Sammlung

Prinzregentenstrasse 3

The most important collection in Europe devoted to twentieth-century design. Its abundant holdings are presented in regular exhibitions on special themes.

Established in 1925 as a Department of Commercial Art within the Bavarian National Museum, the collection became an independent **State Museum of Applied Art** in 1981. Its 22,000 handcrafted and mass-produced objects cover the fields of textile design, ceramics, porcelain, metal products, furniture, and mechanical appliances. The poster collection alone contains 10,000 items. The aim of the museum is to help improve taste by presenting the best in past and contemporary design, in exhibitions selected from the museum's own holdings or arranged in collaboration with other modern design collections. A new building is now in the planning stage.

99 State Prehistorical Collection, Museum of Pre- and Early History
Prähistorische Staatssammlung, Museum für Vor- und Frühgeschichte

Lerchenfeldstrasse 2

A fascinating encounter with Celts, Romans, and Teutons, in an outstanding and attractively arranged collection that focuses on Bavaria.

A Roman citizen, living in the village of Happing near Rosenheim, Upper Bavaria, fell in love with a slave girl, set her free, married her, only to have her taken from him by death – a love story told on a gravestone. How the legionaries of Marcus Aurelius dressed, bathed, and dined in Regensburg; what surgical instruments were used by a Celtic doctor in Obermenzing, now a district of Munich, long before the birth of Christ; what sort of jewellery Bavarian women wore during the Merovingian period; or that such delightful kitsch as a bronze lamp in the form of a sandalled foot has been around since the second century A.D. – these and other human foibles, customs, and skills are illustrated by a **collection** of archaeological finds ranging from about 100,000 B.C. to 800 A.D. Ample space, careful arrangement and lighting, and lucid descriptions lend a magic and eloquence to everything on view, be it a mosaic floor or a prehistoric corpse.

An offshoot of the Bavarian Academy of Sciences, the Museum of Pre- and Early His-

State Prehistorical Collection: Face-piece from a Roman parade helmet, c. 150 A.D.

Merovingian clasp, from Wittislingen, 7th century.

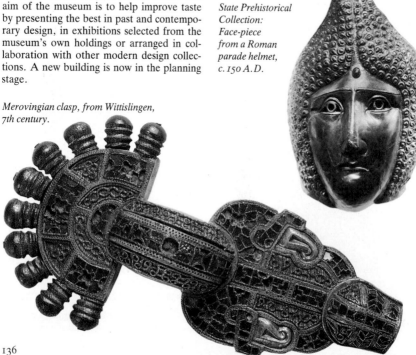

tory was founded in 1885 and provisionally housed at various sites until 1975, when it received its present **building** adjacent to the English Garden. This striking structure of glass and steel, with its gradually darkening protective layer of rust (architects: von Werz, Ottow, Bachmann, Marx), provides ideal spaces for the museum's three main sections, Prehistory, the Roman Era, and the Early Middle Ages. Its regular special exhibitions treat the prehistory of far-off lands, and also show selections from the museum's own extensive foreign collection, for which no permanent display rooms are yet available.

Mosaic from a Roman villa in Westerhofen near Eichstätt (detail), c. 300-320 A. D.; Celtic amber nacklace, 6th century B. C.; pitcher and cup, 800-700 B. C. (below).

100 Monastery Church of St. Anne
Klosterkirche St. Anna

Sankt-Anna-Platz 21

The first Rococo church in Munich and Old Bavaria, an important early work by Fischer with decoration and furnishings by Asam and Straub. A historical ambience convincingly restored.

This church was built to celebrate the arrival of the much-loved elector, Max III Joseph. Begun in the year of his birth, 1727, and completed in 1733, it marked the advent of the Rococo in Munich – straight walls and right angles in the **interior** gave way to sinuous curves and openings, with the nave and central space combining to form a graceful oval. This innovative architecture, by J. M. Fischer, was inspired by churches in Austria and Bohemia. C. D. Asam contributed a light-flooded ceiling fresco of *St. Anne in Her Glory* which seems to let in the open sky; the sculptures and stuccowork are elegant creations of E. Q. Asam and Straub. That little of this glory remained after the war is hardly conceivable in view of the successful architectural reconstruction by Schleich and the convincing restoration by Manninger of the paintings on the basis of color photographs.

Among the furnishings that partially survived the Second World War are the tabernacle with its strikingly beautiful adoring angels by Straub, and the chancel with a figure of Christ the Judge from Straub's workshop. Of C. D. Asam's altar paintings, only those on the foremost side altars could be saved. The remaining altar paintings and sculptures have been reconstructed or renovated. The narrow Rococo **facade,** likewise rebuilt by Schleich, projects only slightly from the monastery building, which was originally erected for the Brotherhood of St. Jerome and has belonged to the Franciscans since 1827.

Destroyed in the war and rebuilt: Monastery Church of St. Anne, by Johann Michael Fischer.

Parish Church of St. Anne.

IOI Parish Church of St. Anne
Pfarrkirche St. Anna

Sankt-Anna-Platz 5

A romantic architectural fantasy in the Rhenish style.

Not the monastery church with its delicate charm, but the forceful masses of the parish church (1887-92) dominate Sankt-Anna-Platz. Its architect, Gabriel von Seidl, took his cue from the Romanesque basilicas of the Rhineland. The frescoes were done by R. von Seitz (apse) and Becker-Gundahl (transept) around the turn of the century. The

Apocalyptic Christ with bow and olive branch above the western portal, by F. von Miller (1910), is noteworthy for its unusual iconography.

102 Schack Gallery
Prinzregentenstrasse 9

A tip for connoisseurs, this important private gallery of the nineteenth century harbors one of the largest collections of German Romantic art in existence.

The inscription and coat of arms on the facade (by Littmann, 1907-08), as well as the Prussian Neoclassical style of its architecture, indicate that this building was donated to the city of Munich by Kaiser Wilhelm II. The treasures it houses were amassed by Count Schack (1815-94), a widely travelled man of the world who belonged to the north German intimates of King Max II and was an avid collector and impassioned supporter, friend, and often savior of many Munich artists, including Feuerbach, Böcklin, and Lenbach.

Count Schack bequeathed the **collection★** in his mansion on Brienner Strasse to the Kaiser, who generously left it in Munich. Such popular canvases as Lenbach's *Shepherd Boy,* Böcklin's *Villa by the Sea,* and Spitz-weg's *Farewell,* have always been the main attraction of the Schack Gallery, but they should not be allowed to outshine the lesser known, delicate compositions by Dillis, Klenze, Schleich, and Morgenstern. Also interesting are the copies of Old Masters by young masters – commissions from Schack which enabled fledgling artists to make their journeys to Italy and Spain.

Schack Gallery: Moritz von Schwind, The Morning Hour *(above) and* Hermit Watering a Knight's Horses, *after 1860 (center); Eduard Schleich the Elder,* Lake Starnberg with Starnberg Castle, *c. 1862 (below).*

Angel of Peace.

103 Angel of Peace
Friedensengel

Prinzregentenstrasse

The focus of Prinzregentenstrasse and perfectly integrated in the natural surroundings, this monument is a high point of Historical Revival architecture.

This decorative combination of bridge, terrace, and monument perfectly integrates the River Isar landscape into the city. Coming

from downtown, the visitor crosses **Luitpold Bridge**, a stone and steel construction by Theodor Fischer (1900), adorned with reclining figures that personify the four groups of the Bavarian population – the Bavarians, Swabians, Franconians, and the inhabitants of the Palatinate. Beyond the bridge rises **Prince Regent Terrace**, with fountain, retaining walls, and a sweeping double stairway – a composition in the Roman manner by Hildebrand and Möhl (1891). The crowning Peace Monument, popularly known as the **Angel of Peace★**, is a later creation of 1896-99. The classical models that inspired it were the Erechtheon Temple on the Acropolis in Athens and Paionios's statue of the goddess of victory at Olympia.

The monument commemorates the twenty-five years of peace that followed the Franco-Prussian War of 1870-71. Portrayed on the round reliefs on the columns of the hall are leaders of the period: emperors William I, Frederick III, and William II; the members of the Wittelsbach family Ludwig II, Otto, and Luitpold; Chancellor Bismarck; and the generals Moltke, Roon, von der Tann, Hartmann, and Pranckh. The gold mosaics in the hall, early examples of the Secession style, are allegorical depictions of Peace, War, Victory, and the Blessings of Civilization.

104 Villa Stuck Museum
Prinzregentenstrasse 60

A luxurious artist's residence of the fin de siècle, now a museum with changing exhibitions.

This fairytale dwelling was owned by an artist with a career to match – Franz von Stuck

Stuck's Amazon *outside the artist's villa.*

Prince Regent Terrace (Luitpold Terrace) with Peace Monument.

(1863-1928). Born a provincial miller's son, this highly talented and classically good looking artist was spoiled by early success, raised to the peerage, and celebrated as a prince among Munich painters. He designed the entire **villa★** including its interiors, the opulent main building in 1897-98 and the more functional studio building in 1913-14. Their unusual blend of Neoclassicism and Art Nouveau seemed just as revolutionary at the time as the spear-wielding Amazon in front of the entrance.

Inside, the reception and living rooms shimmer with gold mosaics and wall-paintings à la Pompeii, coffered ceilings and polychrome panelling, marble-framed reliefs and

Villa Stuck: The residence of 1897-98 and adjacent studio, added in 1913-14.

Villa Stuck Museum: Reception room (above) and Guardian of Paradise *(below), which brought the artist 60,000 gold marks at the 1889 Crystal Palace Exhibition.*

friezes in the classical manner, copies of famous Greek, Roman, and Renaissance sculptures, and, of course, the artist's own paintings, including a version of *Sin,* whose sultry eroticism distracted an entire generation.

Now run by the Stuck Jugendstil Foundation, the museum presents exhibitions of turn-of-the-century and modern art in the numerous, less ornate rooms of the villa.

105 Prince Regent Theater
Prinzregententheater

Prinzregentenstrasse 82

A remarkable festival theater inspired by Bayreuth and built during the reign of Prince Regent Luitpold. Birthplace of the Munich Opera Festival.

King Ludwig II dreamed of building a great festival theater for Richard Wagner, high on the bluff above the River Isar, with a grand avenue leading to the composer's home on Brienner Strasse. As for Wagner, he dreamed of a democratic theater, without tiers or vestibule, and realized his dream in Bayreuth. Decades later, in 1900, a Munich theater director was inspired by Wagner's ideas to commission this somewhat simplified version of the Bayreuth theater. Behind its Neoclassical **facade** by Littmann is a steeply raked **auditorium★**, whose seats are arranged amphitheater-style – a rarity in Germany – and whose decoration was based on the kind of Renaissance grotesque that is typical of the Prince Regent period (1886-1912).

Inaugurated in 1901 with Wagner's *Mastersingers,* the theater soon established a tradition of Wagner performance, featuring the greatest singers of the day, which led to the founding of the Munich Opera Festival. The world premiere of Pfitzner's *Palestrina,* conducted by Bruno Walter, took place here in 1917, followed by such daring drama premieres as Wedekind's *Herakles* in 1919 and Hofmannsthal's *The Tower* in 1928. After the last war, the State Opera had its home here and, in 1948, touched off Munich's first postwar theater scandal with its premiere of Egk's *Abraxas*. From then on, modern music from Stravinsky to Orff had a firm place in the repertoire. A highpoint of the Opera Festival, which was resumed in 1950, was Hindemith's new opera, *Die Harmonie der Welt* ("The Harmony of the World"), conducted by the composer in 1957. Munich is eagerly anticipating the reopening of the renovated theater, scheduled for 1988.

106 Hildebrand House
Maria-Theresia-Strasse 22

A late nineteenth-century artist's residence now accommodating a department of the State Library devoted to Munich and its history.

Like Stuck's and Lenbach's villas, the **studio and residence** of Adolf von Hildebrand (1847-1921) was a focus of artistic life in Munich around the turn of the century. A gifted sculptor who did much to shape the aspect of modern Munich, Hildebrand had his house built to his own specifications in 1897-98 – three wings capped by a mansard roof and set off by a tower with spiral staircase, a design based on country houses of the South German Baroque. Its grounds and rooms are still graced by many of the artist's original works.

Since its restoration in 1977, the Hildebrand House has accommodated the State Library's departments of Monacensia and Manuscripts. For information on Munich and environs, the **Monacensia** is unrivalled, containing over 90,000 volumes in addition to periodicals, maps, and plans. The **Manuscript Department** harbors autographs, manuscripts, and bequests by and from writers, artists, and scholars of the Munich region.

Hildebrand House (Monacensia Library).

107 St. George's Church
Bogenhauser Kirchplatz 1

A charming Rococo village church containing works by Günther and Straub. Its cemetery is the last resting place of many men and women who were prominent in the city's cultural life.

It is a surprise to come across this little onion-domed country church in central Munich – and to find on the plain crosses and gravestones in its **cemetery** such names as Wilhelm Hausenstein, a famous man of letters, Hans Knappertsbusch, the conductor, and the writers Oskar Maria Graf, Annette Kolb, and Erich Kästner. There is also a monument

Prince Regent Theater.

Prince Regent Theater: The amphitheater in its original state.

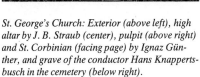

St. George's Church: Exterior (above left), high altar by J. B. Straub (center), pulpit (above right) and St. Corbinian (facing page) by Ignaz Günther, and grave of the conductor Hans Knappertsbusch in the cemetery (below right).

dedicated to four victims of the Nazi regime, among them Father Alfred Delp, rector of St. George's, who was hanged in 1945.

The village of Bogenhausen dates from ancient times, and its **church** was built during the Romanesque period. An architect of the Fischer School, perhaps Trischberger or Giessl, completely redesigned it in 1768. Straub's high altar★, with an equestrian figure of St. George, is the latest Baroque "stage-set" altarpiece in existence (1770); the pulpit★, with coquettish angel, and the emphatic *St. Corbinian*★ on the right side-altar are among Günther's last works (1773); the painted stucco ornament is from the close of the Rococo period. Most of the other figures and the *Töring Epitaph* are from the workshops of Straub and Günther. The ceiling frescoes are by Helterhof, a pupil of Zimmermann.

Maximilianstrasse, Gasteig, Deutsches Museum

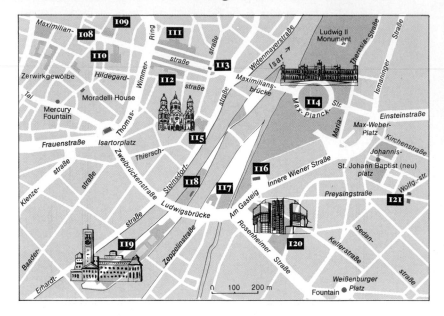

108 Maximilianstrasse

An elegant boulevard lined by galleries, fine shops, and theaters, in an architectural style that is unique in Europe.

Although King Max II was, above all, a devotee of science and scholarship, he did pay tribute to the Wittelsbach tradition of support for the arts, particularly with the street that bears his name (built 1852-75). Its combination of modern iron-and-glass construction with pointed arches derived from English Gothic and Italian arcade architecture has gone down in art history as the Maximilian Style. Its creator, Bürklein, was less fortunate, for after a moment in the limelight, he succumbed to mental illness. There is no telling what he would have made of the brutal bisection of his street by a modern throughway, the Thomas-Wimmer-Ring.

Half a metropolitan boulevard populated by *flâneurs* and window-shoppers, half a grand composition with tree-lined forum and Max II Monument [No. 113], Maximilian-

Above: Four Seasons Hotel.
Facing page: Maximilianstrasse, elegant
shopping street and promenade in one.

strasse culminates beyond the Isar bridge in the soaring facade of the Maximilianeum [No. 114]. Not unjustly described as "stage-set architecture," its rhythmic sequences of columns and arches are nevertheless very effective. Luxurious shops, art galleries, cafés, and theaters lend the street an urbane atmosphere, accentuated by fashionable travellers arriving at the Four Seasons Hotel [No. 109], actors rushing to rehearsals, and opera fans waiting in line for tickets.

109 Four Seasons Hotel

Hotel Vier Jahreszeiten

Maximilianstrasse 17

The oldest and most renowned grand hotel in Munich.

Statues of the seasons and the continents, and busts of a hotel manager and his wife, adorn this facade in the Maximilian Style [see No. 108] designed by Gottgetreu, built in 1857, and since shorn of much of its decoration in the course of several renovations. The hotel's gourmet restaurant was opened by Alfred Walterspiel, whose claim to fame rests on his having brought French cuisine to Germany, around the turn of the century.

Maximilianstrasse, with Max II Monument and Maximilianeum (Bavarian Parliament) in the distance.

IIO Munich Playhouse

Münchner Kammerspiele

Maximilianstrasse 34-35

Germany's only Art Nouveau theater, with a long tradition of support for avant-garde drama.

Not the ubiquitous chandeliers, but small lamps in the shape of tiny blossoms illuminate this **auditorium**, and the sinuous lines of stems and tendrils, leaves and flowers, proliferate everywhere, from balcony railing to door handles. Built by Littmann in 1900-01, the Playhouse is pure Jugendstil, the German version of Art Nouveau. Its interior was designed by the best-known Munich protagonist of this style, Richard Riemerschmid, and restored in all its delicately hued glory in 1970 by his son Reinhard.

After an inaugural performance of Sudermann's *Johannes*, a hearing was accorded to the most advanced playwrights of the day – Ibsen, Hauptmann, Strindberg, Shaw, and Schnitzler – and in 1908 scandal was courted

Government of Upper Bavaria: detail of facade.

Munich Playhouse, foyer.

Munich Playhouse, the only Art Nouveau theater in Germany.

and reaped with performances of Wedekind's *Spring Awakening* and Thoma's *Moral*. The Munich Players moved to the present premises in 1926 under the great director, Falckenberg, who supplemented their classical repertoire with avant-garde plays from Brecht to Kaiser. A long list of the finest actors and actresses in Germany made the Playhouse the most exciting stage outside Berlin. Since the Second World War, it has continued this tradition under the general management of Engel, Schweikart, and Everding. Such events as Fritz Kortner's production of *Waiting for Godot* (1954), Brecht's *The Good Woman of Setzuan* directed by Schweikart with the author's assistance (1955), Schweikart's staging of Arthur Mil-

ler's *The Crucible* (1955), or the world premieres of Orff's *Astutuli* (1953) and Marieluise Fleisser's *Der starke Stamm* ("The Strong Tribe"; 1950) made drama history.

III Government of Upper Bavaria
Regierung von Oberbayern

Maximilianstrasse 39

A fine example of the Gothic Revival variant known in Munich as the Maximilian Style.

These Neo-Gothic government offices on the north side of the landscaped area on Maximilianstrasse were designed by Bürklein and built in 1856-64. The long facade is beauti-

State Museum of Ethnology, Maximilianstrasse (above).

fully accented in the vertical by applied orders, soaring cathedral windows, and arcades, for whose graceful stone construction the architect took full advantage of modern iron framework and expanses of glass.

II2 State Museum of Ethnology
Staatliches Museum für Völkerkunde

Maximilianstrasse 42

The second largest museum of ethnology in Germany, surpassed only by that in Berlin. Parts of its huge collection are on permanent view, and are supplemented by special exhibitions.

The inscription over the museum's porch, "In Honor of my People and as an Example to Them," does not refer to its present exotic collections but to Bavarian craftsmanship – for the building was originally designed to house the Bavarian National Museum [No. 97]. A work by Riedel of 1856-63, the **facade** was intended to complement the government offices across the way, but its adaptation of the English Perpendicular Style seems rather awkward by comparison.

The collection of the **Museum of Ethnology,** housed here since 1926, has a history that stretches back to the Renaissance, when rhinocerous horns consorted with fine Chinese porcelain in the Wittelsbach chambers of curiosities, the *Wunderkammern.* The present focus on non-European ethnography dates from the museum's foundation in 1868. Many fascinating **collections** brought together by famous explorers found their way to Munich – parts of James Cook's estate, relics gathered in Alaska, Siberia, and the South Pacific on a Russian sailing expedition around the world led by Krusenstern, those brought back from the Amazon Basin by the Munich scientists Spix and Martius, from the Himalaya region by the Schlagintweit brothers, and from South America by the

State Museum of Ethnology: Persian vase with Cufic inscription, 13th century.
Left: African relief depicting a Benin warrior, 18th century.
Below: The demon king Ramana abducts Sita in his chariot, India, 18th century.

Facing page:
Ritual gala uniform of a Chinese officer, late 19th century (below left), and head of a Buddha, India, 15th century (center).

Monument to King Max II.

113 Max II Monument
Max-II.-Denkmal

Maximilianstrasse

An elaborate monument to a self-effacing king, who once admitted that he would rather have become a professor.

From high atop his pedestal, the king casts a bronze eye along his boulevard, at his feet allegorical figures representing the four virtues of a ruler and, above them, four little angels holding shields with the arms of the four population groups of Bavaria, the Bavarians and Swabians, the Franconians and the inhabitants of the Palatinate. The rather pompous monument was designed by Zumbusch and cast by Miller in 1875.

Among the other monuments in the **garden** are ones to Count Rumford, physicist and philanthropist (by Zumbusch), and to the philosopher Friedrich Wilhelm von Schelling (Brugger).

Monument to Benjamin Thompson, Count Rumford, Maximilianstrasse.

114 Maximilianeum
Max-Planck-Strasse 1

Architecture as a dramatic backdrop for a grand avenue. Seat of the Bavarian Parliament.

The "great national building" that Max II envisaged on the Isar heights as a worthy culmination to his avenue, turned out to be a rather romantic and, when viewed from a distance, shimmeringly unreal piece of display architecture. The **elevation** is composed of a central tower with flanking galleries, towers, and arcades, and ornamented with busts, statues, and a mosaic (originally a painting by Piloty). In the course of its long construction (1857-74), the architect, Bürklein, was

widely travelled Princess Therese of Bavaria. These treasures were supplemented by such collections as Duke Maximilian of Leuchtenberg's of objects from the Arctic and sub-Arctic regions, and Mother Superior Xaveria Berger's of Indian art, formed during her missionary service. Many research expeditions and acquisition trips have been undertaken by the museum's directors in our own century.

The immense collection now comprises a total of 300,000 objects, with emphases on Africa, Central and South America, Oceania, and South, South East, and East Asia. Although naturally only selections are on permanent view, the range is astonishing enough – from an African pipe bowl to an American Indian tepee, from Persian miniatures to a Greenland kayak, from a Brazilian shrunken head to a Buddha statue. Everyday utensils combine with samples of artistic skill to give a comprehensive picture of each culture represented. The artists of the Munich Blue Rider may have been the first in the twentieth century to derive direct inspiration from these compelling objects, but they certainly will not be the last.

The Professional Association of Visual Artists, an important group on the modern German art scene, has its permanent exhibition space in the east wing.

Maximilian Bridge with Pallas Athena and Maximilianeum, seat of the Bavarian Parliament.

requested to convert his pointed arches into round ones, transforming Neo-Gothic into Neo-Renaissance; he died two years before the project was completed.

In 1876 the building became the home of the Maximilianeum Foundation for Gifted Bavarian Students, which is now located in the extension to the rear. Since 1949 it has been the seat of the Bavarian House of Representatives and Senate. Among the surviving original **furnishings** are frescoes by F. and W. Kaulbach, Seibertz, and Kreling; they may be viewed by prior arrangement with the caretaker's office.

The building provides an impressive backdrop for the statue of Pallas Athene (by Drexler, 1906) on **Maximilian Bridge,** which was built by Zenetti in 1864 and renovated by Thiersch in 1905, and has fine Art Nouveau ornament on its parapets. The rocky ground on the east bank of the Isar, which caused Bürklein so many difficulties during the construction of the Maximilianeum, was landscaped soon after by Karl Effner. **Maximilian Park** has a striking monument to Ludwig II by Rückel (1967), commemorating the king's festival theater project, which was to be located in this area.

View of Maximilian Park.

Monument to King Ludwig II.

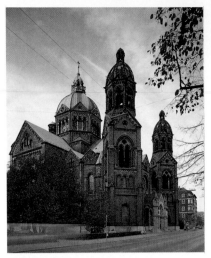

St. Luke's Church.

Müller's Public Baths.

115 St. Luke's Church – *St. Lukas*

Mariannenplatz 3

Historical Revival church architecture at its most effective.

The **exterior** of this striking Protestant church on the left bank of the Isar is dominated by "Romanesque" towers set at an angle to the main body of the church and by a central "Renaissance" cupola, while the **interior** is in the early Gothic style. In its mixture of various historical styles, the building reflects the self-consciousness of an Age of Education. Designed by Albert Schmidt and erected in 1892-97, St. Luke's is a favorite venue for concerts of sacred music.

116 St. Nicholas's Church on the Gasteig

St. Nikolai am Gasteig

Innere Wiener Strasse 1

An intimate ensemble of ecclesiastical buildings across from the Gasteig Arts Center.

Rural St. Nicholas's was once the **church** of a leper colony located far outside the city walls. Renaissance stuccowork, an early Baroque altarpiece, and fine Baroque paintings highlight the beautifully restored building. The adjacent **Altötting Chapel** was built in 1820 on the site of a Baroque structure, but was not converted into its present state until 1926. The **Crucifixion group** at the entrance was originally part of a sequence of sculptures and shrines which stretched along the old Salt Road across the way in imitation of Christ's carrying of the cross to Golgotha. Mary and Joseph are Baroque figures by Luidl (1721); the bronze crucifix is by Panzer (1959).

117 Müller's Public Baths

Müllersches Volksbad

Rosenheimer Strasse 1

Once the most modern indoor bathing establishment in Europe, these baths are still unique for their Art Nouveau design and decor.

It was a full 180 years before the first royal baths in Munich (in Nymphenburg Palace Park; see p. 175) were joined by an establishment open to the public. Donated by a citizen of Munich, Karl Müller, and built by Hocheder in 1897-1901, the **interior** is of an opulence that puts today's public swimming baths to shame. The two halls are justly famous for their relief stuccowork depicting the sun and aquatic animals in a style that manages to combine Neo-Baroque with Art Nouveau without seeming flamboyant. Art Nouveau also characterizes the **exterior,** which extends along the River Isar near Ludwig's Bridge and whose highly original tower is visible from afar. While the Ladies' Pool is still just that, the Gentlemen's Pool has since been opened to both sexes; Saturday is nude bathing day.

St. Nicholas's Church with Altötting Chapel.

Gentlemen's Pool in Müller's Baths, a fantastic mixture of Art Nouveau and Neo-Baroque.

Father Rhine Fountain, at Ludwig's Bridge.

118 Ludwig's Bridge and Father Rhine Fountain

Ludwigsbrücke,
Vater-Rhein-Brunnen

The place where the city of Munich was born.

This was probably the site of the crossing over the River Isar that Henry the Lion established in 1158. Having destroyed the bridge further to the north, which lay under the jurisdiction of the Bishop of Freising, Henry set up Munich's first market and mint, and so began the long history of the city.

The present **bridge,** which had many predecessors, was build in 1935. Two of its seated figures, allegories of River Shipping and Industry by Eberle and Kaufmann, date from 1892, while the figure of Art, by Dietz, is a much later addition of 1979.

On the limestone island accessible from the bridge is a park with Adolf von Hildebrandt's **Father Rhine Fountain,** created for the city of Salzburg in 1902. Removed from its original site in 1919, the fine bronze figure, inspired by classical models, was brought to Munich and installed on a replica of the original fountain and pedestal.

Deutsches Museum,
Floor Plans

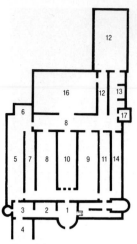

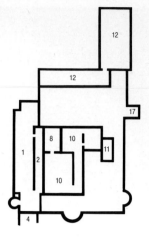

Ground Floor

1 Entrance Hall
2 Natural Resources
3 Mining
4 Crude Oil and Natural Gas
5 Refining
6 Welding, Cutting,
  and Soldering Techniques
7 Machine Tools
8 Engines and Motors
9 High-tension Electricity
10 Shipping
11 Hydraulic Engineering
12 Land Transportation:
   Carriages, Bicycles, Railroads
13 Mining Railroads,
   Model Railway,
   Tunnel Building
14 Roads and Bridges
16 Aviation
17 Tower

Basement

1 Mining
2 Ore Preparation
4 Oil and Gas
8 Motors/Steam Engines
10 Shipping
11 Hydraulic Engineering
12 Motor Vehicles

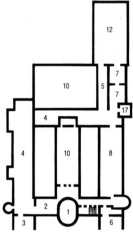

First Floor

1 Hall of Honor
2 Scientific Instruments
3 New Energy Sources and
  Technology
4 Physics
5 Atomic and Nuclear Physics
6 Applied Chemistry
7 Musical Instruments
8 Scientific Chemistry
10 Aviation
12 Communications
   Technology
17 Tower

Second Floor

1 Ceramics
2 Glass
3 Paper
4 Writing and Printing Methods
5 Photography
6 Textiles
7 Space Travel
8 Mechanical Toys
9 Altamira Cave
17 Tower

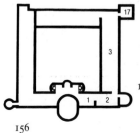

Third Floor

1 Weights and Measures
2 Chronography
3 Agricultural Engineering
17 Tower

Fifth Floor

18 Astronomy

Sixth Floor

19 Planetarium

Deutsches Museum with (from left to right) Exhibition Building, Library, Convention Hall.

119 Deutsches Museum
Museum Island/Museumsinsel

The leading museum of technology on the Continent and, with about 1.5 million visitors each year, the most popular museum in the Federal Republic of Germany. A treasure-trove of human discovery and invention, and a must for every visitor to Munich.

Though its cornerstone was laid during the imperial era, in 1906, the Deutsches Museum was not inaugurated until 1925, under the auspices of the new republic. Its founder, Oskar von Miller, canvassed the entire country for donations and, in 1903, founded a "Museum of Masterworks of Science and Technology" with the declared intention of putting science at everyone's fingertips. It was an unprecedented idea at the time – machines would be shown in operation, physical experiments be demonstrated, and a

Deutsches Museum: First motorized car by Karl Benz, 1886, in the Motor Vehicles Hall (above) and Otto Hahn's worktable with experimental set-up to split uranium atoms, 1938 (below).

Deutsches Museum:
1 S 3/6 passenger locomotive, J. A. Maffei
   Co., Munich, 1912.
2 Loading coal trucks in a 19th-century mine.
3 Planetarium.
4 Rotary drill for oil prospecting, c. 1960.
5 View of the new Aviation Hall, opened in
   1984.
6 Hall of Shipping and Navigation.
7 Motor Vehicles Hall with vintage cars.

3

1

2

4

5

6

phenomenon like electricity explained by a tangible shock. Miller's conception was so successful that this wonderful world of technology is now the most popular museum in the Federal Republic of Germany – a museum where children rapidly become experts and grown-ups become children again.

The core of the great **complex** – the Exhibition Building, with its Meteorological Tower – was built to designs by Gabriel von Seidl in 1908-14: a stately Neo-Baroque edifice that has since become just as much a Munich landmark as New City Hall. The extensions planned from the outset, a Library Building

7

(1932) and a Convention Hall (1935), were designed by Bestelmeyer in the Neoclassical style typical of the 1930s. A Motor Vehicle Building was added in 1938 and a Hall of Aviation and Space Travel in 1979-82.

Today's museum presents a dazzling spectacle, with 16,000 items in an exhibition space of almost 43,000 square feet. The hypothetical visitor who stopped for a moment before each of the exhibits would require over a month to see them all! Our recommendation is that you select points of interest from the huge **collections★** beforehand, whether it be Foucault's Pendulum, a demonstration of the earth's rotation you would otherwise have to go to Leningrad to see, or a Faraday Cage that has survived countless 300,000-volt lightning flashes. You can also stand at the helm of an ocean liner and work the rudder, marvel at the primitive equipment that Otto Hahn used to split the atom for the first time in 1938, or experience the sensation of weightlessness in a space-flight simulation chamber.

In addition to such classical departments as those devoted to motors and engines, mining, road, bridge and waterway engineering, physics, chemistry, electrical engineering, and photography – not to mention a collection of musical instruments where technology meets art – the latest developments in such modern fields as space travel, atomic and nuclear physics, electronics, and automation and computer technology are illustrated in a way intelligible to the layman. Among the museum's main attractions are a full-scale replica of a nineteenth-century mine; the aviation hall, which was redesigned in 1984; the new exhibition spaces for motor vehicles and

Gasteig Arts Center: Detail of facade.

ships, which were reopened after conversion in 1986; and the model railway, with its 800 feet of track on a 430-square-foot layout.

Enthusiasts, researchers, and specialists will feel particularly attracted by the extensive study collections, which contain a total of 50,000 items. Whatever your passion – autographs or documents, plans or corporate trademarks, watermarks or ornate paper, portraits or visual documents, medallions or commemorative coins – you are sure to discover treasures here. An Aviation and Space Travel Archive and a Film and Recorded Sound Archive offer an abundance of valuable source material on the history of technology, much of it available only here.

120 Gasteig Arts Center
Kulturzentrum am Gasteig
Am Gasteig

A modern temple of the muses dedicated to all the arts, especially music.

This modern, brick-red fortress was built in 1985 on the site where the old Salt Road once descended a steep incline ("Gacher Steig," or Gasteig for short) to the customs officer's gate. Its connection with the most evanescent of the arts, music, may not be immediately apparent, yet behind the polygonal "apse" that towers menacingly over the River Isar is a concert hall complete with foyers and great staircase. Like the rest of the building, it is constructed from rough-cast concrete, glass, and brick facings that consciously allude to Munich's Cathedral. The wood-panelled auditorium of **Philharmonic Hall,** opening out like a great seashell, has an intimate atmosphere despite its seating capacity of 2,500, and, indeed, is the only really lucid space in this labyrinthine building by architects Raue, Rollenhagen, Lindemann, and Grossmann.

The extensive complex on Rosenheim Hill is centered around an open-air forum, with stairs and ramps giving access to the various sections of the building. Besides Philharmonic Hall, the Arts Center houses the Carl Orff Hall, with a stage for drama productions; the Black Box studio theater; the Richard Strauss Conservatory, with a small concert hall and classrooms; the Adult Education Center; and the central branch of the Municipal Library. Founded in 1843, the Municipal Library contains 400,000 volumes all told, with a reference section numbering 130,000 volumes and a reading room with 700 periodicals.

Its many events in the fields of music, theater, and cinema, together with the educational opportunities it offers, have made "The Gasteig" a popular and lively center. And the view of the towers of Munich to be had through the windows of its "apse" is one of the finest in town.

Gasteig Arts Center: Philharmonic Hall, auditorium seating 2,500.

121 Üblacker House and Kriechbaum Cottage

Üblacker-Häusl, Kriechbaumhof

Preysingstrasse 58 and 71

Interesting survivors of public housing in old Munich suburbs.

Although Preysingstrasse begins in a rather staid urbanity, it ends with little one-storey houses with dormer roofs – old dwellings of a type built by the city during the eighteenth century and sold cheaply to working-class families who could not afford to live in Munich itself. The Haidhausen district, formerly known as "Broken Glass Hill," still contains a number of these cottages. This one, restored and authentically furnished, now serves as a **Public Housing Museum** and presents regular special exhibitions.

Across the way is the **Kriechbaum Cottage**, which was removed from its original site in 1978 and restored here in 1986. This almost

300-year-old building is the last surviving example of the wooden architecture once so typical of the rural districts of Au and Haidhausen. Its characteristic outside staircases and arcades, decorative as they are, were actually built to make the most of the limited space. The house now contains the offices of the Young Alpinists Association.

Üblacker House:
A dwelling once typical of the area.

Central Station, South Cemetery, Theresa Meadows

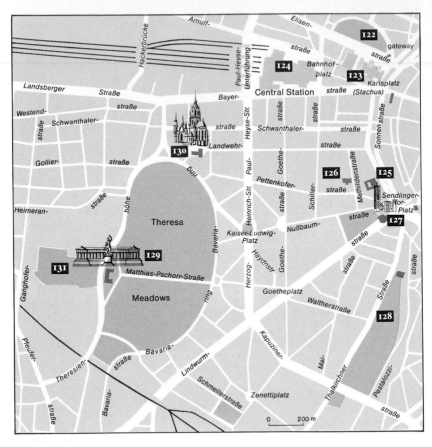

Gateway to the Old Botanical Garden.

122 Old Botanical Garden
Alter Botanischer Garten

Between Elisen- and Sophienstrasse

An island of calm in the downtown rush.

"Flourishing genera cast on inspiriting soil were here united at the beck of King Maximilian Joseph, 1812" – a free rendering of Goethe's Latin on the **gateway** across from the Courts of Justice. The poet wrote these verses at the behest of the Academy of Sciences when their members were unable to come up with a suitable dedication. Designed in a foursquare Neo-Grecian style by Herigoyen (1812), the portal once led to a Botanical Garden laid out by Sckell and

View over Karlsplatz ("Stachus") to the Courts of Justice, by Friedrich von Thiersch, 1891–98.

planted by von Schrank, which was transferred to Nymphenburg in 1914 [No. 136]. A huge Crystal Palace stood on this site from 1854; used for industrial and then for art exhibitions, it was destroyed by fire in 1931 together with many irreplaceable paintings. The present **park,** with Park Café and Neptune Fountain (by Wackerle), was landscaped by Troost in 1937.

123 Courts of Justice – *Justizpalast*
Elisenstrasse 1a and Prielmayerstrasse 7

A monumental Neo-Baroque building and one of the most imposing specimens of Historical Revival courthouse architecture on the Continent.

With its bulging central bay topped by allegorical figures, the facade of the Courts of Justice dominates Karlsplatz. Although definitely in the heavy imperial manner of late nineteenth-century Germany, the building does have a certain dashing brilliance. Its architect, Thiersch, skillfully wove a variety of architectural motifs from the Baroque period into a basically Neo-Renaissance design. His cupola in glass and iron, by contrast, was an innovation at the time (1891-98). The vestibule, stairways, and courtrooms were all restored in a simplified form after the Second World War.

With its clock-towers and stepped gables, the **New Court Building** to the rear (Prielmayerstrasse 5; ill., p. 164), likewise designed by Thiersch and built in 1905, is in the Neo-Gothic style often used for public buildings at the time. Its brickwork is very much in the local tradition, alluding directly to the Cathedral.

Old Botanical Garden: Neptune Fountain.

163

Munich Central Station and skyline by night, seen from Hacker Bridge.

New Court Building (described on p. 163).

I24 Central Station – *Hauptbahnhof*
Bahnhofsplatz 2

Hectic activity behind an impassive facade – Munich's main station is the second busiest in the Federal Republic in terms of annual passenger traffic.

Begun in 1847 by Bürklein and completed by Graff in 1884, Munich's first railroad station consisted of a loose collection of iron-girdered sheds, pavilions, arcades, and terminal buildings. Today's station has been under construction since 1950. Its **main facade,** a grid design by Gerbl with a glass mosaic by R. Geiger, was constructed in 1955-1960 in front of the new **Station Building** (1953) and was followed in 1959-60 by the **Platform Building.** A thorough modernization, begun in 1983, is expected to be finished by 1990.

I25 Postal Savings Office
Postgiroamt

Sonnenstrasse 24

A fine specimen of Munich's Maximilian Style of architecture.

Like a section of Maximilianstrasse gone astray, this **facade** presents a row of tall windows with flat pointed arches, separated by slender pilasters that lend the brick structure a lacy lightness. Designed by Bürklein, the building was erected in 1853-56 as a kind of trial run in the Maximilian Style [see No. 108]. It served as an Obstetrics Hospital, before being converted into a post office in 1929. The statue before the entrance, *Man with Pigeons,* is by Martin Mayer (1979).

Postal Savings Office, 1853-56.

126 St. Elisabeth's Church
Mathildenstrasse 10

The last Rococo church in Munich.

The design of this church by J.M. Fischer (using his favorite centralized groundplan), its furnishings by Ignaz Günther, and the frescoes by Matthäus Günther, all date from about 1760. Restoration work after severe bombing in the Second World War included the **interior** (without the frescoes), the high altar (partially reconstructed), the graceful pulpit, and the imposing **facade** of 1790, an extremely late Rococo design that already contains a strong admixture of Neoclassical stringency.

Facade of St. Elisabeth's Church, 1790.

St. Matthew's Church:
Interior (below left) and exterior (right).

127 St. Matthew's Church
St. Matthäus
Nussbaumstrasse 1

A modern church that dominates Sendlinger-Tor-Platz.

The curves and dips of its roofline have earned this episcopal Protestant church the irreverent nickname of "Martin Luther's Roller Coaster." The campanile and the church itself, with asymmetrical exterior forms on a centralized groundplan, were designed by Gustav Gsaenger and built in reinforced concrete in 1953-55 as a replacement for the original St. Matthew's, which had been demolished by the Nazis. One of the first churches constructed after the war, it has had great influence on modern ecclesiastical architecture in Munich. The apse mosaic was created by Angela Gsaenger.

128 South Cemetery
Südlicher Friedhof
Thalkirchner Strasse 17

An historical cemetery with the graves of many famous personalities of the eighteenth and nineteenth centuries in styles ranging from Neoclassical to Art Nouveau.

Gabriel von Seidl, who loved opulence in both his architecture and his life, lies here beneath a simple cast-iron cross. Sckell, the famous landscape gardener, shares an all-too narrow stone with his nephew, the painter Rottmann. And the great Neoclassical architect Karl von Fischer had to make do with the thin edge of a monument. Although the tombs of Klenze, Gärtner, and Schwanthaler may be flamboyant, and those of Liebig and Miller rich but reserved, most of the great Munich citizens who lie here are chiefly remembered for their achievements. The

brewers and entrepreneurs, by contrast, have had themselves immortalized larger-than-life, one in his fur coat, another with his arm around the Madonna ...

South Cemetery is a chronicle of Munich history. Once the last resting place of poor people and plague victims, it became a general municipal cemetery in the nineteenth century. Its sarcophagus-shaped plan of 1818-21 was extended by a square addition in the Italian manner in 1845. The connecting hall and central fountain were designed by Gärtner. No longer used for burials, the cemetery, with its lovely old tres, invites a quiet stroll.

St. Stephan's, the cemetery chapel, was built in the seventeenth century and contains eighteenth-century altarpieces.

129 Theresa Meadows – Hall of Fame – Bavaria Statue
Theresienwiese – Ruhmeshalle – Bavaria

For two weeks every year, this is the site of the biggest and most uproarious fair in the world, the Oktoberfest.

When Crown Prince Ludwig married Theresa of Saxe-Hildburghausen on October 17, 1810, the occasion was celebrated by a horse-race, held on meadows that, at the time, lay far outside the city limits. Theresa gave the Meadows their name and the marriage celebrations gave rise to the famous annual Oktoberfest, one of the largest and most colorful public festivals in the world, which is still accompanied every two years by an agricultural exhibition. The temple on Theresa Hill, a Hall of Fame presided over

by a personification of Bavaria, and the Bavaria Ring, originally an elliptical race-course around the Meadows, were inspired by the romantic patriotism that followed the defeat of Napoleon. Perhaps no other place in Munich better illustrates its dual character of rural town and seat of monarchy.

Hall of Fame★ Sited on the natural plateau above the Meadows is one of Klenze's finest buildings – a three-part Doric temple erected in 1843-53 to accommodate a pantheon of renowned Bavarians. The seventy-seven busts now on display extend from the late medieval painter Martin Schongauer to the turn-of-the-century writer Ludwig Thoma. On the cornice above the colonnades are reliefs depicting the Goddess of Victory and scenes from the history of art and science, religion and trade. Allegories of the Bavarian provinces adorn the pediments above the two wings. All of the sculptural work was executed to the designs of Ludwig Schwanthaler. In the ancient Greek manner, the temple frames a colossal statue: the figure of Bavaria, who stands atop a long flight of steps leading down to the Meadows.

Bavaria★ Klenze wished to have her wrapped in diaphanous Greek drapery and the king envisaged her as an imperious Roman; but Ludwig Schwanthaler made a Teutonic amazon of her. Concealed inside the awe-inspiring goddess are steps leading up to the crown, which not only affords a wonderful view over the city, but also enables the workmanship to be examined in detail. The statue, created in 1843-50, is a brilliant achievement of iron casting from the Munich foundry of Ferdinand von Miller and Stiglmaier. Bavaria is sixty feet tall, tips the scale at about seven-and-a-half tons of iron cannon

A peaceful fall day in the historical South Cemetery.

Theresa Hill, with Klenze's Hall of Fame and Schwanthaler's statue of Bavaria.

Bavaria Statue lit up at night.

Marble busts of the great in the Hall of Fame.

salvaged from foundered men-of-war, and was cast in six sections – an adventurous and difficult undertaking. But there were moments of comic relief, too. When they hoisted her head up from the pit, the watching crowd was astonished to see Miller's foundrymen and children clamber out!

130 St. Paul's Church
Sankt-Pauls-Platz 11

A late Gothic Revival church in a beautiful urban setting.

A striking focal point on the north side of Theresa Meadows, St. Paul's Church was built in 1892-1906 in the suburban residential area that developed here around the turn of the century. The building was partially financed by the neighborhood's well-to-do inhabitants. As the Historical Revival was

Oktoberfest on Theresa Meadows: Fairgrounds by night (above) and scene in a beer tent (below).

nearing its end, the architect of Munich's New City Hall, Hauberisser, created this soaring basilica with a **twin-towered facade** and an impressive dome-capped spire in free adaptation of models in the Rhenish Gothic style. The **interior,** lucidly proportioned in warm sandstone, once contained fine contemporaneous works of art. A few of these have survived: the *Altarpiece of the Virgin* by Hackl to the right, the *St. Joseph Altarpiece* by Buscher to the left of the choir, and a *Pietà* by B. Schmitt in the War Memorial Chapel. The Crucifix in the choir arch is a modern work of 1960, by Filler.

131 Exhibition Park

Ausstellungspark
Theresienhöhe 15

International fairgrounds set in a spacious landscaped park.

E. von Seidl, Bertsch, and other architects laid out the exhibition grounds in 1908 as a pleasant park with a variety of buildings for exhibition and recreational purposes, including a very popular Artists' Theater that was destroyed in 1944. Today it is an enormous area with modern high-capacity structures whose exhibition space totals about twenty-five acres. Among the fairs held here on a regular basis are the Analytica, Bauma, Ispo, Ikofa, International Crafts Fair, etc.

St. Paul's Church.

Exhibition Park, the site of international trade fairs.

Neuhausen, Nymphenburg, Blutenburg, Pipping

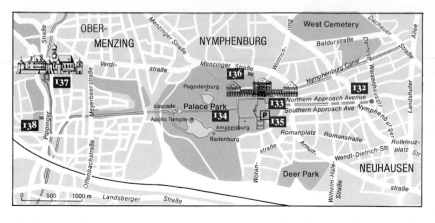

St. Hubert Fountain: Archer, by Hildebrand.

132 St. Hubert Fountain

Hubertusbrunnen

Waisenhausstrasse

A masterpiece of the Historical Revival style.

The Nymphenburg Canal, diverted in 1701 from the River Würm near Pasing, runs through the palace park and crescent, flows on between the approach avenues to the palace, and ends in a pond in front of the St. Hubert Fountain in Neuhausen. The

graceful, pavilion-like **Pump House★** by Hildebrand (1907) would seem to have been created specially for this site, although it was actually intended for the English Garden and stood in front of the Bavarian National Museum for many years. Also by Hildebrand are the fine bronze sculptures symbolizing both the hunt and the ages of man: the Stag of St. Hubert★ inside, and the Wood Nymph★, Hunter★, Amazon★, and Archer★ in the niches (1911-17).

133 Nymphenburg Palace

The summer residence of the Bavarian electors and kings. A bold Baroque design with a frontage almost 800 yards in length and with interiors in styles ranging from High Baroque to Neoclassical. Birthplace of the "Fairy-tale King," Ludwig II, and site of Ludwig I's Gallery of Beauties.

The history of this brilliant Baroque palace began when Elector Ferdinand Maria presented the new country house of Nymphenburg to his wife Henriette Adelaide on the birth of his heir, Max Emanuel. When Max Emanuel ascended the throne he enlarged his mother's chateau, by symmetrical additions, into a great **palace complex★** that looked out upon a landscaped garden interspersed with fanciful pavilions [No. 134]. As unfortunate in political affairs as he was enthusiastic about architecture, Max Emanuel inspired the artists whom he had brought with him from France, or who had worked at the French Court, to feverish activity, at both Nymphenburg and Schleissheim [No. 145]. Among those who invested their talents in these two grand palaces were the architect Effner, the sculptors de Groff and Dubut, the cabinetmaker Pichler, the fresco-painter Amigoni, and the landscape architect Girard.

The original building by Barelli and Zuccalli (1664-74), consisting of a central cube

Nymphenburg Palace: View from the east, on the approach from town.

with terraced flights of steps, was later redesigned by Effner. The galleries were added in 1704; then, from 1715 on, the four staggered pavilions, followed by the royal stables to the south and the orangery and hermitage to the north. The **crescent,** a semicircle of residences for court officials extending at a radius of 1,600 feet around the garden and fountains on the side of the palace facing the city, was built from 1729 to 1758. It was an architectural coup of unparalleled boldness at the time. (The central building on the north side has housed the Porcelain Manufactory since 1761.)

Nymphenburg Palace

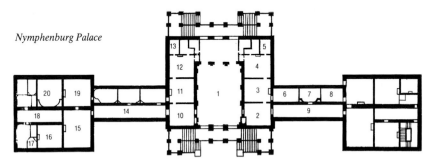

1 Great Hall
  ("Steinerner Saal")

North wing

2 First Antechamber
3 Second Antechamber
4 Former Bedroom
5 North Cabinet
6 Max Emanuel's Gallery of Beauties
7 Coats of Arms Room
8 Karl Theodor Room
9 North Gallery

South wing

10 First Antechamber
11 Second Antechamber
12 Bedroom
13 Chinese Lacquer Cabinet
14 South Gallery
15 King Ludwig I's Gallery of Beauties
16 "Maserzimmer"
17 Cabinet
18 Small Gallery
19 Blue Salon
20 Bedroom

The center and culmination of the **interior** is the Great Hall★ (**1**), whose opulent Rococo decoration includes a principal fresco, *Nymphs Paying Homage to the Goddess Flora,* which celebrates the spirit of the place. The swirling stucco is by Zimmermann

Helene Sedlmayr, from Ludwig I's Gallery of Beauties.

(main hall) and Feichtmayer (gallery) and dates from 1757. Points of special interest in the northern rooms are Pichler's white and gold panelling (**2**); Brussels tapestries (**3**); Max Emanuel's Small Gallery of Beauties, with nine portraits by Gobert of ladies-in-waiting to Louis XIV (**4**); Max Emanuel's turning workshop (**5**); the views of towns by Beich in the gallery (**9**); and the elector's Large Gallery of Beauties, with five young ladies who owe their striking family resemblance to a request that Gobert model their features on those of Louis XIV's daughter, the subject of the first portrait (**6**).

The southern rooms include ceiling frescoes by Triva (**10, 11, 12**), a Chinese Lacquer Cabinet with lacquerwork by Hörringer and stucco by Feichtmayer (**13**), and, in the gallery, views of Bavarian palaces by Beich (**14**). Yet the main attraction is naturally Ludwig I's Gallery of Beauties★ (**15**). These thirty-six noblewomen and burghers' daughters, fashionable ladies and old-fashioned country girls, sat for Stieler between 1827 and 1850. Among them are the king's loves Helene Sedlmayr, the cobler's daughter who has gone down in history as "The Lovely Munich Girl," and the "Spanish" dancer Lola Montez, whose affair with the king caused his downfall. However, the collection was

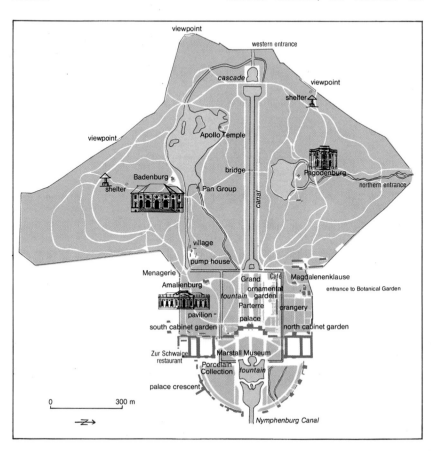

Nymphenburg Canal

Nymphenburg Palace: Great Hall, with stuccowork and frescoes by Johann Baptist Zimmermann.

Cascade in the Palace Park.

intended not as a beauty contest, but as a record of current ideals of feminine loveliness. A high point in the sequence of Neoclassical rooms (**16-20**) is the chamber in which King Ludwig II was born on August 25, 1845 (**20**).

134 Nymphenburg Palace Park and its Pavilions

Nymphenburger Schlosspark und Parkschlösser

An enormous park, created by one of the finest landscape architects of the period and of such variety as to provide a lesson in European landscape design from the formal Italian garden and the French grand parterre to the English landscape garden.

As the palace grew, so did the **park★** to its west. In 1715 Girard began to remodel the original small, geometrically arranged Italian garden into an ornamental park in the French Baroque manner, in which Venetian gondolas glided along the canal and courtiers danced among the boskets. A hundred years

Amalienburg: The loveliest Rococo pleasure-seat, a masterpiece by Cuvilliés.

passed, the gardener's and the king's ideal shifted from nurture to nature, and Sckell transformed and extended the park into an English landscape garden. What he gained in naturalness, however, was paid for by the loss of the clear relationship between park, palace, and pavilions.

An impressive central axis is still provided by the canal, which extends from the *grand parterre* to the distant cascade and, on the opposite side of the palace, continues between the lanes of a broad approach. The French garden in front of the palace and the marble cascade, both authentic Baroque creations, are populated by statues of ancient gods and goddesses by Boos, Straub, Marchiori, Volpini, and de Groff. Basins and fountains, lakes and ponds, bridges, pavilions, miniature and ornamental gardens (with coffeehouse) lend the park a fascinating variety. Its gems are four small, free-standing buildings that were once surrounded by

superb formal gardens – the Amalienburg and Badenburg to the south of the canal, and the Pagodenburg and Magdalenenklause (Magdalene's Hermitage) to its north.

Amalienburg★

A Rococo gem of the first order.

The Rococo splendor of this hunting lodge (built in 1734-39) was the gift of a melancholy prince, Karl Albrecht (Emperor Charles VII from 1742 to 1745), to his wife Amalia, a daughter of Emperor Joseph I. In a ground-plan that ingeniously combines rectangle and circle, the walls of the building swing out with incomparable grace in a convex curve on one side, which is matched by a concave one on the other. Every detail, from the curved projections above the windows to the crown on the roof, reveals the infallible hand of a master – Cuvilliés the Elder. Stepping inside, one enters a dream – the circular Hall of Mir-

Pagodenburg: Embodiment of the intimate late Baroque Maison de plaisance.

Badenburg: An indoor swimming pool of the late Baroque period.

Hall of Mirrors, Amalienburg: An etherial fantasy in the Bavarian national colors, silver and blue.

rors*, whose carvings, stucco ornament, and mirrors seem to dissolve the solid walls. The silver-chased decor contains imaginative depictions of the pleasures of hunting, gardening, and dining, as do the other rooms – the Blue Cabinet, the *retirade,* the Hunting Room (with paintings by Horemans), and the Pheasant Room. The jewel-like brilliance of stucco by J.B. Zimmermann and carving by Dietrich envelops all these rooms. Even the kitchen, with its blue-and-white and multi-colored Delft tiles, is exquisite.

Badenburg*

The first heated "indoor swimming pool" of the modern age.

Bathing as recreation and courtly spectacle – that was the original purpose of the "Bathing Pavilion." The bath itself is a tiled, heated pool – a rarity at the time – and occupies the lower part of the room. A spectator's gallery runs around the upper part of the room, which contains a ceiling fresco by Bertin whose gods and nymphs were reflected in the

175

water below. Set in the brilliant white of the banqueting hall are mythological figures in stucco by Dubut and a fresco by Amigoni. The building was designed by Effner and erected in 1719-21. It was simplified somewhat by Klenze in the nineteenth century.

Pagodenburg★

Rococo à la chinoise – the most individual and intimate of Max Emanuel's buildings.

French outside, Far Eastern inside, the "Pagoda Pavilion" was the first of the four pavilions to be erected in Nymphenburg park (by Effner, in 1716-19) and is, perhaps, the loveliest. Its unique groundplan – an octagon with square extensions on four sides – gave rise, in the upper storey, to two hexagonal salons with niches and to a Chinese Cabinet★, exquisite in design and decoration. In comparison, the blue and white central salon on the ground floor, with its Dutch faience tiles and ornamental painting by Gumpp, seems decidedly European.

Magdalenenklause

This memento mori *of a prince who loved life's pleasures is one of the first artificial ruins in the history of European landscape gardening.*

A symbol of transience to offset the earthly delights embodied in the elector's three pavilions in the park, this artificial ruin is a purposely timeless conglomeration of Romanesque, Gothic, and Moorish forms. The chapel is an anchorite's grotto in tufa, seashells, and pebbles; the living quarters are monastically plain. Although it was dedicated to the lovely penitent, Mary Magdalene, the prevailing melancholy mood of the hermitage (built by Effner in 1725-26) was meant to help the aging Max Emanuel achieve self-denial. By the time it was dedicated in 1728, however, he was dead.

135 Marstall Museum and Porcelain Collection

Marstallmuseum, Porzellansammlung

South wing of the palace

The royal stables and coach house contain a museum of transportation in the grand manner.

The main attractions of the museum are the state coach built for the marriage of Ludwig II, which never took place, and the king's state and "nymph" sleighs – gleaming fairy-tale conveyances designed by the director of the Court Theater, Seitz. Equally splendid is the Baroque coronation coach★ built in Paris by the Goblin firm in 1741 for Elector Karl Albrecht's coronation as emperor. The two Munich coronation coaches made for Max I Joseph (1813 and 1818), more graceful and certainly more maneuverable, are creations in the Empire style by Ginzrot of Strasbourg,

with figurines by Franz Jakob Schwanthaler. By this time such *grandes carosses* had almost relinquished the roads to smart coupés, many fine examples of which are on view here. Wintertime once meant sleighrides in such fabulous craft as the Rococo sleigh by Straub, built in 1740. Harnesses, embroidered saddlecloths, sets of sleighbells, and related paintings and designs round off the display.

Housed in the columned rooms of the former royal stables, the collection of horse-drawn vehicles can hold its own with those in Vienna, Lisbon, and Leningrad. And like them, it has a long tradition, extending back to the Reiche Remise (ornate coach house), which Elector Maximilian I installed on the eastern side of the Residence in the early seventeenth century.

Nymphenburg Porcelain – Bäuml Collection★

A Mecca for everyone who loves fine china, this collection of original Nymphenburg pieces is a worthy counterpart to the Meissen collection in Lustheim Palace.

Since 1986 some 1,200 pieces of "Old Nymphenburg," from the Rococo period to Art Nouveau, have been on view in the rooms over the Marstall Museum. They include Bustelli's delightfully costumed Commedia dell'arte players★ and his enchanting pastoral scenes; Auliczek's charming figurines of the four seasons; miniature versions on porcelain of famous paintings in the Alte Pinakothek; elegant and opulent sets of state tableware with amorous scenes; portraits of the royal family; and depictions of architecture and landscape. These and many, many more provide a wonderfully colorful and complete his-

Porcelain Collection: Mars, *by Auliczek, c. 1770.*

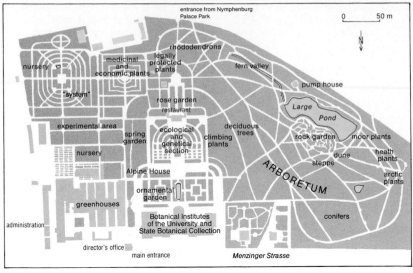

Plan of the Botanical Garden, Menzinger Strasse, Nymphenburg.

Majolica Cockatoo by Josef Wackerle, 1914.

tory of the Nymphenburg Porcelain Manufactory since its founding in the year 1747.

Surprisingly, this priceless collection began as a matter of necessity. In 1888 Albert Bäuml leased the ailing Nymphenburg enterprise from the state and, finding that even the production specimens had been sold, went off in search of them. The younger members of his family then began collecting systematically, reaping such praise from experts that they decided to make their treasures available to the public.

136 Botanical Garden

Botanischer Garten

Menzinger Strasse 65

Fascinating at every season, Munich's Botanical Garden is one of the largest and most beautifully landscaped in Europe: an aesthetic and an educational experience – and a perfect place to relax.

In 1914 the Old Botanical Garden on busy Karlsplatz was superseded by the present one in Nymphenburg. Karl von Goebel commissioned the landscape architect Holfelder to lay out this sixty-acre **park,** paying equal attention to scientific and aesthetic criteria – a guideline that has continued to inform all subsequent alterations.

In front of the building containing the Botanical Institute of the university and the State Botanical Collection lies the **Ornamental Garden,** an ornamental bed whose blaze of color changes with the seasons, from spring tulips, hyacinths, and pansies to dahlias, asters, and zinnia in late summer. The playful majolica figures were designed by Wackerle in 1914 and produced at the nearby Nymphenburg Porcelain Manufactory.

The **Ecological and Genetical Section** illustrates how plants adapt to humid or dry soil and atmospheric conditions, the different types of pollination, the propagation of fruit and seeds, and genetic laws in general. The first months of spring find the **Spring Garden** and the flowers on display in the windows of the **Alpine House** in full bloom, followed in summer by the roses nearby, although the oldest and noblest varieties of rose are gathered in the **Rose Garden** behind the café. No less dazzling in the months of May and June is the **Rhododendron Bower** to the south, which boasts over 150 species.

To the east of the garden's central axis are a selection of the most important plants protected by law in Germany, a section devoted to economic plants (from grain and legumes to herbs and spices), one with medicinal plants grouped according to the substances they contain and the uses to which they are put, and, finally, the "system," which illus-

Botanical Garden: Ornamental garden, with restaurant.

trates the evolution of plants and their diversification.

In the **arboretum** to the west deciduous trees are to be found in the southern section, conifers in the northern. Grouped around the Large Pond are areas demonstrating the geographical distribution of plants, in conditions ranging from arctic and steppe to heath, moor, and dune, and including a rock garden with mountain flora from around the world.

With 6,000 species, the **greenhouses** are among the most amply endowed in Europe. To give just a hint of their abundance: arboreal lilies and leafy succulents, palms and large-stem succulents are gathered in Halls A, B, and C, exotic orchids in House 1, and the stunning Victoria water lilies in House 3. House 5 and 6 offer a range of African succulents and small cacti, as well as succulents and large cacti from the Americas, while Houses 9 and 12 contain palm ferns and tropical ferns.

which, however, could destroy the charm of the whole. The **manor house** now accommodates the International Youth Library, the tower gate houses a small museum devoted to the writer Erich Kästner, and the outbuildings contain a concert hall and a restaurant.

The finest feature is the **Chapel**★ of the Most Holy Trinity, a work by the same masons' lodge that built Munich Cathedral. This simple brick building is gracefully topped by a domed turret and ornamented with a painted tracery frieze and coats of arms. The gleam of light on gold pervades the delicate interior, with its webbed vaulting and filigree altarpiece superstructures. The altarpieces are by the Polish artist Jan Polack, *the* painter of the Late Gothic period in Munich. His rendering of the Throne of Mercy in the main altarpiece★ is unforgettable: the crescent curve of Christ's body resting in the lap of God is flanked by The Coronation of the Virgin and The Baptism of Christ, while the reverse sides of the wings

137 **Blutenburg Castle**
Schloss Blutenburg

A Late Gothic jewel in its own right, this island castle has a chapel of great artistic value.

Preferring "lovely ladies, doves, and the music of the lute" to the internecine conflict that rent the House of Wittelsbach, Duke Sigismund relinquished his coregency and retired to his beloved Blutenburg. This **hunting seat**★ was built in 1431-40 by his father, Albrecht III, on an old fortified island in the River Würm. Sigismund added a chapel in 1488, and later periods brought many less fortunate alterations and additions, none of

Rhododendron blossoms in the Botanical Garden.

Blutenburg: Interior of the Late Gothic chapel with altarpieces by Jan Polack.

depict Duke Sigismund and his name saint. The glowing colors and dramatic compositions set off such delightful details as the attributes held by the Evangelists in the predella. The same master's touch is seen in the altarpieces on either side of the choir arch.

An unknown follower of Grasser created the superb sculptures on the walls: statues of the apostles and of the Risen Christ, as well as the famous Blutenberg Madonna★, a pious burgher woman in a cloak draped in lovely folds, very reserved in her sorrow. The stained glass windows – perhaps designed by Grasser – depict events from the Life of Christ with the Wittelsbach coat of arms above each scene. Like everything in the church, the surviving fragments of wall-paintings – probably by Polack – date from 1488-1495. The chapel is all of a piece, everything from the tiny figures in the superstructures of the altarpieces to the emblazoned corbels contributing to the unity of the whole. The spirit and inwardness of the Late Gothic era have seldom found such pure expression.

Blutenburg: Lovely island castle in the River Würm.

138 St. Wolfgang's in Pipping

Pippinger Strasse 49a

A village church donated by a duke and perfectly preserved in every detail of its Late Gothic decoration and furnishings.

A short distance up the River Würm from Blutenburg Chapel stands Duke Sigismund's rural church in the hamlet of Pipping. Its Late Gothic charm is almost a match for that of the chapel in terms of glowing color, delicate tracery, and finely carved sculpture. The spire once signalled refuge to pilgrims on their way to St. Wolfgang in the Salzkammergut, Austria. Thanks to expert restoration, the beauties of the **interior** seem as fresh as the day they were created – the main altarpiece, with its central sculpture of St. Wolfgang healing and its painted wings depicting scenes from his vita with great immediacy in realistic Salzkammergut landscapes; the frescoes of the Passion and of the Death of the Virgin in the choir; the carved side altars, with images of the Virgin with Sts. Wolfgang and Leonhard (left) and Christ with Sts. Anthony and Lawrence (right); and the perspective wall-painting of the stone pulpit's soundboard, a playful piece of *trompe-l'œil*. Opinions differ as to the authorship of all these works, but it is certain that Duke Sigismund employed Munich artists. The architect was probably Jörg von Halsbach; the church and its altarpieces date from 1480-85.

St. Wolfgang's in the village of Pipping.

The Blutenburg Madonna *in the chapel at Blutenburg.*

Pipping Church: Late Gothic altarpiece.

Olympic Park, BMW Museum, Luitpold Park

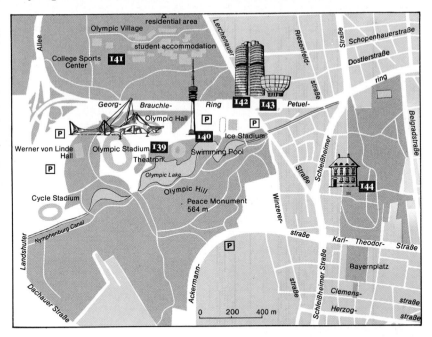

139 Olympic Park

Site of the XXth Summer Olympics in 1972, this beautifully landscaped park is accentuated by a spectacular suspension roof over its main sports facilities. The Olympic Stadium now hosts more athletic events annually than any other stadium in West Germany. Its pool has been called "Europe's loveliest indoor-outdoor swimming pool."

This area, formerly known as Oberwiesenfeld, was once the site of Munich's first airport, where the original Zeppelin landed in 1909. It was also a training ground for the Bavarian Army, and a favorite spot for generations of kite-flying boys and girls. After the Second World War, the vacant fields provided just the features that Munich needed to win the 1966 competition for the next Summer Games – they were close to town, easily accessible, and green.

Facing page:
Enjoying the sun at Olympic Stadium.

The transformation of the amorphous terrain into a landscape garden was planned by Behnisch and Partners and carried out in 1968-72. A 200-foot-high pile of rubble, the remains of bombed-out Munich, became **Olympic Hill,** and the arrow-straight Nymphenburg Canal was excavated to form a meandering chain of lakes. These features, plus improved access roads, have since made this recreation area into one of the country's most popular and attractive, hosting Federal League soccer games and world championships, ice-skating revues and congresses, theater and concerts, rock and pop festivals, sports-car shows, speedway races, swimming meets, six-day bicycle races – sporting and social events of every possible description.

Beneath Olympic Tower [No. 140], the **Suspension Roof★**, an engineering marvel of breathtaking beauty, spreads over the three main park facilities: the **Olympic Stadium,** which seats 75,000 spectators; the **Olympic Hall,** a multipurpose structure with a capacity of 14,000; and the **Olympic Swimming Pool,** with five pools and seats for 2,000 spectators. All three were also designed by Behnisch and Partners and built in 1968-72. To the east lies the **Ice Stadium,** a 1967 design by Schütze which was expanded in 1972 to seat 7,000, and an adjacent open-air skating rink which received an elegantly arched tent-roof in 1983 (by Ackermann and Partners, and Schlaich and Partners). To the west is the **Olympic Cycle Stadium** (1970-72, by Schürmann) which seats 5,000. North of the main facilities, on the other side of the ring road,

Olympic Tower (951 feet high).

141 Olympic Village
Olympisches Dorf

Between Georg-Brauchle-Ring,
Lerchenauer and Moosacher Strasse,
and Landshuter Allee

Conceived to provide its inhabitants with "better views, less noise, and more greenery," this modern residential complex was superbly planned for a change in function after the Olympic Games.

The 1972 Games were touted as an "Olympics of short distances," which was particularly true of the proximity of the Olympic Village to the competition areas. Crossing Georg-Brauchle-Ring, you come first to the former **Women's Village** (1969-71, by Wirsing and Eckert), homes for 1,800 female athletes which now serve as student accommodations and which have been imaginatively decorated by their inhabitants. Behind them lies the **Men's Village** (by Heinle, Wischer and Partners), designed to house 9,000 Olympic competitors and now used as a residential quarter. Between the two complexes, at 31 Connolly Strasse, two **memorial plaques** in German and Hebrew recall the terrorist attack on the Israeli team, which interrupted the Games so horrifyingly on September 5, 1972.

142 BMW Headquarters
BMW-Verwaltungszentrum

Petuelring 130

A convincing merger of aesthetics and functionalism, of the arts of engineering and architecture – a modern building that everyone likes!

It was both an original and an appropriate idea to design the offices of an automobile company in the shape of a fanciful four-cylinder engine. Arranged cloverleaf style, the four round, nineteen-storey towers are cantilevered to a central core that is visible at the top. The aluminum-clad structure, illuminated by continuous bands of windows, rises seemingly weightlessly above a long, low factory building. The complex, including the museum [No. 143], was designed by the Viennese architect Schwanzer, and built in 1970-73.

143 BMW Museum
Petuelring 130

No car or motorcycle fan should miss this imaginatively staged show illustrating the history of the Bavarian Motor Works and their epoch-making vehicles.

A perfect complement to the towering BMW headquarters building, this graceful silver chalice, 135 feet in diameter, houses the company's museum. Inside the windowless spaceship, a spiral ramp leads visitors from exhibit

lies the Olympic Village [No. 141], while an open-air theater in the Greek mode, the **Theatron,** nestles on the lakeshore to the south. Atop Olympic Hill, a 1972 sculpture (by Belling) symbolizes rebirth and peace in a flowerlike composition consisting of war debris. At the foot of the Hill, outside the Cycle Stadium, is a graceful bronze sculpture, *Girl Doing a Handstand,* by Martin Mayer (1972).

140 Olympic Tower – *Olympiaturm*

The tallest television tower in the Federal Republic, with a fabulous panoramic view.

On a clear day – which, in Munich, means especially when the *föhn* wind is blowing – you can see up to 250 miles of the Alps from this tower: from the Dachstein across to the peaks of Switzerland. Built in 1965-68, the 951-foot-high tower has two elevators that whisk an annual 1.1 million visitors at a speed of twenty-three feet per second up to its two **platforms,** at 620 and 630 feet above ground level. Seated in the **restaurant** below (a mere 597 feet high) you can enjoy the view over fine food and drink, as your table, the waiters, and everything else slowly revolve around the tower's axis once every 35, 53, or 72 minutes (open daily from 11 a.m.).

to exhibit. The **display** combines the history of automobile and motorcycle engineering with visions of the future, ranging from a 1928 Dixi car to an aerodynamic coupe, from the famous flat-twin motorcycle of 1923 to today's compact drive system, and from 1920s garage production to computerized robot assembly lines. The presentation is brilliant: car models and automobile components revolve soundlessly, and slides and video films flicker over the monitors along the way. The whole culminates in a dazzlingly effective cinemascope show. Founded in 1966, the collection is rearranged every few years to shed light on different aspects of the company's development.

BMW Headquarters and Museum, with automotive design of the future (below).

144 Luitpold Park
with Bamberg House
Karl-Theodor-Strasse and
Brunnerstrasse 2

A Munich park with an architectural feature from the town of Bamberg in north Bavaria.

This **park** in the north of town, which was laid out in 1911 to celebrate the ninetieth birthday of Prince Regent Luitpold, has since grown into a landscape garden of some eighty acres. It includes Schwabing Hill, another of the sites where the debris of bombed Munich came to rest, recalling the city's demise in the Second World War and providing a view of it as it has arisen from the ashes.

The story of **Bamberg House,** located at the west end of the park, is one worth telling. Workers discovered a cache of Baroque busts, heads, herms, stone eagles, and broken ornaments here in 1910. These had belonged to a mansion in the town of Bamberg, owned by a Mr. Böttinger. When his heirs went bankrupt, the house was demolished, and what remained of its facade came to Munich by circuitous paths in 1900. An architect by the name of Rank agreed to buy the pieces and donate them to the city in return for a commission to build a lodge into which they could be incorporated. The lodge was erected in 1912 – a structure in the Franconian Baroque style decorated by an anonymous Munich sculptor. Bamberg House has since been restored to its original function as café and restaurant, with a garden terrace and furnishings in 1920s style. It also contains a delightful Gallery of Cartoons and Caricatures, which puts on popular exhibitions.

Schleissheim and Lustheim Palaces

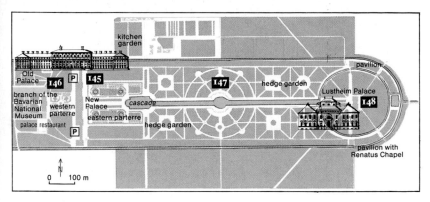

145 New Schleissheim Palace

Elector Max Emanuel's Versailles, the embodiment of an absolute ruler's dreams and a memorial to a man whose reigning passion was art.

Max Emanuel, the "Blue Elector" who joined the Austrians to fight the Turks and then joined the French to fight the Austrians, may not have brought Bavaria much luck in the political arena, but he did give Munich the glory of two Baroque palaces – Schleissheim and Nymphenburg.

Although Max Emanuel's imperial reveries led him to conceive Schleissheim as a gigantic royal residence, debts and exile forced him to reduce his plans – with charming results, it has to be admitted. The **New Palace**, begun in 1701 by the aging Zuccalli and continued by the French-trained Effner from 1719 to 1726 (vestibule and stairwell are nineteenth-century additions, by Klenze), is an exuberantly elaborate structure in the late Baroque and the Rococo styles. Extremely elongated in its proportions – the **facade** is a full 1,100 feet long – and divided into a central tract, connecting wings, and corner pavilions, the building looks west toward the Old Palace,

State Gallery, New Schleissheim Palace: The Merry Party, *by Gerard van Honthorst, 1623.*

New Schleissheim Palace: Eastern facade with ornamental garden in the French style.

and east over the park to the focal point of Lustheim Palace.

The elegance of French architecture, evident outside in the placement and proportions of the windows, comes into its own in the **interior**. The colonnaded entrance hall, the spectacular staircase, the Great Gallery, the festival and banquet rooms, and the residential suites all abound in airy stuccowork and brilliant frescoes and paintings. "Victory Over the Turks" – this battlecry is commemorated everywhere on the upper floor of the central tract. J.B. Zimmermann's wonderful stucco sculpture features Turks' heads, war trophies, and slaves as atlantes. Max Emanuel is extolled in the guise of his Roman predecessor, Aeneas, in the frescoes by Ami-

goni. This Venetian artist replaced Asam when the latter's "trial fresco" in the vault of the staircase★, *Venus with Vulcan,* was rejected by Max Emanuel because his portrait (to Venus's right) displeased him. Beich's paintings also celebrate the victory over the Turks, in two huge battle scenes in the light-flooded Great Hall★ and in nine smaller ones in Victory Hall★. This latter is a Baroque gem, with its Hercules herms by Dubut and Regency decor from Pichler's workshop. Allegories of princely rule adorn the elector's apartments, decorated in gold throughout, on the upper floor of the southern tract, while allegories of peace and nature are set off by the silver decor of the electress's apartments in the northern wing.

New Schleissheim Palace: Floor Plans

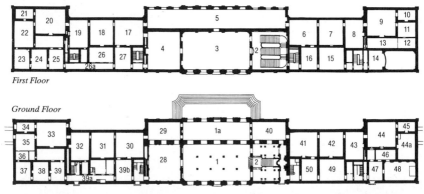

First Floor

Ground Floor

1 Entrance Hall, **2** Staircase, **3** Great Hall, **4** Victory Hall, **5** Great Gallery, **6-10** Elector's Apartments, **11** Netherlandish Paintings Cabinet, **12** Oratory, **13** Upper Sacristy, **14** Choir, **15-16** Chambers, **17-20** Electress's Apartments, **21** Chamber, or Upper, Chapel, **22-27** Gallery Rooms, **28** Dining Hall, **29** Northern Antechamber, **30-33** Gallery Rooms, **34** Stuccowork Cabinet, **35** Turnery Room, **36-39** Gallery Rooms, **40** Southern Antechamber, **41-44** Gallery Rooms, **45** Blue Cabinet, **46** Lower Sacristy, **47** Chapel Vestibule, **48** Maximilian Chapel, **49-50** Chambers.

The Great Gallery★ between the two residential suites was once one of the finest picture galleries in Europe, for which Max Emanuel alone acquired over 1,000 paintings. Later divested of its greatest works by the Alte Pinakothek, the New Palace was reopened in 1978 as the **State Gallery of European Baroque Painting**. With over 300 works all told, the Gallery itself contains paintings of all schools, while the apartments have Flemish and Dutch paintings on the upper floor, and French, Spanish, German, and Italian works on the ground floor. High points are the works by Rubens, Brueghel the Younger, van Dyck, Honthorst, Poussin, Ribera, Rottmayr, Maulpertsch, Desmarées, and Sandrart.

146 Old Schleissheim Palace

A rare specimen of a late Renaissance country residence.

Across from the opulent elector's palace stands the country seat of a duke, a late Renaissance **building** with an attractive porch and an interior decorated with paintings by Candid. After being severely damaged during the Second World War, it was partly restored, partly rebuilt in 1972. The original residence, built for Maximilian I by Schön the Elder in 1616-23 with extensive outbuildings, replaced the unassuming country house of Duke Wilhelm V, around which was a circle of nine hermitages – wooden cottages in the shape of chapels for meditation and worship. Christian piety is also the hallmark of the **Weinhold Collection,** a branch of the Bavarian National Museum now on display here. This extensive collection of artifacts

pertaining to popular Christian faith all over the world – exhibited in 250 showcases under the title "The Gospels in Homes Around the World" – centers on the Catholic countries of South America, Mexico, and Poland, but also includes ecumenical pieces.

Old Schleissheim Palace: Central tract with western parterre.

147 Schleissheim Palace Park

A Baroque park pure and unalloyed, apart from Herrenhausen the only one of its kind in Germany.

The central axis of these lovely grounds is formed by a broad canal, which issues from the circular canal around Lustheim Palace and ends in a cascade in the basin in front of the New Palace. The two lateral canals, which determined the length of the New Palace facade, meet to form a semicircle behind Lustheim. The boskets and paths between the canals are arranged geometrically, in circles, squares, and radiating lines.

New Schleissheim Palace: Elector's bedroom, with bed of state.

Lustheim Palace, Schleissheim Palace Park.

148 Lustheim Palace in Schleissheim Palace Park

Zuccalli's most personal creation, this influential "pleasure seat" was adorned with ceiling frescoes in an unprecedented style. It houses the Ernst Schneider Collection, the largest collection of Meissen porcelain in West Germany.

This residence and hunting lodge encircled by a canal was intended as an "island of love" for Max Emanuel and Maria Antonia, the emperor's daughter who became his wife in 1685. But sadly, its main fresco, *Jupiter Crowning Diana as Goddess of the Chase,* which bears Maria Antonia's initials, was destined to look down much longer on the elector's union with Therese Kunigunde Sobieska of Poland, for in 1692 Maria Antonia died in childbirth, after a short, unhappy marriage.

With Lustheim, Zuccalli rang in the courtly **palace architecture** of the late Baroque period with tremendous verve. Built in 1684-88, its central section is flanked by four projecting tracts, corresponding inside to a lofty main hall and four two-storey apartments. The ceiling frescoes, by Rosa, Trubillio, and Gumpp, are superb accomplishments of *trompe-l'œil,* with Diana and her entourage hovering above painted architectural perspectives supported by illusionistic atlantes.

The present treasure of Lustheim Palace, displayed throughout its rooms, is the **Ernst Schneider Collection of Meissen Porcelain★**, which was donated to the Bavarian National Museum in 1968. This extraordinary collection comprises 1,800 pieces from the heyday of the Meissen manufactory in the eighteenth century, and ranges from early tableware by Böttger, *chinoiseries* by Höroldt, and Kändler's renowned animal figurines to porcelain from the time of the Seven Years War.

Girard, a pupil of Le Nôtre, conceived of the garden as a site for festivities and diversions, long, narrow, and capable of being taken in at a single glance. He created this park in 1715 with the aid of drawings done by Zuccalli in 1684. Restoration work on the park is still underway.

Collection of Meissen Porcelain: Vase with relief ornament, c. 1720 (left), and sugar bowl, c. 1735-45 (below).

Facing page: Aerial view of Schleissheim Palace and Park.

Neu-Bogenhausen, Berg am Laim, Ramersdorf, Perlach

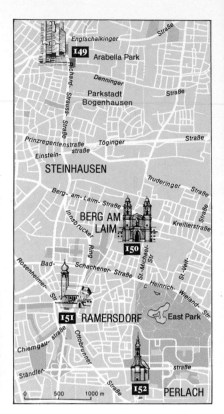

Administrative Headquarters of the Hypo Bank

149 Administrative Headquarters of the Hypo Bank

Hypo-Bank-Verwaltungszentrum

Arabellastrasse 12

A daring skyscraper design that dominates the city's northeastern area.

Munich's only "skyscraper" – 374 feet high – is rather unusual in being located at a considerable distance from downtown. Though not without a certain pretentiousness born of new affluence, the design is impressive – three prismatic elements contrasted with four tubular towers, all linked by broad bands from which the lower stories are suspended and on which the upper ones rest. The polished aluminum surfaces lend a feeling of lightness and elegance to the building, which was designed by the architects W. and B. Betz and erected in 1975-81.

150 St. Michael's in Berg am Laim

Clemens-August-Strasse 9a

One of the most delightful of all Bavarian Rococo churches, by masters of the first rank. A perfect unity of architecture by Fischer, sculpture by Straub, and painting by Zimmermann.

Clemens August, Max Emanuel's son, was partial to festivities and a patron to the best artists of the day: Balthasar Neumann, Cuvilliés, and Johann Michael Fischer. As Elector and Archibishop of Cologne, to whose territory Berg am Laim ("clay ridge") then belonged, he had this **building★** created for a Brotherhood and Knights' Order of St. Michael. It took over twenty years to erect (1735-58) owing to intrigues between Kögelsberger, Head Architect of Munich, and Fischer, Architect to Bavaria and the Electorate of Cologne, who finally prevailed.

The church itself shows no signs of this dissension. Fischer's **interior★** is composed of a series of oval and octagonal spaces of varying size, the octagons fitted with niches flanked by angled corner columns. The vaulting is extremely varied, and light from the beautifully arched oriel windows lends a shimmering weightlessness to the whole. The frescoes and the statuary, the stuccowork and the color harmonies transform the interior into a throne room for the Prince of Angels, St. Michael. Exuberant groups of putti are headed by two particularly delightful figures on the high altar: a little girl playing the lady and a little boy dreaming of being the Old Man of the Sea. Actually, these putti represent the Virgin Mary reading and Tobias with the fish!

St. Michael's: The most significant Rococo church in Munich to have survived in its original state.

St. Michael's: Putto as Tobias on the high altar.

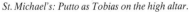

In his three light-flooded ceiling frescoes★, Zimmermann (who also did the stuccowork) depicts St. Michael's three appearances on Monte Gargano. From west to east, these are, over the congregational area, *The Institution of the Pilgrimage* (with Elector Clemens August under a sunshade in the procession); over the area reserved for the Knights' Order, *St. Michael Intervening in Battle for the People of Siponto;* and, over the altar, *The Consecration of the Grotto.* The central theme of the legend, *St. Michael Defeating the Dragon,* is represented in the altar painting by J. A. Wolff (1694).

All the altar superstructures and figures in the church are by Straub and his workshop. The glorious high altar★, flanked by finely

193

Detail of fresco in the main cupola, representing the procession from Siponto up to Monte Gargano. The church's donor, Elector Clemens August of Cologne, walks beneath the sunshade.

proportioned statues of the archangels Gabriel and Raphael, has a tabernacle representing the table in the inn at Emmaeus. Especially beautiful among the other altars are those without columns – an elegant type invented by Straub and Günther – and the Immaculata and St. John of Nepomuk altars fronting the main arch. These contain paintings by Zimmermann, as well as the finest of the twelve apostle figures: St. John and St. Jacob the Elder. The pulpit, attached to a

pillar of the main arch in the usual Rococo manner, is a graceful creation by Hassler, surmounted by St. Michael bearing a flag with the Bavarian colors. In the vestibule are two compelling Baroque statues of saints by Straub's teacher, Faistenberger.

Sadly, the stately twin-tower **facade★** has been somewhat cramped in its effect by new buildings. But a royal church in a village of 200 souls – that was overdoing things somewhat even in those days.

St. Michael's in Berg am Laim: Twin-tower facade (left) and pulpit canopy (right), with a patriotic St. Michael displaying the Bavarian flag.

151 St. Mary's in Ramersdorf
Aribonenstrasse 9

One of the oldest pilgrimage churches in Bavaria, this Late Gothic building has a Baroque interior with fine works by Grasser, Polack, and others.

Ever since the fourteenth century pilgrims have come to this church to worship the Mother of God and the Holy Cross. Accordingly, the focal point of the Baroque high altar is a miraculous image of the Virgin Enthroned as Queen of Heaven, dating from 1465 and now attributed to the Late Gothic master, Kriechbaum. Pilgrims are blessed with a relic of the Cross, preserved in a crucifix worn by Emperor Ludwig the Bavarian that is housed in an exquisite monstrance. When closed, the wings of the altarpiece* on the north wall of the nave display paintings by Polack representing the donation of the relic to Ramersdorf by one of the Emperor's sons; when open, they show reliefs by Grasser, depicting the Crucifixion and various Passion scenes (1483).

Other superb works include the *Madonna of the Protecting Cloak* (1503) on the south wall and votive paintings in the choir, one of which (by Kager, 1635) is consecrated to the thirty-two Munich citizens who were taken hostage by King Gustavus Adolphus of Sweden during the Thirty Years' War. The heavy Baroque ornament, with its stucco panelling and elaborate altars, contrasts with the plain Gothic lines of the exterior, whose graceful, onion-domed tower presides over the village.

152 St. Michael's in Perlach
Pflanzeltstrasse 1

An exquisite rural church of the late Baroque period.

St. Mary's, Ramersdorf: The Virgin Enthroned.

Part of Munich's charm lies in the old village churches on the city outskirts, most of which were refurbished during the Baroque era. This one was built in 1732 by Mayr, Fischer's father-in-law, on the site of a Romanesque church. Stuber painted the nave fresco, *The Fall of the Angels,* and Zächenberger the choir frescoes of *St. Michael on Monte Gargano* and *The Trinity in the Guise of Three Men* (both restored using photographs). Widmann contributed a moving St. Michael (1796), on the high altar. The side altars contain Late Gothic depictions of St. Kolomann and The Virgin and Child with St. Anne, and late Baroque images of the Crucifixion and St. John of Nepomuk.

Pilgrimage Church of St. Mary, Ramersdorf.

St. Michael's in Perlach.

Thalkirchen, Forstenried, Geiselgasteig, Grünwald

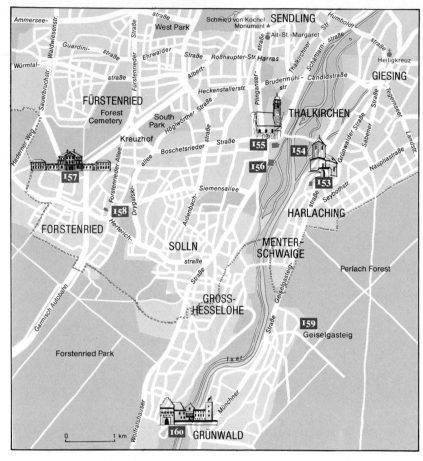

St. Anne's, Harlaching: A Rococo frame.

153 Pilgrimage Church of St. Anne in Harlaching

Wallfahrtskirche St. Anna in Harlaching

Harlachinger Berg 30

A Rococo church with original decoration and the last fresco painted by Zimmermann.

This little church, hidden among trees high up on the bank of the Isar, has been the goal of a St. Anne pilgrimage since the early eight-

Hellabrunn Zoo: Elephant enclosure with Elephant House, whose dome made architectural history.

eenth century. The somewhat boxy **building** was erected around an earlier core – the tower – in 1751-61, possibly by J. M. Fischer. In the **interior,** events from the Life of the Virgin are related in various forms of the Rococo style: in a ceiling fresco by J. B. Zimmermann; in the high altar, with its Late Gothic miraculous image of the Virgin and Child with St. Anne; and, especially delightful, in two side altars with picture frames within frames★, an ingenious way of filling the space originally intended for larger paintings. The lion, elector's crown, and imperial crown on the right inner frame allude to the emperorship of the Wittelsbach Dynasty, which dates the altars to about 1742-52. They, like the pulpit, reveal a master's touch, perhaps that of Ignaz Günther.

Outside the church is a **Claude Lorraine Monument** donated by Ludwig I in 1865. The great French painter was once thought to have lived in Harlaching Palace, which earlier occupied this site. Actually, although he may have passed through Munich at some time, his sojourn here is a legend that arose out of various cases of mistaken identity. Yet Ludwig was so obsessed with art that he was ready to believe almost anything.

154 Hellabrunn Zoo
Siebenbrunner Strasse 6

The first geographical zoo and still the largest zoo of any kind in Europe, with about 4,500 animals of 460 species in a beautifully landscaped habitat.

A forest bar awaits the weary traveller on his 300-yard jaunt from Europe to America, and a beer garden provides refreshment between African zebras and Asian deer. The idea of organizing a **zoo**★ not by species but by conti-

nent was Hagenbeck's (of circus fame), and it brought the Berlin zoologist Heinz Heck to Munich. Set up in 1911 and closed owing to lack of funds in the period of inflation after the First World War, Hellabrunn Zoo opened its doors again in 1928 and was soon a resounding success. Its name derives from the former Palace of Hellabrunn in the Upper Isar meadows which, together with the high eastern bluffs, provided an ideal natural site for a park. The first animal enclo-

Ring-tailed lemurs from Madagascar.

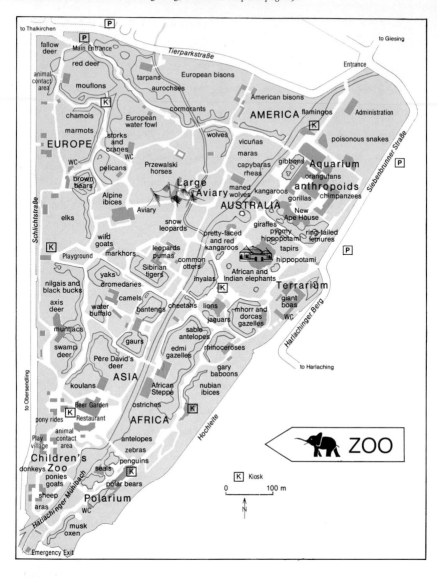

to Thalkirchen

to Giesing

fallow deer

Main Entrance

red deer

Tierparkstraße

Entrance

animal contact area

mouflons

tarpans

European bisons

aurochses

American bisons

cormorants

AMERICA

flamingos

Administration

chamois

European water fowl

wolves

vicuñas

poisonous snakes

marmots

maras

EUROPE

storks and cranes

WC

capybaras

gibbons

Aquarium

Przewalski horses

rheas

orangutans

pelicans

WC

anthropoids

brown bears

Large Aviary

maned wolves

kangaroos

gorillas

chimpanzees

Alpine ibices

Aviary

AUSTRALIA

New Ape House

elks

snow leopards

giraffes

pygmy hippopotami

ring-tailed lemures

wild goats

leopards pumas

pretty-faced and red kangaroos

tapirs

Playground

markhors

common otters

hippopotami

yaks

Sibirian tigers

inyalas

African and Indian elephants

Terrarium

nilgais and black bucks

dromedaries

camels

cheetahs

lions

giant boas

axis deer

water buffalo

bantengs

jaguars

mhorr and dorcas gazelles

WC

muntjacs

gaurs

sable antelopes

swamp deer

edmi gazelles

rhinoceroses

Harlachinger Berg

Père David's deer

gary baboons

to Harlaching

koulans

ASIA

African Steppe

nubian ibices

to Obersendling

Beer Garden

ostriches

Restaurant

pony rides

AFRICA

Hochleite

Play village

animal contact area

antelopes

zebras

Children's Zoo

penguins

donkeys

seals

ZOO

ponies

goats

polar bears

sheep

aras

Polarium

WC

musk oxen

Emergency Exit

K Kiosk

0   100 m

N

Schlichtstraße

Siebenbrunner Straße

Harlachinger Mühlbach

Hellabrunn Zoo: Red flamingos from Central America and the Antilles at the Flamingo Pond.

sures, designed by Emanuel von Seidl and built in 1910-14, were wooden or masonry structures with thatched roofs, and included an **Elephant House** with the world's first cantilevered concrete and glass dome.

A full-scale modernization of the zoo, by architect Jörg Gribl, has been underway since 1972. Its new landmark is the huge **Large Aviary,** a fine steel net suspended tent-like over a 53,821-square-foot area at the park's center. The Anthropoid Station and the **New Ape House,** which contains a variety of breeding species in pavilions without interior bars, are also recent additions. Penguins, seals, and polar bears have received a **Polarium,** while the **Children's Zoo** offers a play village, a pony riding track, and a meadow where children can pet a variety of animals.

During the 1930s Heinz Heck succeeded in rebreeding such extinct species as the aurochs and wild horse, thus creating "living models" of these breeds. At that time, it was already obvious that the zoo of the future would have to be devoted to the care and protection of endangered species. In the meantime, the European bison, the brown bear, the Cretan wild goat, a number of species of leopard, the water buffalo, and the Père David's deer – to name only a few – are no longer, or only rarely, to be found in their natural habitats, and can be studied only in zoos. This fact has made Hellabrunn the focus of extensive research activity.

Among the zoo's most popular celebrities are the orangutan twins Hella and Bruno, born in captivity in 1969 and since the progenitors of a new generation, and Tanga the hippopotamus, a distinguished elderly lady just over fifty. From an ancient African family, Tanga was born in Leipzig, but has been a resident of Munich ever since her toddling days.

155 St. Mary's in Thalkirchen
Fraunbergplatz 1

A medieval village and pilgrimage church with Baroque and later additions, containing notable works of art by Erhart and Günther.

This "church in the valley" (*Thalkirchen*) was long the parish church for villages scattered along the left bank of the Isar. Its beginnings reach back to the thirteenth century, as the **exterior** reveals. Steep Gothic roofs are set off by a helmeted Baroque spire and by a Neo-Baroque hexagonal annex with dome – a successful synthesis of styles from the building periods of c. 1400, 1700, and 1908.

The annex by G. von Seidl, its Neo-Baroque stucco carrying overtones of Art Nouveau, opens into the Baroque **nave** with elaborate stucco decoration and an Assumption fresco by J. A. Wolff (1696). The high altar in the **choir** is a true masterpiece, com-

St. Mary's, Thalkirchen: Late Gothic Madonna.

bining the exuberance of Rococo with the inwardness of the Late Gothic style. Its richly carved miraculous image of the Virgin and Child (1482)★ is probably by the renowned Michael Erhart, a woodcarver from Ulm. In 1760 Ignaz Günther added the angel gracefully descending to crown the Virgin with a wreath, and placed the group in front of a gloriole in an elaborate, columned structure. Günther's figures of St. Joachim and St. Anne, between the columns, are flanked by Erhart's statues of the bishops St. Ulrich and St. Corbinian over the side passages.

Also noteworthy are a Crucifix of 1744, a cartouche with the Munich coat of arms and the *Münchner Kindl,* and a number of votive images.

St. Mary's in Thalkirchen: The Baroque tower.

156 Asam Estate, "St. Mary Anchorite"
Asam-Schlössl "Maria Einsiedel"

Maria-Einsiedel-Strasse 45

The country residence of Cosmas Damian Asam, reflecting the taste and self-confidence of a highly successful Baroque artist and providing a rare

Asam Estate, "St. Mary Anchorite."

example of the facade painting once common throughout Munich.

The prosperous C. D. Asam, twice married, father of numerous children, and resident of Theatinerstrasse in the center of town, acquired this country estate in 1724. After adding an upper storey to the house and installing a studio in the projecting gable, he set to work on the **facade** and, in the manner then widespread in Munich, covered it with paintings of architectural perspectives, saints, and allegories. Named "St. Mary Anchorite" after the Swiss pilgrimage church to which Asam had contributed frescoes, the opulent residence once included several outbuildings, a geometrically arranged garden, and a chapel by the artist's brother, Egid Quirin.

After the Second World War, the interior and facade paintings were restored by Schleich. Adorning the main facade are depictions of the Virgin and Child, Moses, Borghese fencers, and angels on clouds. The balcony railing contains the artist's initials, CDA, twice intertwined.

Church of the Holy Cross, Forstenried: The Romanesque Crucifix.

157 Fürstenried Palace
Schloss Fürstenried

Fürstenried 1

A miniature Nymphenburg Palace by Effner.

Now cut off by a sweeping autobahn, the central axis of Fürstenried Park, lined with old linden trees, was directly aligned with Munich Cathedral five miles away. The original **palace complex,** grouped around a stately middle tract, was created by Effner for Max Emanuel in 1715-17. After serving a series of Wittelsbach rulers as a hunting lodge, it became an asylum for King Otto, brother of Ludwig II, who was mentally ill and spent the years 1883 to 1916 here. Much altered, the palace is now a religious institution.

Fürstenried Palace: Central tract.

158 Parish and Pilgrimage Church of the Holy Cross, Forstenried
Pfarr- und Wallfahrtskirche Heiligkreuz in Forstenried

Forstenrieder Allee 180a

This church's Romanesque Crucifix is the only masterpiece of that era still located in a Munich church.

The **Forstenried Crucifix,★** a compelling image of Christ, His eyes wide with inward torment, His body emaciated yet beautiful in its austerity of form, has understandably been the subject of many legends. Art historians consider the Romanesque sculpture, which was probably made in Seeon Monastery in about 1180 and remained in Andechs (see page 230) until 1229, the earliest crucifix in which Christ's feet are placed not side by side but on top of one another.

While the origins of the **church** go back to about the year 1000, the present building dates from the fifteenth century. The interior was redesigned in the Baroque and Rococo periods, and recently extensively restored. There are fine statues of Christ and the Virgin (1708) by Fassbinder on the engaged piers, and figures of the twelve apostles by an anonymous artist (1670).

159 Bavaria Film Tour, Geiselgasteig Movie Town

Bavariafilmplatz 7

A fascinating look behind the scenes in the Hollywood of Europe.

Whether you stretch out in a director's chair or get a taste of submariner's claustrophobia in *The Boat*, ride a racing snail through *The Never-Ending Story* or marvel at the feats of stuntmen and the tricks of special-effects artists, the one-and-a-half hour walk and ride with the Film Express through Munich's Television and Motion Picture Town is an experience to remember. Founded in 1909 and now a film location of international renown, Geiselgasteig has hosted great stars, from Albers to Lancaster and Dagover to Loren; famous directors, from Hitchcock to Fassbinder; and lasting works of the motion-picture art from *Cabaret* to *Fathers and Sons*. (Open daily from March 1 to October 31, 9 a. m. to 4 p. m.)

Geiselgasteig Movie Town: Bavaria Film Tour.

160 Grünwald Castle

Burg Grünwald

Grünwald, Zeillerstrasse 3

On an Isar Valley site redolent with history, this late medieval castle commands the river from a bluff. Today it houses a branch museum of the State Prehistorical Collection.

Not far from the former Roman castellum on the Isar heights rises another **castle,** not awesomely battlemented, but with roofs delicately poised above the trees and an eastern gateway whose gable bears colorful coats of arms. Built to control an Isar crossing-point and to oversee the collection of ferry toll, Grünwald Castle became the seat of an ancient noble family from Andechs in the twelfth century and, from the thirteenth to the seventeenth century, served as a hunting lodge for the House of Wittelsbach. In 1487 the building was converted and enlarged for the marriage of Duke Albrecht and Kunigunde, the Emperor's daughter (hence the family arms on the gable). It was degraded to a prison and powder magazine in the eighteenth and nineteenth centuries, before becoming a private residence in 1879. Since 1977 the castle has belonged to the State of Bavaria which, after shoring up the undermined bluff, partially rebuilt and partially restored it.

Some of its buildings now house the **Castle Museum.** The exciting history of the castle itself is related in an exhibition in the Large Tower, the top of which affords a wonderful view of the Isar Valley and the Alps. A room in the east wing presents special exhibitions on prehistorical subjects, while the west wing contains a "lapidarium" – a fascinating collection of milestones and gravestones, altars and sacred images, frescoes and objects of daily use, which evokes the shades of Roman civilization in this and other regions of the Empire.

Remains of Roman entrenchments may be seen in the southern part of Grünwald, which lies just outside the city precincts.

Grünwald Castle with Prehistorical Museum seen from the high left bank of the Isar.

Places of Interest
at a Glance

Heiligkreuz in Giesing, by Dollmann,
the architect of Ludwig II's fabulous castles.

Churches

Alt-St. Margaret, Plinganserstrasse 1 [see map on p. 196]. Baroque and Rococo structure erected over the remnants of a village church demolished in 1705 during peasant uprising against Austrian occupation ("The Bloody Christmas of Sendling"). Architect: Zwerger, 1711-12. Altars by Grässl, 1710.

Erlöserkirche (Protestant), Ungererstrasse 13 [map on p. 123]. Art Nouveau building

Heiligkreuz in Fröttmaning.

along Romanesque lines, dramatically sited at the end of Leopoldstrasse. Architect: Theodor Fischer, 1899-1901. Mural by Koegel, 1903-04, destroyed during the Second World War and since partially restored.

Erscheinung des Herrn, Terofalstrasse 68 [map inside back cover]. A modern church whose roof supports provide a dominant interior accent. Architect: Eisele, 1969-70.

Heiligkreuz in Fröttmaning, Kranzberger Allee 66 [map inside back cover]. Probably Munich's oldest church, with tower over the apse. Romanesque in origin, converted in fourteenth century, and again, in the Baroque manner, in 1736. Significant twelfth- and thirteenth-century ornamental paintings.

Heiligkreuz in Giesing, Ichostrasse 1 [map on p. 196]. Brick building on Giesing Hill, its tall spire a landmark in the cityscape. Only Neo-Gothic church in Munich to have survived the Second World War almost undamaged. Architect: Dollmann, 1866-86. Fine contemporaneous sculptures.

Herz-Jesu-Klosterkirche (Monastery church of the Niederbronn Sisterhood), Buttermelcherstrasse 10 [map inside front cover]. Reinforced concrete structure of original design that exerted great influence on modern ecclesiastical architecture in Munich. Architect: von Branca, 1955.

Karmelitenkirche, Karmeliterstrasse 1 [map inside front cover]. First Baroque church building in Munich, donated by Maximilian I in gratitude for the victory over the Swedes in the Battle of White Mountain (1620). Architect: Schinnagl, based on designs by Asper, 1657-60. Richly decorated eastern facade simplified in 1802. Destroyed during the Second World War, rebuilt in simplified form. Limited accessibility.

Mariahilfkirche in der Au, Mariahilfplatz 42 [map inside back cover]. Munich's first church in Romantic Neo-Gothic. Major work of Ohlmüller, a pupil of Fischer; completed 1831-39 by Ziebland. Originally decorated with stained glass by Hess, Schraudolph, and others. Bombed out during the Second World War; rebuilt, not very sensitively, in simplified form.

St. Johann Baptist (old), Kirchenstrasse 39 [map on p. 127]. Old parish church of Haidhausen. Two-aisle Late Gothic building around Romanesque nucleus; Baroque conversion 1700, by M. Gunetzrhainer. Interior largely Baroque. Crucifix, c. 1520. Old cemetery to the north.

Facing page: Richard Strauss Fountain (Neuhauser Strasse).

St. Maximilian soaring above the left bank of the Isar on Auenstrasse.

St.Johann Baptist (new), Johannisplatz 22 [maps on pp. 127, 146]. New parish church of the Haidhausen district. Neo-Gothic; interior using engaged piers in Gothic forms. Architect: Berger, 1852-74. Neo-Gothic stained glass windows, designed by Bradl, 1903-18.

St.Johann Baptist in Johanneskirchen, Gleissenbachstrasse 2 [map inside back cover]. Romanesque apse-tower church with

Herz-Jesu-Klosterkirche (von Branca, 1955).

fortifications, built c. 1200; enlarged and converted in Baroque style in 1688. High altar★ by Iganz Günther includes outstanding sculptures of St. Zacharias and St. Elizabeth.

St.Joseph, Josephsplatz [map inside back cover]. First Historical Revival church in Munich to be based on Baroque rather than on medieval architecture. Architect: Schurr, 1898-1902. Rebuilt after the Second World War without decoration; stucco elements added in more recent restoration.

St.Maximilian, Auenstrasse 1 [map inside back cover]. Majestic Neo-Romanesque basilica based on north Italian models; a landmark located on the left bank of the Isar. Architect: H. von Schmidt, 1895-1905. Striking high altar by B. Schmitt. Apse mosaic by Becker-Gundahl.

St.Nikolaus in Englschalking, Flaschenträgerstrasse 1 [map inside back cover]. Early Gothic, thirteenth-century village church incorporating Romanesque core. Superb Baroque altar, 1695, and Late Gothic statuary.

St.Nikolaus in Freimann, Heinrich-Groh-Strasse 11 [map inside back cover]. Romanesque and Early Gothic church with tower over the apse, altered in the sixteenth and nineteenth centuries. General restoration in 1984, including architectural painting on tower.

St.Sylvester, Biedersteiner Strasse 1a [map on p. 123]. Rural Gothic church converted to Baroque in 1654-61, and given Neo-Baroque annex in 1926 (architect: Buchert). Major Baroque sculptures, including figure of a bishop, probably by Guggenbichler; statue of St.Thaddeus and busts of St.Benedict and St.Barbara after designs by Günther.

St.Ursula, Kaiserplatz 1 [map on p.123]. Brick basilica with dome and campanile based on Florentine and north Italian early Renaissance models; beautifully sited and integrated in the surroundings. Architect: Thiersch, 1894-97. Important parish church of the then-new district of Schwabing.

Main Jewish Synagogue, Reichenbachstrasse 27 [map inside front cover]. Established in 1931 as Eastern Jewish Synagogue and third Jewish place of worship in Munich. Architect: Gustav Meyerstein, 1931. Devastated in 1938; restored and reconsecrated in 1947. Now main synagogue. The earlier Reformed main synagogue on Herzog-Max-Strasse and the Orthodox synagogue on Herzog-Rudolf-Strasse were destroyed in 1938.

Fountains

Artur-Kutscher-Platz: **Artur Kutscher Fountain,** with theatrical masks, in honor of the theater historian Kutscher. E. Dietz, 1968 [see map on p. 123].

Crystal Palace Fountain (Weissenburger Platz).

Norn Fountain (Maximiliansplatz).

Brienner Strasse 11/13 (Luitpold Block): **Prince Regent Luitpold Fountain.** Henselmann, 1983 [maps inside front cover and on p. 95].

Finanzgarten (Galeriestrasse): **Heinrich Heine Fountain.** Stadler, 1962 [map inside front cover and on p. 95].

Frauenplatz: **St. Benno Fountain.** Henselmann, 1972 [map inside front cover].

Hackenstrasse (Radspieler House): **Radl Fountain.** A. Rauch, 1967 [map inside front cover].

Lenbachplatz 7 (Maxburg courtyard): **Moses Fountain,** Henselmann, 1955 [map inside front cover].

Lilienstrasse: **Augia Fountain,** with allegory of the suburb of Au. Schwanthaler, 1848 [map inside back cover].

Pine Cone Fountain (Prinzregentenstrasse).

Fisherboy Fountain (Viktualienmarkt).

"Harmless" Statue.

Marstallplatz (eastern entrance of Residence): **Crown Prince Rupprecht Fountain.** Bleeker, 1961 [map inside front cover].

Maximiliansplatz (Ash Grove): **Norn Fountain.** Netzer, 1907 [maps inside front cover and on p. 95; ill., p. 205].

Maximiliansplatz (eastern section of park): **Karl Amadeus Hartmann Memorial Fountain,** in honor of the Bavarian composer. Stadler, 1971 [map inside front cover].

Neuhauser Strasse 51: **Richard Strauss Fountain.** With scenes from *Salome.* Wimmer, 1962 [map inside front cover; ill., p. 203].

Prinzregentenstrasse 28 (pump house in front of Ministry of Economics): **Pine Cone Fountain.** Wackerle, 1937 [map on p. 127; ill., p. 205].

Tal 13: **Mercury Fountain.** F. von Thiersch and Kaufmann, 1911 [map inside front cover and on p. 146].

Königinstrasse: **Snake Fountain.** E. Dietz, 1958 [map on p. 123].

Viktualienmarkt: **Fisherboy Fountain.** Taschner, 1934 [map inside front cover; ill., p. 205].

Wedekindplatz: **Wedekind Fountain.** Filler, 1959 [map on p. 123].

Weissenburger Platz: **Crystal Palace Fountain,** in the Maximilian Style (see p. 146); formerly located in front of the Crystal Palace. Voit, 1853. [map inside back cover; ill., p. 205].

Monuments

Galeriestrasse, between Finanz- and Hofgartenstrassen on the way to Prince Carl Mansion: **"Harmless" Statue.** A marble, Grecian adolescent (original in Residence Museum) by Franz Jakob Schwanthaler, 1803. Conceived as "Genius of Rural Life" for the English Garden. Its jocular title derives from the verses inscribed on the tablet: "Harmless / wander here / Then return refreshed / to every duty" [map on p. 95].

Kaiser-Ludwig-Platz: **Emperor Ludwig Monument** in the midst of a small garden. An equestrian statue of Ludwig the Bavarian (1282-1347) with two squires on massive pedestal surrounded by balustrade. Two bronze reliefs depict the Battle of Gammelsdorf (1313, victory over the Habsburgs) and Field Marshal Seyfried Schweppermann, to whom the Emperor presented two eggs after the battle, saying, "To each one egg, to the pious Schweppermann two." Monument donated by Matthias Pschorr, designed and cast by Ferdinand von Miller, 1905. Drew protests from the clergy, who objected to a monument in honor of an emperor who had been excommunicated by the Pope and to locating it, of all places, in front of a school [map on p. 162].

Lindwurmstrasse/Plinganserstrasse: **Schmied von Kochel,** legendary popular hero of "The Bloody Christmas of Sendling" (1705), which took place on this site. Architecture by Sattler, figure by Ebbinghaus, 1906-11 [map on p. 196].

Maximiliansplatz park on either side of Max-Joseph-Strasse: **Max von Pettenkofer,** Ruemann, 1909; **Justus von Liebig,** Wagmüller, 1883; to the left of Wittelsbach Fountain, **Goethe,** E. Dietz, 1962; on Platz der Opfer des

Richard Wagner Monument.

Nationalsozialismus, **Schiller,** Widnmann, 1863 [map inside front cover and on p. 95].

Prinzregentenstrasse, green area adjacent to Prince Regent Theater: **Richard Wagner,** Waderé, 1913 [map on p. 127].

Promenadeplatz, green area: **Christoph Willibald Gluck,** Brugger, 1848; **Orlando di Lasso,** Widnmann, 1848; **Elector Max Emanuel,** Brugger, 1861; **Lorenz Westenrieder,** Widnmann, 1854 [map inside front cover].

Schönfeldstrasse 3/5: Statue of horses, dedicated to the **Cavalry,** Bleeker, 1960 [maps on pp. 95, 123].

Facades

Damenstiftstrasse 4: **Trischberger House,** former residence of Master Builders Trischberger and Widmann. Stately Neoclassical edifice of 1800 incorporating earlier building on this site. Lovely decoration in Empire Style. Rebuilt, with reconstructed stucco, in 1957 [map inside front cover].

Hackenstrasse 7: **Radspieler House.** In the seventeenth and eighteenth century, palace of the Princes of Rechberg, where Heinrich Heine stayed in 1827-28. Acquired in 1848 by the Radspieler family. Combines two existing seventeenth-century buildings; converted and given Neoclassical facade by Métivier, who also created the interior furnishings in 1817. Its Garden Court – with fountain by Boos – is the sole surviving example of an early Munich courtyard planted with trees [map inside front cover].

Hackenstrasse 10: **House "Zur Hundskugel".** Former residence of the sculptors Straub and Boos. Simple three-storey domicile of the eighteenth century, presumably built in 1741 by J. M. Fischer. The relief over the west portal depicting six dogs playing with a ball (replica) gave the house its name. Facade once adorned by a bust of the Virgin, by Straub, which is now in the National Museum [map inside front cover].

Hotterstrasse 18: **Restaurant "Zur Hundskugel".** Oldest restaurant in Munich, established 1440. House in typical old Munich style, with steep, single-slope roof, dormer windows, and arched windows in gable [map inside front cover].

Hochbrückenstrasse 8: **Moradelli House.** Old Munich middle-class residence of the sixteenth century, heightened in the seventeenth century. Noteworthy arcaded yard with wooden balcony around three sides. Restored and partially reconstructed in 1969, by Schleich. Modern facade paintings by Kaspar [maps inside front cover and on p. 146].

Ledererstrasse 3: **Zerwirkgewölbe** (Game-Dressing Vaults). Medieval building with interesting groined vaults. Originally a ducal

Maxburg tower and Wittelsbach Fountain.

falconry, built in the thirteenth century and altered in the fifteenth century, then Court Brewery for a time. Used from 1808 as a storage room for game taken on royal hunts – hence the building's present name. Now a specialist grocer, who also stocks game [map inside front cover and on p. 146].

Lenbachplatz 7: **Maxburg.** Originally the "Wilhelmine Fort" of Duke Wilhelm V, built by Schön the Elder in 1593-96. During the latter half of the seventeenth century, residence of Duke Maximilian Philipp, or "Maxburg" for short. Since destroyed, except for the tower on the north side. The present complex houses Departments of Police and Justice. Architects: Pabst and Ruf, 1953-55 [map inside front cover].

Munich's oldest inn: "Zur Hundskugel."

Practical Tips

Musical Life

Munich's concert-going public would seem to have an insatiable appetite for music. The Gasteig Arts Center is the bastion of the city's musical activities, but it has by no means replaced the time-honored **concert venues** of Hercules Hall in the Residence and the Convention Hall of the Deutsches Museum. Moreover, concert life continues to flourish in churches such as St. Luke's,

Organ of St. Michael's Church.

St. Mark's, St. Michael's, and St. Boniface's; in Schleissheim and Nymphenburg palaces, Blutenburg Castle, and the Fountain Court of the Residence; in Lenbach House and in a host of other places. The rock and pop scene is to be found in the Olympic Halle, the Circus Krone, and the Alabama-Halle, which offers a particularly attractive and varied program.

Munich also has a large number of **music pubs** (*Musikkneipen*). At the time of writing, classical music can be heard only in the Mariandl, where home-style cooking and chamber music – often performed by very talented young musicians – are perfect partners. Political songs, rock, pop, and jazz are performed in countless pubs. Unterfahrt (in Haidhausen) provides jazz of international quality in programs that change almost daily (from 9 p.m.) and in jam sessions on Sunday mornings (11 o'clock, admission free). Singer-songwriters, folk music, and jazz can be heard in Kaffee Giesing. In Schwabing, the Domicile is once again booking renowned jazz bands, while La Cage aux Folles and the Schwabing Podium both take a nostalgic look at the jazz of former days. The Allotria con-

centrates on mainstream and Dixieland, and presents a Rock and Roll *Frühschoppen* (lunchtime drink) at 12 a.m. on Sundays. Thursday is Rock and Roll day at the Rigan Club, which otherwise concentrates on jazz from the Fifties to the present day performed by a mixture of well-known bands and up-and-coming combos. Crash is known for hard rock, whereas Live-Club-Vogue encompasses most sectors of the current music scene.

Music of other cultures is presented in an especially enlivening way in the Freies Musikzentrum München, although it is not a pub. In La Cumbia and La Peseta Loca, Latin American music can be heard, often played by exciting groups.

Music

Alabama-Halle, Schleissheimer Strasse 418, tel. 3513085
Allotria, Türkenstrasse 33, tel. 285858
Circus Krone, Marsstrasse 43, tel. 558166
Convention Hall of the Deutsches Museum, Museumsinsel 1, tel. 298430
Crash, Lindwurmstrasse 88, tel. 773272
domicile, Leopoldstrasse 19, tel. 399451
Freies Musikzentrum München, Ismaninger Strasse 29, tel. 4706314
Gasteig Arts Center, Rosenheimer Strasse 5, tel. 4181-0
Hercules Hall, Residenzstrasse 1, tel. 224641
Kaffee Giesing, Bergstrasse 5/9, tel. 6920579
Künstlerhaus, Lenbachplatz 8, tel. 592625
La Cage aux Folles, Kaiserplatz 4, tel. 331861
La Cumbia, Taubenstrasse 2, tel. 658501
La Peseta Loca, Oberländerstrasse 3b, tel. 772845
Live-Club-Vogue, Drygalsky-Allee 117-Gulbranssonstrasse, tel. 7918109
Mariandl, Goethestrasse 51, tel. 535158
Olympiahalle, Spiridon-Louis-Ring 7, tel. 306131
Rigan-Club, Schleissheimer Strasse 393, tel. 3542525
Schwabinger Podium, Wagnerstrasse 1, tel. 399482
Unterfahrt, Kirchenstrasse 96, tel. 4482794

Music in Churches
St. Bonifaz, Karlstrasse 34
St. Lukas, Mariannenplatz
St. Markus, Gabelsbergerstrasse 6
St. Michael, Neuhauser Strasse 52

Music in Castles and Palaces
Blutenburg, Seldweg, tel. 939933
Nymphenburg, Schloss Nymphenburg 1, tel. 179081
Schleissheim, Oberschleissheim, tel. 3150212

Fashion and Antiques

Maximilianstrasse is the bird of paradise among Munich's fashion streets – every shop window presents an array of colors. There is, for example, the distinguished elegance of Gucci, the extravagant Loden designs of Resi Hammerer, the breezy sportiness of the English House, the distinctive cottage style of Polo Ralph Lauren, the Parisian pep of Saint-Laurent, the cool and classical Jil Sander (around the corner), Moshammer's snob appeal, Bagheera's wild luxury, and much more besides. And alongside all this are the high-quality perfumes, chocolates, china, jewellery, glass, and leather goods – only the best will do. The extravagance continues at right-angles to Maximilianstrasse, amid the marble and glass of **Residenzstrasse** and the courts behind it. This is the home of the world-famous Dietl, who is no longer just a "tailor of divine trousers," of Bogner's, and of other traditional Munich establishments. The arcades between Residenzstrasse and Theatinerstrasse are a paradise for accessories.

Around the **Luitpold Block**, and on **Wittelsbacherplatz** and **Maximilianplatz**, the sartorial elegance of Italian and French designers appears between select furniture and antique shops. The splendid displays are a real feast for the eyes.

Theatinerstrasse and its side streets are not quite as intimidating. Many long-established fashion houses are situated here which rapidly adapt international trends to the demands of Munich style – Loden Frey, Sartorius, Maendler, and Eden, for example. That does not exclude the bizarre, as can be seen at Maja of Munich.

The empire of the textile kings – from Ludwig Beck right by New City Hall to the clothing departments of Oberpollinger – centers on the streets that run fom **Marienplatz to the Stachus** and from **Marienplatz to Sendling Gate**. These streets are a place of pilgrimage for every eager shopper.

Schwabing is the place to look for – and find – the latest ideas in fashion. The boutiques jostle with each other for space on **Leopoldstrasse** and **Hohenzollernstrasse**. Sweetheart cultivates a film-star image with its sparse but artistic display, whereas the Leopoldmarkt goes in for the teenager look – to name just two of the most extreme examples on the "Boulevard Leopold." Fantastic, distinguished, or daring fashions can be found at Lady Jane and Lord John in **Kurfürstenstrasse**, at M.H. Mistral in **Feilitzschstrasse**, and at Schmalor in **Siegesstrasse**. Most of the things on sale here can be found at much cheaper prices in the countless second-hand boutiques.

Munich's individual contribution to fashion continues to be the **rustic look**, with its Loden coat (*Lodenmantel*) and its traditional Bava-

Shop windows on Sendlinger Strasse.

rian costume (the *Dirndl* for women, the *Trachtenanzug* for men). Raised to the level of an Alpine *haute couture,* this apparel has completely undermined international fashion laws. Dinner jackets in the *Trachtenanzug* style and floor-length silk evening gowns in the *Dirndl* mode are worn at even the most formal official and festive occasions. Who cares about the "purity" of local tradition when elegance and Alpine flair are what count? The latter can be found at Dirndl-Königin in Residenzstrasse, Dirndl-Ecke on the Platzl, or Schöne Münchnerin on Petersplatz. Most large fashion houses have a *Trachten* department. Loden Frey has the best range of *Dirndls,* jackets, capes, *Gamsbarthüte* (hats with goat bristle tufts), and every kind of accessory. A shop specializing in inexpensive goods of this type is the Isartaler-Trachtenkammer Haslinger in the Rosental. Adler's in the Elisenhof (opposite Central Station) is the cheapest of all.

Munich's reputation as an important center for **antiques** dates well back into the nineteenth century. Fall is the best time to look for nostalgic wares. The *Deutsche Kunst- und Antiquitätenmesse* (German Art and Antiques Fair) takes place in October and November in the Haus der Kunst, and October also sees the *Internationale Kunst und Antiquitäten München* fair in the Regina Haus. In the same month, the Deutsches Museum hosts the *Süddeutsche Antiquitäten- und Kunstwoche* (South German Antiques and Art Week), which also takes place in January and March. In addition, there are the fall auctions of such famous Munich dealers as Karl und Faber, Wolfgang Ketterer, Rudolf Neumeister, Hugo Ruef, and Josef Weiner.

Several times during the year art and antique dealers display their treasures in the Pschorrkeller on Theresa Hill and in the Salvator-Keller on the Nockherberg. Three times a year, in May, July, and October, the Auer Dult comes alive. This colorful market takes place around the Mariahilfkirche – antique hunters can sometimes strike a lucky bargain. If you manage to miss all of these events, just treat Munich as one large fair. Your quest is made easier by the fact that antique and art dealers are concentrated in certain areas of town.

Prannerstrasse and Ottostrasse are bursting at the seams with this kind of shop. In **Prannerstrasse** one can find first-class dealers in china, furniture, fixtures and fittings, clocks, and sculpture. In the Kunstblock on **Ottostrasse**, the shops specialize in Indian art, nineteenth- and twentieth-century painting, silver tableware, table cloths, carvings, antique sculpture, coins, archeological finds, glass, jewellery, and furniture, while the art galleries concentrate on contemporary art. In Ottostrasse itself, you can also find furniture, china, pewter, paintings, old prints, and folk art from Austria and the Alpine regions. The Galerie Handwerk at No. 15 holds exhibitions where you can buy pottery, glass, and textiles, often of extraordinarily good design. In **Fürstenstrasse**, an alley between Oskar-von-Miller Ring and Theresienstrasse, the emphasis is on glass old and new, English furniture and silver, French lamps and furniture, and Italian tables and chairs.

The house of Bernheimer on Lenbachplatz, founded in 1864, laid the foundations for Munich's reputation as a city renowed for antiques. However, it transferred all business to its London branch at the end of 1987.

Other important dealers in the neighborhood are: Böhler, with sculpture and Old Master paintings (Pacellistrasse); the Galerie im Bayerischen Hof (Promenadeplatz); Balogh (Residenzpassage) and Dr. Bühler (Theatinerhof), with paintings of the much sought-after Munich School of the nineteenth century; Hermann (Theatinerstrasse), with rare oriental carpets; Caroll (Residenzstrasse), which specializes in the eighteenth century; and Ledebur (Brienner Strasse), with English art and antiques.

The three stories of the Antic-Haus in Neuturmstrasse accommodate many antique dealers.

The shops in **Westenriederstrasse** near the Viktualienmarkt go in less for select wares than for rustic goods. They sell mainly country-style furniture (*Bauernmöbel*), folk art, curiosities, and all sorts of odds and ends – which may include a good find or two. This area is also the place to go for Art Nouveau.

In Schwabing, antique dealers are particularly numerous on **Kurfürstenstrasse, Türkenstrasse**, and **Schellingstrasse**. They concentrate on Art Nouveau and Art Deco, and on folk art from Asia, South America, and Africa. One can also find jewellery from far-flung markets, various handicraft items, and ritual objects.

Schwabing is also the main area for **second-hand bookshops**. In Schellingstrasse, bookworms will find a lavish supply of fiction and non-fiction at Kitzinger's, while Hauser's deals in books and prints, and Köbelin's in children's books and volumes on Bavarian subjects ("Bavarica"). In Türkenstrasse, Monika Schmidt specializes in prints and maps, and Hammerstein in illustrated books of the nineteenth and twentieth centuries. In Amalienstrasse, Wölfle offers choice books and prints from the fifteenth to the twentieth century. Ackermann in Ludwigstrasse is another good address for connoisseurs, while Hugendubel on Salvatorplatz has one of the largest second-hand book departments in the center of town.

Bavarian Gifts and Souvenirs

The last day spent in a foreign city means not only a sad farewell, but also the unavoidable hunt for souvenirs. Those who are extravagant by nature will already have ordered clothing in the *Trachten* style (see page 209) or have visited the display and sales rooms of the Nymphenburg Porcelain Manufactory on Odeonsplatz in order to select a dinner service or a vase bearing the diamond pattern of the Bavarian coat of arms. Those who love art and have friends who would appreciate Munich's museums also have an easy job: they can buy a copy of an Antique head after a visit to the Glyptothek, a copy of a small Greek vase in the State Collection of Antiquities, or one of a hippopotamus in the State

Collection of Egyptian Art. And in most of the picture galleries they will find high-quality reproductions of the famous paintings of which Munich is so proud.

In and around the city center items can be found which, ranging from the very expensive to the very cheap, will make ideal souvenirs from the Royal Kingdom of Bavaria. Designed in the **folk art** tradition and often decorated in the traditional blue and white colors of Bavaria, such articles may be bought, for example, at Wallach's. Things to look out for are: *Fatschenkinder* (models of the baby Jesus in His swaddling clothes), paintings on glass, *Spanschachteln* (small wooden boxes) from Berchtesgaden, pewter and pottery, traditional cloth, and braid trimmings. A Bavarian cupboard may be rather difficult to pack, however! In the Münchner Heimatwerk department of Beck's store, quality items may be found, ranging from traditional cloth and jewellery to amulets and old prayer books, and from felt hats to the traditional Bavarian *Haferl* shoes. Or would you prefer a small Bavarian lion made of stone? You will find it in the Beck-Dult. A good selection of *Gewürzsträusse* (bunches of spices, herbs, and flowers), country-style dolls, and beer mugs will be found in the Münchner Geschenkstube. In the Blaudruckerei am Viktualienmarkt you can order something very special: country-style linen (*Bauernleinen*) with blue patterning known as *Blaudruck*. Table cloths, napkins, and tea-towels are some of the exquisite articles to be had.

Traditional and handsome items made from wood, tin, glass, clay, or cloth can be acquired in two branches of the old firm of Radspieler in the center of town. The same kinds of wares can be found in different variations at Charivari and at the Bayerische Kunstgewerbe-Verein.

A whole universe of **pewter** figures is available at Babette Schweizer, a shop affiliated with Germany's oldest pewter factory, in Diessen on the Ammersee lake south of

A most exquisite souvenir or gift: Nymphenburg porcelain.

Munich. Soldiers, folk figures, statues of saints, and sacred objects add up to a real Bavaria *en miniature*. Similar items can be purchased from Mory in New City Hall, alongside pewter dishes manufactured according to old traditions.

Just about the whole of Bavaria seems to have been cast in **wax**, with a proliferation of sacred, rural, and historical scenes, coats of arms of cities and rulers, and highly ornate candles the size of organ pipes. Munich's oldest wax-work is that of St. Peter's, established in 1577 and now run by Sebastian Wesely. Just as broad a selection is to be found at Wachszieher am Dom and nearby at Koron-Kerzen.

The Etcetera, in a side street off Maximilianstrasse, is known all over the city for its crazy and ingeneously witty **Bavarian curiosities**. This is a "speciality shop where you find everything you've never been looking for" – for example, a Bavarian-Prussian chess game of Ludwig versus Wilhelm, an Order of the White Sausage, or a watch which goes round the wrong way. The most popular item remains One Square Meter of Bavarian Soil – exactly what this is we will not divulge. There is also a range of fine jewellery, glass, et cetera.

Delicacies always make appropriate gifts: fine chocolates, for example, beautifully wrapped as only Munich knows how and bearing the name of one of the famous confectioners (see Coffeehouses). Those who are looking for something with more of a "kick" will certainly relish original Bavarian mead: a honey wine made from herbs and hops from the Hallertauer, which melts on the tongue leaving a sweet spicy taste. This is the main attraction of the Honig-Häusl on Viktualienmarkt.

Weisswürste (white sausages) do not make good souvenirs, since local custom decrees that they be eaten before midday! If one disregards the "Weisswurst Aquator" – an imaginary line separating the Franconians from the inhabitants of Old Bavaria – then the Franconian varieties of sausage (for example, Kräuter-Leberwürste or Würzburger Knäutele) still belong to Bavaria. You can buy them in the Fränkische Wurst-Häus'le on Viktualienmarkt and in the Fränkische und Westfälische Wurstwaren in Dienerstrasse.

Addresses

Bayerischer Kunstgewerbe-Verein, Pacellistrasse 7
Beck-Dult, Dienerstrasse 20
*Blaudruckerei am Viktualienmarkt –
Traditionsreiche Volkskunst* (owner: Johanna Henkenjohann), Frauenstrasse 12
Charivari-Kunsthandwerk, Brunnstrasse 3 (in the Asamhof)
Etcetera Spezialitäten-Handlung, Wurzerstrasse 12
Fränkische und Westfälische Wurstwaren Clasen, Marienplatz 8 (entrance on Dienerstrasse).
Fränkisches Wurst-Häus'le, on Viktualienmarkt
Honig-Häus'l, on Viktualienmarkt
Koron-Kerzen, Mazaristrasse 1
Ludwig Mory Kunsthandwerk, Marienplatz 8
Münchner Geschenkstube, Marienplatz 8
Münchner Heimatwerk, Beck's department store, Burgstrasse 2
Nymphenburg Porcelain Manufactory, salesroom: Odeonsplatz 1; central office: Nördliches Schlossrondell 8, Nymphenburg Palace
Anna Otter Honig-Fachgeschäft, on Viktualienmarkt
Radspieler, Furniture, furnishings, cloth: Hackenstrasse 7; folk art, silk, fashion, glass, pottery, cooking utensils: Residenzstrasse 23
Babette Schweizer (owner: Ilse Schweizer), Maxburgstrasse 4

Intimate surroundings at the Grüne Gans.

Wachszieher am Dom, Sporerstrasse 2
Wallach Volkskunst und Trachten, Residenzstrasse 3
Sebastian Wesely Wachswaren, Rindermarkt 1

International Cuisine

Recently, Munich has been reaching for the stars: the stars in the Michelin sky. In 1986, fifteen Michelin stars were awarded to the city's restaurants – two three-star awards and nine one-star awards. Admittedly, these "constellations" are somewhat unreliable, and the only astronomical thing about them are the prices. Some tips regarding **gourmet temples** in Munich follow, including restaurants with stars, those without stars, those still without stars, and those no longer with stars.

People who know where to eat go to Aubergine, the restaurant of Witzigmann, Germany's first three-star chef. You will not regret the financial gamble. Most agree that the far more spacious and theatrically furnished Tantris is also top class. In the Käfer-Schänke, it is not only the extensive menu that counts, but also the high society that gathers just to be seen. Le Gourmet offers plush surroundings, panache, and phenomenal truffle tortellini. The Preysing-Keller tempts the palate with exquisite cuisine that is a feast for the eyes as well and also has an excellent wine list. The cuisine of Kay's Bistro, run by Witzigmann's pupil, is ambitious, but the smart-set clientele is more impressed by the decor and the famous visitors. In the Grüne Gans, on the other hand, a small group of committed individualists enjoy *haute cuisine* by candle light.

With its nostalgic elegance, the Walterspiel lives on its cosmopolitan reputation. The Königshof offers classical cuisine with an ambitious style all of its own. The Halali, formerly furbished in Russian leather, and the once soberly middle-class Weinhaus Neuner today bring a breath of fresh air to the tradition of "fine" cuisine. Zum Klösterl, where actors congregate, serves Austrian, Bohemian, and Mexican food.

In Schwabing one can enjoy crayfish or seaweed under crystal chandeliers at La Mer, rabbit supreme at Savarin, and wild breast of duck wrapped in savoy at La Coquille (which is also a suitable place for a cosy tête-à-tête, incidentally).

In gourmet language "international" means, to all intents and purposes, "French" or, at the very least, "having a French touch." Yet special mention must be made of two restaurants serving **French** regional specialities: the Bistro Terrine with Alsatian cooking and the Bouillabaisse with Provençal cuisine. The Austernkeller has oysters flown in from Britanny, while Chesa-Rüegg and Walliser Stuben maintain the related Swiss cuisine.

Italian chefs are not at all bothered by the niceties of *haute cuisine*; they simply rule foreign gastronomy all over the city. If you can read Italian, know how to enjoy Italian food, and are good at spending money, you will enjoy Da Pippo's pasta creations in Bogenhausen. The intimate Galleria, hidden away in the center of town, complements the art on its walls with the culinary art on its plates. Some of the most distinguished Italian cooking to be found in Munich is served in pleasant surroundings at the Janus-Keller in Schwabing. Gattopardo's, too, is excellent.

Staying with the Mediterranean for a moment, **Greek** restauranteurs have set up their headquarters in Haidhausen. Kytaro, Korfu Lotus, and Olympia are just three of the many Greek restaurants in this part of town, while Schwabing boasts Zorbas, with its pleasant garden. Among the **Yugoslavian** restaurants, Opatija is both the oldest and the most distinguished and comfortable.

Whoever wants to speak, or at least hear, **Czechoslovakian** when eating loin roast and *powideltatschkerln* will head for the Goldene Stadt carrying a well-filled purse, or to St. Wenzel or the Praha with a slightly lighter one. Lovers of **Hungarian** cuisine will make a similar distinction between the Piroschka-Csarda (with tsigane music) and the Puszta-Csarda. Excellent **Russian** food is served at the Datscha.

A trip to the Far East is only a stone's throw away in each area of Munich. The oldest and most distinguished **Chinese** restaurant is the Tai-Tung, the most easy-going and comfortable the Peking. Experts hold that the food served at Lotos and Fung Wah is the least Europeanized. **Japanese** cooking has established itself thanks to Daitokai, where each table has its own chef, and to Mifune, where you can eat sitting on mats. The prices, however, are not exactly floor-level. Mekong was the first of Munich's increasingly popular **Vietnamese** restaurants. Finally, there is Trader Vic's, which serves **Polynesian** food until late at night.

Whoever sets store by traditional **English surroundings** complete with fireplace and candle light, but does not wish to forego French and Italian cuisine, will have to make sure to get one of the forty seats at Eaton Place. If you want to give the other extreme a try, and eat with your fingers in the **medieval manner,** you will find a boisterous, positively feudal atmosphere in the Welser Küche.

Festive atmosphere in the Königssaal of Mongelas Mansion (Hotel Bayerischer Hof).

Daitokai, Nordendstrasse 64
Datscha, Kaiserstrasse 3
Eaton Place, Mariannenstrasse 3
Fung Wah, Prinzregentenplatz 11
Galleria, Ledererstrasse 2
Goldene Stadt, Einsteinstrasse 177
Grüne Gans, Am Einlass 5
Halali, Schönfeldstrasse 22
Il Gattopardo, Georgenstrasse 67
Janus-Keller, Elisabethstrasse 12
Käfer-Schänke, Prinzregentenstrasse 73
Kay's Bistro, Utzschneiderstrasse 1
Königshof, Karlsplatz 25
Korfu Lotos, Rosenheimer Strasse 98
Kytaro, Innere Wiener Strasse 36
La Coquille, Römerstrasse 15
La Mer, Schraudolphstrasse 24
Le Gourmet, Ligsalzstrasse 46
Lotos, Konrad-Celtis-Strasse 33
Mekong, Lachnerstrasse 1
Mifune, Ismaninger Strasse 136
Olympia, Kellerstrasse 29
Opatija, Brienner Strasse 41
Peking, Lindwurmstrasse 167
Piroschka-Csarda, Prinzregentenstrasse 1
Praha, Rossmarkt 3
Preysing-Keller, Innere Wiener Strasse 6
Puszta-Csarda, Volkartstrasse 15
St. Wenzel, Ungererstrasse 67
Savarin, Schellingstrasse 122
Tai-Tung, Prinzregentenstrasse 60
Tantris Restaurant, Johann-Fichte-Strasse 7
Trader Vic's, Hotel Bayerischer Hof, Promenadeplatz 4
Walliser Stuben, 40, Leopoldstrasse 33
Walterspiel, Hotel Vier Jahreszeiten, Maximilianstrasse 17
Weinhaus Neuner, Herzogspitalstrasse 8
Welser Kuche, Residenzstrasse 27
Zum Klösterl, St.-Anna-Strasse 2
Zorbas, Königinstrasse 34

Addresses

Aubergine Restaurant, Maximiliansplatz 5
Austernkeller, Stollbergstrasse 11
Bistro Terrine, Amalienstrasse 89
Bouillabaisse, Falkenturmstrasse 10
Chesa-Rüegg, Wurzerstrasse 18
Da Pippo, Brahmsstrasse 32

Bavarian Cooking

Bavaria was divided into three parts in its past. A fourth division has been caused by the white sausage (*Weisswurst*), which has split the Bavarians into those who consider it to be delicious and those who find it to be tasteless. Total agreement exists, however, about the qualities of other traditional local delicacies: *Leberkäs* ("livercheese," which contains neither liver nor cheese!), *Schweinshaxe* (roast leg of pork), *Surhaxe* (pork pickled in spicy sauce), *Schweinsbraten mit Semmelknödel* (roast pork with bread dumplings), *Kalbslüngerl* (lungs of calf), *Kutteln* (tripe), *Blutwurstgröstl* (potatoes and blood sausage fried together), *Leberknödelsuppe* (liver dumpling soup) or *aufgeschmalzene Brotsuppe* (bread soup with fried onions), *Dampfnudeln* (steamed jam dumplings), *Auszogne* (flat doughnuts), and *Zwetschgendatschi* (plum cake). Such local food is served in any number of guises – as "superior home-style cooking," "home-style cooking," "traditional cooking," etc. The menu will usually allow you to choose standard German dishes as well.

The Straubinger Hof prepares traditional local food in the classical Munich way. *Filet in Bier-Kümmel-Sauce* (fillet of beef in beer sauce), *Briesmilzwurst* (a type of beef sausage meat), *Kaiserschmarrn* (scrambled pancake with raisins) – the menu is long, and the portions large. *Weisswürste* may be ordered from 9 a.m. onwards. The Braunauer Hof has a similar cuisine, but it, too, is usually very crowded. A table as long as a race track, beer in mugs with lids, two beer gardens, and delicious food are what Zum Dürrbräu has to offer. The Bratwurstherzl, behind the Church of the Holy Ghost, opens at 8 a.m. It is especially favored by those who work in the Viktualienmarkt, as well as by those shopping there, because of its fine *Bratwürste* (fried sausages) and because of the excellent *Hirnsuppe* (brain soup), *Beinfleisch* (juicy beef or pork), and *Lüngerl* (stewed lung). Traditional Munich fare may also be eaten in the Weisses Bräuhaus in the Tal. Its *Schneiderweisse* – an excellent wheat beer, bottle-fermented in the traditional way – is famous all over the city. Bögner, also in the Tal, is

The classic Munich snack.

Mongelas Mansion; Bavarian and international cuisine is served in its basement restaurant.

similar in character. The rather arty folk-art decor of the Wirtshaus zur Weissblauen Rose cannot disguise the fact that the food is genuinely traditional. The reliable menu of the Nürnberger Bratwurst-Glöckl, a restaurant steeped in tradition, adds a Franconian accent to the prevailing Bavarian one. Its small beer garden reaches right up to the apse of the Cathedral, while in the interior, with its engravings of Munich on the walls, high spirits are well-nigh impossible to tame.

The Augustinerbräu comprises a restaurant, a beer hall, and an *Imbiss* (snack bar) and thus manages to keep more leisurely customers apart from those who wish to eat quickly. This is the case in many beer halls. In the picturesque Muschelsaal (see page 74), one can enjoy home-style cooking in splendid, comfortable surroundings. The Zum Spöckmeier restaurant, with its wooden panelled rooms, exudes old Munich charm and is well known for its excellent traditional cooking. In the Ratskeller, under Neo-Gothic arches, one can eat a very good roast piglet. Actors, lawyers, doctors, politicans from "next door," and well-off travelers form the clientele of the Franziskaner's "Fuchsenstuben." The menu includes everything from *Rahmbeuscherl* (cooked lung, liver, and sweatbread of calf heated in cream sauce) to international (indeed, too international!) cuisine. Its "Brotzeitstüberl" (a Bavarian snack bar) does more justice to Bavarian specialities.

Excellent Bavarian cooking, as well as international cuisine, is served in cultivated surroundings at Zum Bürgerhaus (in the center of town), at the Schlosswirtschaft zur Schwaige (in Nymphenburg Palace), and at the Weichandhof (in Obermenzing).

Breweries, Beer Cellars, and Beer Gardens

Beer gardens are Munich's sacred cows. They are often called beer "cellars" – one sits on, rather than in them. In earlier times brewing was not permitted in summer, so the winter beer was stored in deep cellars in, or on the edge of town, and chestnut trees planted above them for shade. Not surprisingly, this led to beer and food being sold in these places. Restaurant owners, however, protested against the sale of food, with the result that customers could buy only beer and had to bring along their own food. Today, one *may* do so, but does not *have* to, as there is always a menu with hearty dishes. Later, beer gardens without cellars came into being wherever nature permitted.

Of the beer cellars in the center of town, the Augustiner-Keller is cherished most by the inhabitants of Munich. Its majestic chestnut trees give shade to 5,000 seats, many of which "belong" to the regulars. With its arcades and fountains, the beer garden in the Hofbräuhaus is certainly picturesque and, like the rooms inside, would be an attractive place to sit, were it not for the fact that its very notoriety causes it to degenerate into a mass of raucous people swaying to music – a form of enjoyment which has absolutely nothing to do with Munich. By contrast, the Hofbräukeller and Löwenbräukeller – large restaurants with beer gardens – have remained true to Munich tradition. The Salvator-Keller on the Nockherberg even manages to get important politicans to talk to each other, probably owing to its strong, dark *Fastenbier* (Lent beer), which was called Salvator by the Paulaner monks. (All other strong beers followed suit and used this "-ator" ending.) Visitors come in droves to the Salvator-Keller in March, the strong beer season. The Max-Emanuel-Brauerei offers a special attraction besides its restaurant and beer garden: the "Münchner Volkssänger-bühne" (a cabaret with folk singers), which subjects the literature of the world to Bavarian parody – great fun!

The beer garden around the Chinese Tower in the English Garden was depicted by landscape painters of the nineteenth century bathed in sunlight and teeming with life. It is even more turbulent today – a stomping ground for 7,000 people at a time. Also in the English Garden are the Seehaus beer garden on the Kleinhesseloher Lake and, on a much smaller scale, the Osterwaldgarten, a favorite haunt of Munich's students. In the Sankt Emmerams Mühle or in the Grüntal – both in the north of town – members of the smart set are (almost) to themselves. To the south, on the banks of the Isar, is the appealing Menterschwaige. Families, companies, and groups of friends make for the Aumeister, with its 2,000 seats; the Hirschgarten, with 7,000 (a good place if you have children); or the Waldwirtschaft Grosshesselohe, with room for 2,000. Some tips for beer garden veterans: Fasanerie in the Hartmannshofen district; the Schlosswirtschaft in Schleissheim Palace; the Post in Oberföhring; and the Iberl in Solln.

Addresses

Augustinerbräu, Neuhauser Strasse 16
Augustiner-Keller, Arnulfstrasse 52
Biergarten am Chinesischen Turm, Englischer Garten 3
Bratwurstherzl, Heiliggeiststrasse 3
Braunauer Hof, Frauenstrasse 40
Fasanerie, Hartmannshofer Strasse 20
Franziskaner und Fuchsenstuben, Perusastrasse 5
Grüntal, Grüntal 15
Hackerkeller, Schwanthalerstrasse 111
Hirschgarten, Hirschgartenallee 1
Hofbräuhaus, Platzl 9
Hofbräukeller, Innere Wiener Strasse 19
Iberl (with garden), Wilhelm-Leibl-Strasse 22
Kaisergarten, Kaiserstrasse 34
Löwenbräukeller-Biergarten, Nymphenburger Strasse 2
Mathäser-Bierstadt, Bayerstrasse 5
Max-Emanuel-Brauerei, Adalbertstrasse 33
Menterschwaige, Harthauser Strasse 70
Nürnberger Bratwurst-Glöckl am Dom, Frauenplatz 9 (next to the Cathedral)
Osterwaldgarten, Keferstrasse 12
Post (with garden), Oberföhringer Strasse 155
Pschorr-Keller, Theresienhöhe 7
Ratskeller, Marienplatz 8
Salvator-Keller, Hochstrasse 77
Sankt Emmerams Mühle, St. Emmeram 41
Schlosswirtschaft Schleisseim (with garden), Schleissheim, Old Palace
Schlosswirtschaft zur Schwaige (with garden), south wing of Nympenburg Palace
Schwabinger Bräu, Leopoldstrasse 82
Seehaus-Biergarten on the Kleinhesseloher Lake in the English Garden
Spatenhaus-Bräustuben, Residenzstrasse 12
Straubinger Hof (with garden), Blumenstrasse 5
Waldwirtschaft Grosshesselohe, 8023 Grosshesselohe, Georg-Kalb-Strasse 3
Weichandhof (with garden), Betzenweg 81
Weisses Bräuhaus, Tal 10
Wirtshaus zur Weissblauen Rose, Marienplatz 11
Zum Aumeister, Sondermeierstrasse 1
Zum Bögner, Tal 72
Zum Bürgerhaus, Pettenkoferstrasse 1
Zum Dürnbräu, Tal 21
Zum Spöckmeier, Rosenstrasse 9

Coffeehouses and Cafés

In Vienna, the difference between a coffeehouse and a café would be the subject of a philosophical discussion. In Munich, definitions are more clear-cut. A coffeehouse, permeated by the aroma of confectionery, is a place in which you can order a well-earned piece of cake and pot of coffee after shopping, whereas a café is a place where people gather around a table, talk, and read newspapers until late at night, and do not just stick to coffee and cake.

Café Annast: Relaxing in the pleasant surroundings of the Court Garden.

The **oldest coffeehouses** are located mainly in the pedestrian precinct, and offer pastries and chocolates made on the premises with an individual touch (they make good presents!). Among them are the Feldherrnhalle; Arzmiller; Rottenhöfer (Hag); the Kreuzkamm, with its specialities of *Baumkuchen* (pyramid cake) and *Dresdner Stollen* (a light fruit cake); and Rischart's Backhaus, which specializes in strudel. In addition, there is Erbshäuser just to the north of Marienplatz, Zur Schönen Münchnerin opposite the Haus der Kunst, and Wiener on Reichenbachplatz (whose specialities are cakes made without baking powder and vegetable cakes). The once-famous writers' café Luitpold – a coffeehouse/restaurant with its own pastry shop – is now visited mainly by business executives and women carrying shopping bags from fashionable boutiques.

The following cafés stand out because of their **attractive location**: the Café Glockenspiel, overlooking Marienplatz from five floors up and with a good view of the City Hall glockenspiel; Annast, with summer tables in Munich's most attractive spot, the Court Garden and Odeonsplatz; and, in Luitpold Park, the Bamberger Haus café, with its idyllic garden terrace. For theater lovers, the café/restaurant Die Kulisse is also an attractive location – actors meet there. A visit to the Stadtmuseum can be wound up with a coffee in Brum (in the museum itself) or, just opposite, in Bienenkorb. Bookworms from the State Library and the University Library end up in Trötsch's, in the Café an der Uni, or in Schmid's.

Anyone looking for an **original touch** will find it in the Schmalznudel Café Frischut on Viktualienmarkt. Here, a mixed clientele gathers to eat *Rohrnudeln* (a sort of doughnut) and drink coffee between five o'clock in the morning and one o'clock at night. The Schmankerl-Café, also on Viktualienmarkt, serves good strong coffee and Bavarian beer. In the unique atmosphere of the Turmstüberl in the Valentin Museum, over a liver dumpling soup, coffee, and a pastry, it becomes clear that all the world is a stage. The various

types of Viennese coffee can be sampled in the Kleines Wiener Kaffeehaus in the Asamhof. The Villanis Café-Bistro, also in the Asamhof, will serve you *crèpes* until one o'clock at night.

Among the colorful **Schwabing cafés**, the Extrablatt is the place to see and be seen. Names from the gossip columns turn up here in person. If you are really curious about them, just sit around for a bit. Intellectuals, filmmakers, and the young people of Schwabing congregate at the Café Münchener Freiheit and its nearby branch, the Forum. In summer, you can sit under large parasols and enjoy the house's specialities – ice cream, and marzipan in all shapes and sizes. Students frequent the Monopteros, situated between the university and the English Garden, and the Oase in the Amalienpassage. The Café im Studiotheater München attracts actors and all kinds of "characters." With its variety of cakes, lunch menus, and a large choice of breakfast foods, the Höflinger in the west part of Schwabing is also a good bet. It has branches in this and other parts of town.

Of the many cafés in the up-and-coming district of **Haidhausen**, the Café Grössenwahn and the Sedan, as well as the Café Wiener Platz, are the talk of the town. In the first two, smart socialites gather; in the latter, one is more likely to encounter those who cultivate a causal look. In **Nymphenburg**, the Ruffini is an attractive haunt of young people. Run by a cooperative, the service is excellent in this cafe-cum-wine bar/restaurant with an Italian touch.

Addresses

Café an der Uni, Ludwigstrasse 24
Café Annast, Odeonsplatz 18
(also open in the evening)
Café Arzmiller, Salvatorstrasse 2
(Theatinerhof)
Café Bamberger Haus, Brunnerstrasse 2
(also open in the evening)
Café Bienenkorb, Oberanger 26
Café Brum im Stadtmuseum, Sankt-Jakobs-Platz 1 (also open in the evening)
Café Die Kulisse, Maximilianstrasse 26
(also open in the evening)
Café Erbshäuser, Glückstrasse 1
Café Extrablatt, Leopoldstrasse 7
(also open in the evening)
Café Feldherrnhalle, Theatinerstrasse 38
Café Fischbacher, Reichenbachstrasse 10
Café Glockenspiel, Marienplatz 28
Café Grössenwahn, Lothringer Strasse 11
(also open in the evening)
Café Höflinger, Schleissheimer Strasse 85;
and Elisabethstrasse 19/21, Friedrichstrasse 1,
Leonrodstrasse 47
Kleines Wiener Kaffeehaus, Kreuzstrasse 3 a
Café Kreutzkamm, Maffeistrasse 4

Konditorei-Café Kustermann, Lindwurm-strasse 36
Café Luitpold, Brienner Strasse 11
Café Monopteros, Königinstrasse 43
(also open in the evening)
Café Münchener Freiheit, Münchener Freiheit 20; and *Café im Forum,* Münchener Freiheit 7
Café am Salvatorplatz, Salvatorplatz 2
Café Eisenrieder, Ungererstrasse 137
Café Oase, Amalienstrasse 89
(also open in the evening)
Café Rischart's Backhaus, Marienplatz 18
Conditorei–Café Rottenhöfer (Hag), Residenzstrasse 25/26.
Café Ruffini, Orffstrasse 22-24
(also open in the evening)
Café Schmid, Amalienstrasse 97
Schmankerl-Café, Frauenstrasse 7
Schmalznudel Café Frischhut, Prälat-Zistl-Strasse 8
Café Sedan, Gravelottestrasse 7
Café im studiotheater münchen, Ungerer-strasse 19 (also open in the evening)
Café Trötsch, Schönfeldstrasse 24
Café Turmstüberl im Valentin-Musäum, Tal 43
Villanis Café-Bistro, Kreuzstrasse 3b
(Asamhof) (also open in the evening)
Café Wiener Platz, Innere Wiener Strasse 48
(also open in the evening)
Konditorei–Café Wiener, Rumfordstrasse 8a and Sebastiansplatz 12
Café Zur Schönen Münchnerin, Karl-Schar-nagl-Ring 60

Venues for Night Owls

Casual students will sometimes succeed where smartly dressed business people fail, and get past the two bouncers at the doors of P1 – just one aspect of Munich's nightlife that has neither rhyme nor reason. Yuppies, the very chic, and antimacho types between the ages of 20 and 35 (over)populate this up-scale disco which, for quite a long time now, has maintained its position as Munich's number-one trend-setter. In the Park Café one finds a completely different scene. You can take a tranquil afternoon tea at five o'clock, but beware: it livens up later and becomes a tur-bulent disco! Punk ladies, aging social lions, and a sprinkling of young men in Lederhosen are the extreme poles in a very mixed clien-tele.

Here are some further glamorous dives for **disco-freaks.** The Tanzcafé im Seehaus has rapidly made it to the top with its mixture of funk and fun. The older Charly M and East Side both used to be pretty snobby, but now have a younger, more mixed clientele. Hard rock freaks gather in the Sugar Shake, while trend-setters move around a glass dance floor at Maximilian's. Anyone whose taste is black – in music and in people – will make for Cadillac. In the Tanzcafé Grössenwahn, those who share an alternative life-style will feel at home. The Orange Disco, despite its name, does admit non-Bagwhans.

If you are somewhat older and enjoy more **traditional dancing,** you will have problems finding the right place. The elegant night club in the Bayerischer Hof has excellent bands and fine drinks – a good tip for those with a cultivated taste. The Sheraton's night club, the Vibraphone, offers the same degree of luxury, while the tasteful ba-ba-lu is easier on the pocket, if not on the legs! The Lehnbach-Palast, with its crystal and plush opulence, is the place for those who love to move around to the sound of tangos and foxtrots and, now and again, disco music. With its infectious atmosphere, the Ball der einsamen Herzen ("Lonely Hearts' Ball") belies its name night

Munich at night, as seen from the Olympic Tower.

after night. With around 200 visitors, it is not too difficult to exchange your partner for the "right" one. The Philoma, which plays a considerable variety of music, manages to mix active pensioniers with inquisitive adolescents.

Among the **bars**, Schumann's, with its legendary boss Charles and the ultra-cool barmen, ranks as the first star in the night sky of Munich's champagne society. Harry's New York Bar comes a close second, and lives up to its name with original cocktails and excellent pianists. But Madrigal may well have ousted both these bars in the insider's affections, with its successful division into a bistro-restaurant and a piano bar. In any case, the night owls' preferences change like the wind – all of the above may or may not still be true. The Wunder Bar is a favorite haunt of the young and middle-aged intelligentsia. Decorated by students from the Academy of Visual Arts, this basement bar plays recordings of good Fifties jazz and other music. The clientele of Adam's City, with a bar and low-priced restaurant that are open until the early hours, is a colorful mix. Near Goetheplatz (an otherwise deserted area at night), Gratzer's Lobby has, for a long time, exhibited a cultivated taste. It offers a large assortment of wines and you can also get a decent bite to eat. In Schwabing, Gisela, a former cabaret artiste of the Sixties, has recently opened a bar: the Schwabinger Gisela. It is a cosy place for an evening drink.

Typical **hotel piano bars** are the King's Corner Club in the Königshof Hotel, which has an outstanding wine list; Regina's Cocktail Lounge, with an infinite number of whiskies; and the Kamin-Bar in the Holiday-Inn, with its English-style decor.

Insomniacs can find a totally different type of bar in Schwabing: the **Kneipe**, which is a mixture of restaurant, bar, café, and pub. It is usually very full, very smoky, and a good place to meet people. In some cases one can eat late, until two or three o'clock in the morning. The most famous one of all is the Alte Simpl, once the meeting place of Schwabing's artists and writers. Such famous names as Frank Wedekind and Olaf Gulbransson still keep an eye on proceedings, looking down from old photographs on their present-day successors – filmmakers, journalists, actors and actresses, and publishers. If you are not interested in finding a place on this Mount Olympus, then pay a visit to Charivari – although it is probably easier to get a seat on Olympus! La Bohème serves Italian food in elegant domestic surroundings, Mykonos offers Greek fare, and the Alte Ofen provides good home-style cooking amidst grandma's furniture. If you want to play pool, chess, or cards until one o'clock at night, or get an early breakfast at 7 a.m., then try the Schelling-Salon – a traditional, inimitably easy-going *Kneipe*.

In Leopoldstrasse, Feilitzschstrasse, and Occamstrasse, night owls will find an almost unlimited number of opportunities to enjoy themselves: **bistros, pubs, clubs, night-cafés**. Four deserve special mention. The Shalom-Club is a pleasant departure from the norm, in that it entertains its public with Jewish, French, and Spanish songs. In the early hours, the owner himself, a former *chansonnier*, performs with considerable skill. The Drugstore lives up to its cosmopolitan name with an easy-going atmosphere, fine breakfasts for those who get up late, a kiosk with the world's press, and a revue theater upstairs. The Munich combines a French bistro with an American bar, the latter with mute wild west movies accompanied by rather less mute pop music. Its speciality is a Happy Hour, or *L'heure bleue*, between 6 and 8 p.m. In the Kneipencafé Säge one can meet garrulous Bohemian types.

Addresses

Adam's City, Pacellistrasse 2
Alter Ofen, Zieblandstrasse 41
Alter Simpl, 40, Türkenstrasse 57
ba-ba-lu, Ainmillerstrasse 1
Ball der einsamen Herzen, Klenzestrasse 71
Cadillac, Theklastrasse 1
Charivari, Türkenstrasse 92
Charly M, Maximiliansplatz 5
Drugstore, Feilitztstrasse 12
East Side, Rosenheimer Strasse 30
Gratzer's Lobby, Beethovenplatz 2-3
Harry's New York Bar, Falkenturmstrasse 9
Kamin-Bar, Leopoldstrasse 194
King's Corner Club, Karlsplatz 25
Kneipencafé Säge, Feilitzschstrasse 9
La Bohème, Türkenstrasse 79
Lenbach-Palast, Lenbachplatz 3
Madrigal, Herzog-Rudolf-Strasse 1
Maximilian's, Maximiliansplatz 16
Munich, Leopoldstrasse 9
Mykonos, Georgenstrasse 105
Nightclub im Bayerischen Hof, Promenadeplatz 6
Orange Disco, Sunday through Wednesday in California New, Occamstrasse 24; at the weekend in the Theaterfabrik Unterföhring, Föhringer Allee 23.
P1, Prinzregentenstrasse 1
Park Café, Sophienstrasse 7
Philoma, Schleissheimer Strasse 12
Regina's Cocktail Lounge, Maximiliansplatz 5
Schelling-Salon, Schellingstrasse 54
Schumann's, Maximilianstrasse 36
Schwabinger Gisela, Herzog-Heinrich-Strasse 38
Shalom-Club, Leopoldstrasse 130
Sugar Shake, Herzogspitalstrasse 6
Tanzcafé Grössenwahn, Klenzestrasse 43
Tanzcafé im Seehaus (in the English Garden), Kleinhesselohe 3
Vibraphon, Arabellastrasse 6
Wunder Bar, Hochbrückenstrasse 3

Addresses, Opening Hours, Etc.

*Times in [square brackets]
refer to winter opening hours*

Information Bureaus

CITY TOURIST OFFICE
(Fremdenverkehrsamt München):

Central Station, south exit (Bayerstrasse).
Tel. 2391256-7. Open daily, 8 a.m.-11 p.m.

Airport (Munich-Riem), Arrivals Hall.
Tel. 907256 and 2391266. Mon. to Sat.
8.30 a.m.-10 p.m., Sun. 1-9 p.m.

Central office, Rindermarkt 5. Tel. 23911.
Mon. to Fri. 8 a.m.-4 p.m.

**Presse- und Informationsamt der Stadt
München** (City Press and Information
Office), New City Hall, Marienplatz 8,
Room 241. Tel. 2336447. Mon. to Thurs.
8 a.m.-3.45 p.m., Fri. 8 a.m.-2 p.m.

*Gasteig Arts Center: Philharmonic Hall, Richard
Strauss Conservatory, Municipal Library, and
Adult Education Center united under one roof.*

New City Hall: Main portal.

Citizens Information Center on Stachus
(Karlsplatz), ground floor. Tel. 554459.
Mon. to Fri. 8 a.m.-6 p.m.

Jugend-Informations-Zentrum
(Information Center for Young People),
Paul-Heyse-Strasse 22. Tel. 531655. Mon.
to Fri. 11 a.m.-7 p.m., Sat. 11 a.m.- 5 p.m.

Advance Booking for Concerts, etc.

Abendzeitung ticket office, Sendlinger
Strasse 79. Tel. 267024.

abr Theater Booking, Neuhauser Strasse 9.
Tel. (5904) 421-422.

Bavarian State Opera booking office,
Maximilianstrasse 11. Tel. 221316.
Mon. to Fri. 10-12.30 a.m. and
3.30-5.30 p.m., Sat. 10-12.30 a.m.

Convention Hall of the Deutsches Museum,
Museumsinsel. Tel. 298430, 221790.
Mon. to Fri. 3-6 p.m., Sat. 11 a.m.-2 p.m.

Cuvilliés Theater. See Bavarian State Opera.

Gasteig Arts Center, Rosenheimer Strasse 5.
Tel. 4181614. Advance booking in the
"glass hall": Mon. to Fri. 10.30 a.m.-2 p.m.
and 3-6 p.m., Sat. 10.30 a.m.-2 p.m.

Hallo travel agent, in the PEP (Perlach-Ein-
kaufs-Passagen), Thomas-Dehler-Strasse 12.
Tel. 6371044

Hercules Hall in the Residence, evening box
office (entrance from Court Garden).
Tel. 224641.

Lehmkuhl bookshop, Leopoldstrasse 45.
Concert tickets, Tel. 398042.

Max Hieber, Liebfrauenstrasse 1
(next to the Cathedral). Tel. 226571.

Olympic Park. Booking office for events in
the Olympic Hall and Ice Stadium, as well as
for soccer matches in the Olympic Stadium:
Ice Stadium, Tel. 3061357. Mon. to Thurs.
8 a.m.-5 p.m., Fri. 8 a.m.-2 p.m. Also
obtainable from **Münchner Merkur – tz,**
Paul-Heyse-Strasse 2-4 (Tel. 53060), and
Sport-Scheck, Sendlinger Strasse 85 (Tel.
2166252).

Otto Bauer, Marienplatz 8 (in New City Hall,
Landschaftsstrasse entrance). Concert tickets. Tel. 221757.

Radio-Rim, Theatinerstrasse 17.
Tel. 551702/53.

"Old Peter," the tower of St. Peter's Church, offers the finest view of the Old Town.

Residenz-Bücherstube, Residenzstrasse 1. Concert tickets. Tel. 220868.

Studiosus-Reisen, Amalienstrasse 73. Student tickets only. Tel. 280768. Mon. to Sat. 10 a.m.-2 p.m.

Theater on Gärtnerplatz, Gärtnerplatz 3. Tel. 2016767. Mon. to Fri. 10-12.30 a.m. and 3.30-5.30 p.m., Sat. 10-12.30 a.m.

Towers Open to the Public

Bavaria, Theresa Hill. View from the head of the monument. Tues. to Sun. 10-12 a.m. and 2-5.30[4] p.m.

Cathedral, Frauenplatz. Elevator to room at height of 302 ft. in south tower. Daily 9 a.m.-6 p.m. (closed in winter).

New City Hall, Marienplatz (279 ft.). Elevator to the gallery on the ninth floor (230 ft.). Mon. to Fri. 8[8.30] a.m.-6[3.45] p.m.

Olympic Tower (950 ft.), Olympic Park. Elevator to 620-30 ft. Daily 8[9] a.m.-12 p.m. Rotating restaurant.

St. Peter's Church, Rindermarkt. 302-ft.-high tower, with gallery at 187 ft. Mon. to Sat. 8 a.m.-5 p.m., Sun. 10 a.m.-7 p.m. (closed in bad weather).

Fine Views

Maximilianeum at the end of Maximilianstrasse (on the right bank of the Isar). Terrace with view of the Old Town.

Monopteros in the English Garden. View of the Old Town.

Olympic Hill (197 ft.). View of the north-east part of Munich and, on a clear day, of the Alps.

Prince Regent Terrace at the foot of the Angel of Peace (on the right bank of the Isar). View of the Old Town.

Terrace of the Hall of Fame on Theresa Hill. View of the Theresa Meadows.

City Sight-Seeing Tours

(organized by the Münchner Fremdenrundfahrten oHG, Central Station. Tel. 1204/248).
Departure for all tours from the Bahnhofsplatz, opposite the main entrance of Central Station.

Short tour: approx. 1 hour. Daily at 10 a.m. and 2.30 p.m. From May 1 to October 31 also at 11.30 a.m.

Long tour: approx. 2½ hours, including visits to the Alte Pinakothek and the Cathedral, Nymphenburg Palace and the Amalienburg. Daily at 10 a.m., except Mondays.

Tour of the Olympic grounds, including ascent of the Olympic Tower: approx. 2½ hours. Daily at 10 a.m. and 2.30 p.m.

Munich at Night: approx. 5 hours, including visits to three typical Munich establishments. Wed. to Sat. at 7.30 p.m. From November 1 to April 30 on Fridays and Saturdays only.

Flights Over the City

Weather permitting, from the airport at Munich-Riem (organized by Airtrade, Executive Charter- und Reiseservice, Drosselweg 7, 8011 Kirchheim. Tel. 9036434).

Flight over the city: approx. 20 minutes. Sat., Sun., and on public holidays at 9 a.m. or by appointment.

Flight by helicopter (over the city center): approx. 15 minutes. Minimum of three persons. Sat. 11.15 and 12 a.m.

By appointment: **flights over the lakes, Alps, and castles of Bavaria.** Weekends, approx. 20-90 minutes.

Museums, Art Collections, Palaces and Castles, Exhibitions

Alte Pinakothek, Barer Strasse 27. Tel. 2380 5215/216. Tues. to Sun. 9 a.m.-4.30 p.m., Tues. and Thurs. also 7-9 p.m. Admission free on Sundays and public holidays.

Bavarian National Museum. Prinzregentenstrasse 3. Tel. 2168-1. Tues. to Sun. 9.30. Admission free on Sundays and public holidays.

Branch in Old Schleissheim Palace. Tel. 3155272. Folklore collection. Tues. to Sun. 10 a.m.-5 p.m.

Bavarian State Collection of General and Applied Geology, Luisenstrasse 37. Tel. 5 20 31. Mon. to Fri. 8 a.m.-6 p.m. Admission free.

BMW Museum, Petuelring 130. Tel. 38 95/33 07. Daily 9 a.m.-5 p.m.

Castle Museum, Grünwald: see State Prehistorical Collection.

Collection of Meissen Porcelain, Lustheim Palace (in Schleissheim Palace park). Tel. 3 15 02 12. Tues. to Sun. 10-12.30 a.m. and 1.30-5[4] p.m.

Deutsches Museum, Museumsinsel 1. Tel. 2 17 91. Daily 9 a.m.-5 p.m.

German Museum of Hunting and Fishing, Neuhauser Strasse 53. Tel. 22 05 22. Tues. to Sun. 9.30 a.m.-4 p.m., Mon. 7-10 p.m.

German Theater Museum, Galeriestrasse 4 a (Court Garden arcade). Tel. 22 24 49. Library: Tues. and Thurs. 10-12 a.m. and 1.30-4 p.m. Photographic Collection: Tues. 10-12 a.m., Thurs. 2-4 p.m. Archive and Study Collection: by appointment.

Glyptothek, Königsplatz 3. Tel. 28 61 00. Tues., Wed., and Fri.to Sun. 10 a.m.-4.30 p.m., Thurs. 12 a.m.-8.30 p.m. Admission free on Sundays and public holidays.

Haidhausen Museum, Kirchenstrasse 24. Exhibitions on the history of Haidhausen and on the social history of workers and day laborers. Sun. to Wed. 4-6 p.m.

Haus der Kunst, Prinzregentenstrasse 1. Tel. 22 26 51. Exhibitions in the central and eastern sections of the building. Daily 9.30 a.m.-6 p.m., Thurs. to 9 p.m. Western section: see State Gallery of Modern Art.

Hypo-Kunsthalle, Theatinerstrasse 15. Tel. 22 44 12. Changing exhibitions. Daily 10 a.m.-6 p.m.

Alte Pinakothek: A must for lovers of art.

Lustheim Palace: The Ernst Schneider Collection of Meissen Porcelain.

Haus der Kunst: Scene of major international exhibitions.

Munich City Museum: Visitors enjoy a performance on the orchestrion in the collection of musical instruments.

Kunstraum München, Nikolaistrasse 15. Tel. 34 89 20. Changing exhibitions. Tues. to Fri. 3-6.30 p.m., Sat. 11 a.m.-1 p.m. Admission free.

Meter Museum, Stadtwerke Elektrizitätswerke, Franzstrasse 9. Tel. 38 10 13 93. Wed. 9-12 a.m. Admission free.

Munich Art Association, Galeriestrasse 4 c. Tel. 22 11 52. Changing exhibitions. Tues. to Sun. 10 a.m.-6 p.m.

Munich City Museum, Sankt-Jacobs-Platz 1. Tel. 23 32 3 70. Tues. to Sat. 9 a.m.-4.30 p.m., Sun. 10 a.m.-6 p.m. Admission free on Sundays and public holidays. Silbersalon: Historical interiors in the Altes Hackerhaus (administered by the Munich City Museum), Sendlinger Strasse 75 (entrance on Hackenstrasse). Sat. 1-4.30 p.m., Sun. 10 a.m.-6 p.m.

The Residence: Ludwig I's Nibelung Halls.

Munich Firefighting Museum, Blumenstrasse 34. Tel. 238061. Sat. 9 a.m.-4 p.m. and by appointment. Admission free.

Municipal Gallery in Lenbach House, Luisenstrasse 33. Tel. 521041. Tues. to Sun. 10 a.m.-6 p.m. Admission free on Sundays and public holidays.

Museum of Casts of Antique Sculpture, Meiserstrasse 10. Tel. 5591560/557. Mon. to Fri. by appointment. Admission free.

Museum of Chamber Pots – Manfred Klauda Collection, Böcklingstrasse 30. Tel. 1575989. Sun. 10 a.m.-1 p.m., Thurs. 2-6 p.m.

Museum of Sewing Machines and Irons, J. Strobel & Söhne GmbH & Co., Heimeranstrasse 68-70. Tel. 510880. Mon. to Fri. 10 a.m.-4 p.m. Admission free.

Neue Pinakothek, Barer Strasse 29. Tel. 23805195. Tues. to Sun. 9 a.m.-4.30 p.m., Tues. also 7-9 p.m. Admission free on Sundays and public holidays.

Nymphenburg Palace and Pavilions. Tel. 17908/1. *Palace,* with King Ludwig I's Gallery of Beauties: Tues. to Sun. 9[10]-12.30 a.m. and 1.30-5[4] p.m.

Amalienburg: daily 9[10]-12.30 a.m. and 1.30-5[4] p.m.

Badenburg, Pagodenburg, and Magdalenen-klause: Tues. to Sun. 10-12.30 a.m. and 1.30-5 p.m. Closed in winter.

Marstall Museum, south wing of the palace (including **Nymphenburg Porcelain – Bäuml**

Collection): Tues. to Sun. 9[10]-12 a.m. and 1-5[4] p.m.

Old Residence Theater (Cuvilliés Theater), Residenzstrasse 1. Tel. 224641. Mon. to Sat. 2-5 p.m., Sun. 10 a.m.-5 p.m.

Paleontological Museum – Bavarian State Paleontological and Geological Collection, Richard-Wagner-Strasse 10. Tel. 5203361. Mon. to Thurs. 8 a.m.-4 p.m., Fri. 8 a.m.-3 p.m. Admission free.

Public Housing Museum, Überlacker House, Preysingstrasse 58. Tues., Thurs., and Sun. 10-12 a.m., Wed. and Fri. 6-7 p.m.

Residence Museum and Treasury, Max-Joseph-Platz 3. Tel. 224641. Tues. to Sat. 10 a.m.-4.30 p.m., Sun. 10 a.m.-1 p.m.

Schack Gallery, Prinzregentenstrasse 9. Tel. 224407. Daily 9 a.m.-4.30 p.m., except Tuesdays. Admission free on Sundays and public holidays.

Schleissheim Palace and State Gallery in the New Palace. Tel. 3150212. Tues. to Sun. 10-12.30 a.m. and 1.30-5[4] p.m.
Lustheim Palace: see Collection of Meissen Porcelain.
Old Palace: see Bavarian National Museum.

Siemens Museum, Prannerstrasse 10, Tel. 234/2660. Mon. to Fri. 9 a.m.-4 p.m., Sat. and Sun. 10 a.m.-2 p.m. Admission free.

State Anthropological Collection, Karolinen-platz 2a. Tel. 595251. By appointment only.

State Collection of Antiquities, Königsplatz 1. Tel. 598359. Tues. and Thurs. to Sun. 10 a.m.-4.30 p.m., Wed. 12 a.m.-8.30 p.m. Admission free on Sundays and public holidays.

State Collection of Egyptian Art, Hofgarten-strasse 1. Tel. 298546. Tues. to Sun. 9.30 a.m.-4 p.m., Tues. also 7-9 p.m. Admission free on Sundays and public holidays.

State Collection of Graphic Art, Meiser-strasse 10. Tel. 5591490. Mon. to Fri. 9 a.m.-1 p.m. and 2-4.30 p.m. Admission free.

Municipal Gallery: Masterpieces of Early Modern art.

State Gallery of Modern Art, Prinzregenten-strasse 1. Tel. 29 27 10. Tues. to Sun. 9 a.m.-4.30 p.m., Thurs. also 7-9 p.m. Admission free on Sundays and public holidays.

State Mineralogical Collection, Theresien-strasse 41 (Entrance on Barer Strasse, oppo-site the Alte Pinakothek). Tel. 23 94-1. Tues. to Fri. 1-5 p.m., Sat. and Sun. 1-6 p.m.

State Museum of Ethnology, Maximilian-strasse 42. Tel. 22 48 44. Tues. to Sun. 9.30 a.m.-4.30 p.m. Admission free on Sundays and public holidays.

State Numismatic Collection: A Greek coin with the head of Mithridates III (123-87 B. C.) from this important collection.

State Numismatic Collection, Residenz-strasse 1, Tel. 22 72 21. Open Tues. to Sun. 10 a.m.-5 p.m. Admission free on Sundays and public holidays.

State Prehistorical Collection – Museum of Pre- and Early History, Lerchenfeldstrasse 2. Tel. 29 39 11. Tues. to Sun. 9 a.m.-4 p.m., Thurs. to 8 p.m. Admission free on Sundays and public holidays.

Branch at the **Castle Museum, Grünwald,** Zeillerstrasse 3. Tel. 641 32 18. March 1-Nov. 30, Wed. to Sun. 10 a.m.-4.30 p.m.

Stuck Villa Museum, Prinzregentenstrasse 60, Tel. 47 07 086/87. Visits are possible only in conjunction with exhibitions.

The New Collection – State Museum of Applied Art, Prinzregentenstrasse 3. Tel. 22 78 44. Changing exhibitions, Tues. to Sun. 10 a.m.-5 p.m.

Toy Museum, Old City Hall tower, Marien-platz. Tel. 29 40 01. Mon. to Sat. 10 a.m.-5.30 p.m., Sun. 10 a.m.-6 p.m.

Valentin Museum, Tal 43. Tel. 22 32 66. Mon., Tues., Sat. 11.01 a.m.-5.29 p.m., Sun. 10.01 a.m.-5.29 p.m.

Other Sights

Bavaria Film Tour, Bavariafilmplatz 7, Geiselgasteig. Tel. 64 90 67. Guided tour of the film studios: 1½ to 2 hours. From March 1 to October 31: daily between 9 a.m. and 4 p.m.

Botanical Garden, Menzinger Strasse 63. Tel. 1 79 23 10 (administration) and 1 79 23 50 (ticket office). Grounds: daily 9 a.m.-7 p.m. (4.30 in Jan., Nov., and Dec.; 5 in Feb., March, and Oct.; 6 in April and Sept.); greenhouses: 9-11.45 a.m. and 1-6.30 p.m. (4 in Jan., Nov., and. Dec.; 4.30 in Feb., March, and Oct.; 5.30 in April and Sept.).

Glockenspiel in the tower of New City Hall (Marienplatz). Coopers' Dance and Knights Tournament: 11 a.m., 12 a.m., and 5 p.m. (11 a.m. only in winter). The *Münchner Kindl* is put to bed at 9 p.m.

Hellabrunn Zoo, Siebenbrunner Strasse 6. Tel. 62 50 80. Daily 8[9] a.m.-6[5] p.m.

Observatory and Planetarium, Rosenheimer Strasse 145 a. On clear days: Mon. to Fri. 8-10 p.m., Sun. 2-3 p.m. Showings in the planetarium: Thurs. from 8 p.m. onwards.

Olympic Park (see also Advance Booking for Concerts, etc. and Towers Open to the Public). The park surrounding the sports facilities is open to the public at all times. The Olympic Stadium is open daily (except on days when there is an event) from 8.30[9] a.m. to 6[4.30] p.m.

Part of the suspension roof in the Olympic Park.

St. Michael's Church, royal sepulcher: Flowers are laid on the sarcophagi of rulers from the House of Wittelsbach on most important holidays of the year.

Fairs and Markets

Auer Dult. A traditional nine-day fair held three times a year on the Auer Kirchplatz. Stalls open from 8 a.m. to 8 p.m. on weekdays and 10.30 a.m. to 8 p.m. on Sundays, recreation facilities open from 12 a.m. to 8 p.m. (7 p.m. at the Fall Fair).
The *Maidult* (May Fair) begins on the Saturday before May 1.
The *Sommer-* or *Jakobidult* (Summer, or St. Jacob's Fair) begins on the Saturday after the Feast of St. Jacob (July 25).
The *Herbst-* or *Kirchweihdult* (Fall, or Kermis Fair) begins on the Saturday before kermis (third Sunday in October).

Münchner Christkindlmarkt. A Christmas market held on Marienplatz and in Kaufinger- and Weinstrasse every year during the four weeks before Christmas. Weekdays 9 a.m.-7 p.m., Sundays 10 a.m.-7 p.m., Christmas Eve 9 a.m.-2 p.m.
Christkindlmarkts are held at the same time at the Münchner Freiheit in Schwabing, on Weissenburger Platz in Haidhausen, on Rotkreuzplatz in Neuhausen, and in front of the Parish Church in Pasing.

Royal Sepulchers

St. Michael's Church, Neuhauser Strasse 52. Entrances to the Wittelsbach royal sepulcher are near the two easternmost side altars. Open from May 1 to November 2: Mon. to Fri. 10 a.m.-1 p.m. and 2-4.30 p.m., Sat. 10 a.m.-3 p.m.
Sarcophagi of Duke Wilhelm V, Elector Maximilian, King Ludwig II, and numerous other members of the Bavarian and Palatine branches of the House of Wittelsbach.

St. Boniface, Karlstrasse 3.
Tombs of King Ludwig I (right-hand aisle) and his wife Therese of Saxe-Hildburghausen (crypt).

Cathedral, Frauenplatz 1. The bishops' and rulers' tombs in the crypt under the presbyterium are freely accessible.
The oldest Wittelsbach sepulcher in Munich, containing the remains of Emperor Ludwig the Bavarian, of the Bavarian dukes from Ludwig V to Albrecht V, and of King Ludwig III.

Theatine Church of St. Cajetan, Theatinerstrasse 22. The royal sepulcher is entered from the right transept (through the western iron gate). It contains *the sarcophagi of the Bavarian electors from Ferdinand Maria to Karl Theodor, of Emperor Charles VII, of kings Max I Joseph and Otto of Greece, and of Prince Regent Luitpold. The sarcophagi of King Max II and Queen Marie* are in the third chapel of the right aisle. Open from May 1 to Nov. 2: Mon. to Fri. 10 a.m.-1 p.m. and 3-5 p.m., Sat. 10 a.m.-3 p.m.

Trade Fairs and Exhibitions

Bavarian Agricultural Fair (Bayerisches Zentrallandwirtschaftsfest) on Theresa Meadows. Begins, like the Oktoberfest, on the third Saturday in September. Every two years (1988, etc.).

CBR München: Caravan – Boat – International Travel Fair. International exhibition of caravans, boats, and the travel and holiday industries. Annually, in February.

German Art and Antiques Fair (Deutsche Kunst- und Antiquitätenmesse). Annually, around October/November, in the Haus der Kunst.

Handicrafts and the Home (Heim und Handwerk). Handicrafts in the home, with special presentations by individual branches of the handicraft industry. Annually, in November/December.

Igafa: International Fair of the Hotel and Catering Industries. Every two years.

IHM: International Crafts Fair. Trade fair of the handicraft industry. Annually, in March.

Munich Book Fair (Münchner Bücherschau). Presentation of new books published by Bavarian publishers. Annually, around November/December, in the Haus der Kunst.

Munich Comprehensive Exhibition (Grosse Kunstausstellung München). Annually, usually June to September, in the Haus der Kunst.

Guided Tours

Tours of the city and its churches are organized regularly by the **Münchner Bildungswerk,** Dachauer Strasse 5 (for information call 557331/32/33). Tours of the city and its museums are organized by the **Münchner Volkshochschule,** Kellerstrasse 6 (for information call 41806-229/230).

Church Services

with orchestral and choral music in historic churches.

Regularly on Sundays and public holidays in:

Cathedral, Frauenplatz 1, at 9.30 a.m.
St. Michael's, Neuhauser Strasse 52, at 9 a.m.
St. Peter's, Petersplatz 1, at 9 a.m.
Theatine Church of St. Cajetan, Theatinerstrasse 22, at 10.30 a.m.

Festivals, Fun Fairs, Processions, and Pageants

Munich Opera Festival. Annually, from July to August.

Ballet Festival in the National Theater. One week, in either April or May.

Theater Festival of the City of Munich. At various times in May and/or June.

Schwabing Festival, with literary and musical events. Two weeks in June/July.

München narrisch (replacing the old carnival procession on Shrove Sunday) with a changing program in the pedestrian precinct, from Karl's Gate to Marienplatz. The traditional carnival procession has been reinstated in the Giesing neighborhood and is called the "Gaudiwurm."

Strong beer season (Starkbierzeit), usually in the fourth and third week before Easter, with large beer festivals in the beer cellars of Munich's breweries. The Salvator, served in the Salvator-Keller on the Nockherberg (Hochstrasse), is the oldest and most famous strong beer.

May bock season (Maibockzeit), after Easter. The season of spring strong beer.

Spring Festival (Frühlingsfest), held on Theresa Meadows for two weeks at the end of April/beginning of May, with fireworks on the first evening.

Summer Festivals (Sommerfest), held in the Olympic Park for ten days in the middle of August, with fireworks on the last day.

Oktoberfest ("Wies'n"), the world's largest public festival, held on Theresa Meadows from the penultimate Saturday in September to the first Sunday in October. The beginning of the Oktoberfest is marked by:

Munich and Bavarian flags at Festival time.

Wies'n Einzug: festive procession of the beer-tent keepers and breweries on the morning of the Oktoberfest's first day.

Trachten- und Schützenzug: procession of riflemen, of groups in traditional costume and historical uniforms, of bands, and of thoroughbred horses from Bavaria, Germany, and the neighboring European countries on the second day of the festival.

Corpus Christi Procession (Fronleichnamsprozession), organized by the Cathedral parish on the Feast of Corpus Christi (second Thursday after Whitsun). Smaller processions, organized in various Munich parishes, take place on the Sunday after Corpus Christi.

View through Karl's Gate during Carnival.

Excursions

*A selection of the most notable historical
and Alpine towns, churches, and royal castles within
two hours' drive of Munich.*

Dachau Concentration Camp

In 1965 the former concentration camp on the eastern edge of Dachau was set up as a memorial to the 32,000 people who lost their lives there. The crematorium, gas chambers, punishment blocks, barracks, and watchtowers were preserved and a museum established to document Nazi atrocities. An international and a Jewish memorial, together with a Protestant and a Catholic chapel, were erected as places in which to do penitence and honor the dead. On the edge of the grounds stands the Carmelite Penitence Monastery of the Holy Blood, with its simple church.

Augsburg: Perlach Tower and City Hall.

Historical Towns

Augsburg

Founded 2,000 years ago by the Romans, Augsburg was an important center of trade with the Mediterranean in the later Middle Ages and the Renaissance. It owed its prosperity to merchant families like the Welsers and Fuggers, the "bankers of the Empire." The city played a significant part in religious history (Protestants were accorded freedom of worship here in 1530) and was a major center of arts and crafts, with painters such as the Holbeins, architect Elias Holl, and a host of first-class goldsmiths, engravers, and printers.

Renaissance architecture still dominates the city, with aristocratic mansions and patrician dwellings lining the broad main street from the Cathedral (tenth to fifteenth century) to St. Ulrich and Afra (c. 1500). The imposing City Hall (1618), the Perlach Tower (1616), and the Zeughaus (Armory; 1607) were built by Elias Holl, while the three splendid Renaissance fountains are the work of Adriaen de Vries (Mercury and Hercules fountains) and Hubert Gerhard (Augustus Fountain). The Fuggerei was set up in 1525 as a model settlement for needy citizens, and its inhabitants still pay a monthly rent of just DM 1,71 (about one dollar). Among the numerous museums, the German Baroque Gallery and the Roman Museum are particularly fine.

Landshut

The former residence of the dukes of Lower Bavaria is still a picture-book town, with its castle, imposing Minster tower (after Strasbourg Cathedral, the tallest medieval building in existence), and long rows of colorful Gothic houses. A special attraction is the "Landshut Wedding": every four years (1989, etc.) the plays, processions, and tournaments that accompanied the betrothal of Duke Georg to the Polish princess Jadwiga in 1475 are re-enacted in medieval costume.

The dukes resided in Castle Trausnitz, a Gothic and Renaissance building high up above the River Isar (with famous Italian murals in the interior), and in the Stadtresidenz (1543), the only genuinely Italian *palazzo* north of the Alps. St. Martin's Church, built between 1380 and 1500, is one of the most spectacular of Late Gothic hall

St. Martin's, Landshut: View from the castle.

View of Regensburg from the Danube.

churches and contains several fine sculptures, among them a *Virgin and Child* (1520) by Hans Leinberger.

Regensburg

Founded over 1,800 years ago by the Romans, this is the only medieval town in Germany to have escaped war damage. A prosperous royal residence and a bishop's seat, it also hosted the Permanent Diet of the Holy Roman Empire.

Romanesque and Gothic patrician dwellings and towers lend the city an Italianate air. The stone bridge over the Danube (1135), a major technical achievement of the Middle Ages, was the starting point of many a medieval crusade. Of particular note among the numerous churches, which range from the Romanesque to the Rococo period, are St. Peter's Cathedral (erected from 1250 to 1618 in the style of French cathedrals); the Romanesque "Scottish Church" of St. Jacob, with its interesting north portal of c. 1150; and the Alte Kapelle, with a sumptuous Rococo interior. The City Hall contains an authentically furnished torture chamber.

It is well worth taking a motorboat to see the dramatic Danube cutting to the west of the city and to visit the nearby Baroque monastery of Weltenburg, its church a masterpiece by the Asam brothers. Not far away (near Kelheim) is the Befreiungshalle, built by Klenze for the former King Ludwig I to commemorate the wars of liberation against Napoleon. Klenze achieved another imposing landscape effect with his Valhalla (near Donaustauf), a Neo-Greek pantheon of famous Germans perched high above the Danube.

Famous Towns in the Bavarian Alps

Bad Tölz

Already an important center of trade on the Salt Road in the thirteenth century, Bad Tölz became a popular spa after the discovery there of iodine springs in the nineteenth century. Its splendidly painted gabled houses make Market Street one of the most picturesque sights in Upper Bavaria. The town's reputation as a notable cabinetmaking center dates back to the late Middle Ages: examples, including the well-known *Bauernschränke* ("rustic cupboards") may be seen in the Local History Museum in the Altes Rathaus. The parish church of Mariä Himmelfahrt, a Late Gothic hall church, contains several remarkable tombstones.

Two structures above the town are connected with religious customs typical of Bavaria. On November 6 of each year horses are led on a *Leonhardiritt* ("St. Leonard's

Leonhardiritt in Bad Tölz.

Ride"), a pilgrimage to St. Leonard's Chapel (named for the patron saint of horses), to receive benediction. The "Calvary" is a hill arranged to enable the faithful to relive Christ's carrying of the cross to Golgatha, with tiny chapels, steps, and a Crucifixion group.

Bad Tölz's "personal" mountains are the Zwiesel (4,422 ft. above sea level), with a glorious view in all directions, and the Blomberg (4,094 ft.), with a cable-car railway and a popular summer sled run.

Tegernsee

The area around Tegernsee is one of the most popular for hiking and skiing in the Bavarian Alps. The town of Tegernsee on the east side of the lake grew up around the ancient Benedictine monastery (founded in 719), whose far-reaching missionary activities and cultivation of the arts of stained glass, manuscript illumination, poetry, sacred drama, and music made it highly influential. The monastery church of St. Quirin, a Gothic basilica erected on Romanesque foundations, was given a Baroque face-lift by A. Riva in 1684-88 and a Neoclassical facade by Klenze in 1817. Its interior contains frescoes by J. G. Asam, father of the famous Asam brothers, and altar figures by J. B. Straub. A number of small museums recall some of the famous personalities – including the painter Olaf Gulbransson – who lived in the area.

Other delightful places on the lake are Gmund, Wiessee spa, and Rottach-Egern. Trips southward to Wallberg (5,650 ft. above sea level, with cable-car railway), Wildbad-Kreuth, Achenpass (3,087 ft.), Schweigeralm, and Sylvenstein-Stausee can also be recommended.

Summit of the Zugspitze.

A scene on the Tegernsee.

Garmisch-Partenkirchen

Nestling at the foot of Germany's highest mountain, the Zugspitze (9,721 ft. above sea level), Garmisch-Partenkirchen is a world-famous venue for winter sports, with modern sports facilities, cog and cable-car railways, and ski lifts. The town hosted the Winter Olympics in 1936 and the Alpine Skiing World Cup in 1978. The annual New Year's ski-jumping competition attracts many visitors. Its climate has made Garmisch-Partenkirchen a popular health resort, with first-class clinics and some 190 miles of footpaths ideal for walking or hiking. The folklore of the region may be experienced in all its variety in the Werdenfelser Museum, at the local theaters, and during the festivals held in July (Garmisch) and August (Partenkirchen). Both Garmisch and Partenkirchen – the two were merged in 1936 – are notable for the painted decoration of their houses, while the Old Church of St. Martin in Garmisch boasts some fine exterior murals from the fourteenth and fifteenth centuries. The Munich architect G. von Seidl built the Richard Strauss Villa, where the composer lived for many years and in which he died in 1949.

The Zugspitze is accessible by cog or cable-car railway. The finest view of it is to be had from the Wank (5,840 ft. above sea level), while the wildly romantic scenery of the Partnachkamm and Höllentalkamm ought not to be missed.

Mittenwald

The town at the foot of the mighty Karwendel range once lay in the middle of a forest ("mitten im Wald") on the Roman trade route from Verona to Ausburg. During the Middle Ages, log driving on the River Isar was the source of its prosperity. Mittenwald, the "violin town," has been a center of violin making since the seventeenth century, and is the home of a well-known, 100-year-old school for violin construction and of an interesting Violin Museum. The seventeenth- and eighteenth-century house decoration turned the town into a "living picture book"

Sts. Peter and Paul, Mittenwald: Fresco by Günther.

(Goethe). Matthäus Günther created the fine ceiling fresco and altar painting in the parish church of Sts. Peter and Paul, and the Pilgerhaus zum Hl. Geist contains notable figures of saints from the Gothic and Baroque periods.

The western peak of the Karwendel (7,362 ft. above sea level) can be reached by cable-car railway. The waterfalls on the Leutaschkamm and in the Laintalschlucht, as well as the peaceful mountain lakes Terchensee and Lautersee, are within easy walking distance of Mittenwald, whereas it takes about an hour to reach the lookout point on the Burgberg or the inn up on the Aschauer Alm.

Scene from the Oberammergau Passion Play.

Oberammergau

Three things have made this beautiful mountain town famous: the Passion Play, which first took place in 1634 and is now performed every ten years (1990, etc.) to an international audience; the almost 900-year-old tradition of wood carving, whose products are now exported to all parts of the world; and the colorful decoration of its houses, dating from the Baroque and Rococo periods and from the present day. Oberammergau is also an ideal health resort and venue for winter sports. The Passion Play Theater, built in 1900 and seating 4,700; the Heimatmuseum, with its display of masterpieces of local carving; and the Baroque parish church (1736-42), containing frescoes by Matthäus Günther as well as outstanding stuccowork and sculptures are all worth a visit. Also to be recommended are a walk in the Ammergau mountains – to Kofel (4,403 ft. above sea level) or to Ettaler Mandl (5,374 ft.) – and a trip on the Laberberg or Kolbensattel cable-car railways to a height of 5,374 and 4,101 feet respectively.

Königssee: St. Bartholomä and the Watzmann.

Berchtesgaden

Before becoming a Bavarian possession in 1810, the Berchtesgaden region was an independent principality, made rich by salt mining. Its present-day riches are its scenery and art. Old houses, with projecting gable roofs and painted facades, and Gothic and Baroque church towers, dominate the view of the town against the Watzmann massif. The former College of Augustine Canons (founded in 1120), whose provost was also the local prince, became a Wittelsbach palace in 1923, and now houses an extensive museum. The Collegiate Church of St. Peter is a Romanesque and Gothic structure with Baroque furnishings. Highly recommended is a visit to the salt mines where, clad in miners' garb, you can travel on the mine railway and take a raft across the underground salt lake.

The nearby mountain lake and town of Königssee attracts a large number of visitors. Its picturesque pilgrimage church of St. Bartholomä lies at the foot of the breathtaking eastern face of the Watzmann, the highest precipice in the Alps. From the town of Königssee a cable-car railway runs to Jenner, which affords a glorious view at 6,148 feet above sea level. From Berchtesgaden you can take a cable-car railway to the Obersalzberg (3,346 ft.) or walk across to the idyllically situated pilgrimage church of Marie Gern.

Vault in the monastery church, Andechs.

Churches and Monasteries

Andechs

Andechs Monastery attracts a great number of pilgrims – not only the pious, but also people making a pilgrimage to the pleasures of nature, art, and beer-drinking. Legend has it that the pilgrimage church on the "Holy Hill" high up above Herrsching on the Ammersee lake was founded in the tenth century. Its sumptuous interior (1755) contains works by such masters of Bavarian Rococo as J.B. Zimmermann and J.B. Straub. The pilgrims' goals are a miraculous image of the Virgin Enthroned (c. 1460) and a collection of holy relics dating from various periods. The fame of the monastery's brewery, with its popular beer garden, extends far beyond the borders of Bavaria.

The Abbey of Ettal.

Diessen

Behind the restrained nobility of its facade, the former Collegiate Church at Diessen on the Ammersee lake harbors a masterly late Baroque interior (1732-39) by J.M. Fischer, with a striking high altar by Cuvilliés, an elegant pulpit and organ loft by Straub, fine frescoes by J.G. Bergmüller, and notable stuccowork by the Feichtmayr brothers. It is worth taking a walk in the marshy countryside alongside the lake to the east of the town.

Interior of the former collegiate church, Diessen.

Ettal

With its mighty Baroque dome, the Benedictine Abbey of Ettal (founded in 1330 by Emperor Ludwig the Bavarian) sits in an incomparably impressive setting in a mountain valley. In the eighteenth century, the unusual form of the original church – a dodecagonal rotunda – received a shape equally unusual for that time through the addition of a dome and a choir. The result is a uniquely harmonious mixture of the Gothic and Baroque styles. J.J. Zeiller's huge fresco in the cupola, J.B. Zimmermann's Rococo stuccowork, and J.B. Straub's six side altars are all virtuoso works of art. The pilgrimage church was erected to house a miraculous image of the Virgin, a small, fourteenth-century marble statue of Italian provenance. Anyone not intoxicated by the monastery's art treasures is likely to have more success with its famous liqueur!

Altar in Ottobeuren monastery church, detail.

Wieskirche, near Steingaden

This priceless Rococo jewel stands in a large meadow ("Wiese") against a backdrop of mountains and forests. Its light, swirling interior, which seems to defy the laws of gravity; its effervescent stuccowork; and its captivating ceiling frescoes unite to give the best possible idea of that heaven on earth which is Rococo art. The masterpiece of the brothers Dominikus and Johann Baptist Zimmermann, the church was erected in 1746-54 to house a figure of the flagellated Christ which, according to legend, shed real tears and performed miraculous healings. (An extensive restoration of the interior is in progress.)

Wieskirche, exterior view.

Ottobeuren

The 1,200-year-old monastery of Ottobeuren belongs among the finest achievements of Baroque architecture. The monumental

Monastery church of Ottobeuren, exterior view.

twin-tower facade of the church and the symmetrically arranged monastery buildings dominate the little market town situated in a valley in Bavarian Swabia. On his favorite combination of a centralized and a longitudinal groundplan J. M. Fischer erected in 1748-66 a breathtaking interior space of supreme clarity, articulated by columns and pilasters, imaginative stuccowork (by J. M. Feichtmayr), and exquisite color harmonies. J. J. Zeiller's frescoes in the vaulting depict the foundation of the Benedictine order. As a *Reichsstift*, Ottobeuren was subject to the emperor alone, enjoying exceptional privileges and wealth. The Baroque monastery was built under Abbot Rupert Ness, the son of a village smith. The monastery buildings, apart from housing an interesting museum of religious art, are notable for their splendid interiors, which include a room for theatrical performances and a library.

Neuschwanstein amidst the mountains.

Ludwig II's Castles

Linderhof

This most intimate of Ludwig II's architectural fantasies – and the only one in which he actually lived – lies amidst the Ammergau mountains in a park that combines English and French features. G. Dollmann built it in 1870-86 in the so-called Second Rococo Style, basing his design on the Petit Trianon at Versailles. The sumptuously furnished chambers of this lodge-like palace are grouped around four opulent staterooms: the precious Mirror Room; the Bedroom, with its four-poster bed; the Dining Hall, with its mechanically operated tables; and the Audience Chamber, with its canopied throne. The park's main attractions are the artificial grotto, which, complete with wave machine, is illuminated alternately to simulate the Blue Grotto on Capri and the Venus Grotto from Wagner's *Tannhäuser,* and the luxurious Peacock Throne in the Moorish Kiosk, which was transported *en bloc* from the Paris World Fair.

Neuschwanstein

One of the most popular tourist attractions, Neuschwanstein receives well over one million visitors each year. In contrast to Linderhof and Herrenchiemsee, Ludwig II was here dreaming, not of eighteenth-century France, but of the romantic age of German chivalry. Unfinished at the king's death, this picturesque Neo-Romanesque castle perched on a ridge above the Pöllat Precipice was built by E. von Riedel and G. Dollmann in 1869-92. The Minstrels Hall, with paintings of the Parzival legend, and the Throne Room, solemn in the manner of a Byzantine church, form the core of the interior, while the living quarters themselves, complete with

Linderhof, view from the park.

a splendid array of old German furniture, are decorated with Tristan and Lohengrin motifs, particularly the latter's swan. It was in Neuschwanstein that Ludwig was arrested on June 12, 1886, before being taken to Berg on Lake Starnberg, where he died the following day under mysterious circumstances.

Nearby Hohenschwangau Castle was built on the site of a ruined castle in 1833-35 as a summer residence for Ludwig's father, King Max II. Together with Linderhof, this Neo-Gothic building by D. Quaglio, J.D. Ohlmüller, and F. von Ziebland was Ludwig's favorite residence.

Louis XIV. Its interior contains an ornate staircase for court ceremonies; the "sacred domain" of the Gala Bedroom; the 320-foot-long Hall of Mirrors, a festival hall celebrating the monarchy, lit by 1,800 candles, and now used for concerts in the summer; as well as salons, studies, and porcelain chambers. Every single item of the extremely opulent furnishings is of exquisite craftsmanship. Yet the lord of the palace spent only a few days amid all the splendor.

The south wing contains a King Ludwig Museum, with 400 exhibits illustrating the king's life.

Herrenchiemsee

The two islands in the "Bavarian Sea" of Chiemsee have a venerable past. As early as the eighth century, the Fraueninsel (women's island) was occupied by a convent and the Herreninsel (men's island) by an abbey, whose church later became the cathedral of the diocese of Chiemsee. After the secularization of church property in 1803 the Herreninsel was threatened with deforestation, until Ludwig II bought it in 1873 as a suitable site for his long-dreamt-of "Bavarian Versailles." Only the main section of the palace, built in 1878-85 by G. Dollmann and J. Hofmann, was completed. Surrounded by a French garden and a landscaped park, the horseshoe-shaped building of three tracts was erected in the ostentatious spirit of, and as a homage to,

Latona Fountain, Herrenchiemsee.

233

Index

Finis spectaculi!

Photography Credits

Artothek 107, 108 (top left), 109 (center left)
Augustiner-Bräu Wagner KG 74 (bottom)
Bavaria Atelier GmbH 201 (top)
Bayerische Hypotheken- und Wechselbank 192 (left)
Bayerische Staatsbibliothek 118 (top, center)
Bayerische Staatsgemäldesammlungen 22 (top), 108 (bottom, top right), 109 (top, bottom), 110 (bottom), 112, 113, 129 (bottom), 139, 187 (bottom)
Bayerische Verwaltung der staatlichen Schlösser, Gärten und Seen 24 (center), 46 (top right), 47 (top), 49 (top left), 50, 53 (bottom), 54, 56, 172 (top), 174 (bottom right), 177, 188, 189, 190 (top)
Bayerischer Landesverein für Heimatpflege e.V. 15 (2nd from top)
Bayerisches Nationalmuseum 130 (bottom), 132, 133, 134, 135 (top), 190 (bottom)
L. Bernheimer KG 210
Biller, Josef H. 25 (top), 59 (bottom), 117 (center right), 135 (bottom), 165 (bottom left), 174 (bottom left), 194 (top, bottom right), 228 (left), 230 (top left)
Birker, Willi 16 (top left)
BMW Museum 185 (center)
Braunmüller, Robert 211
DAKS London, Munich branch 146 (bottom)
Deutsches Museum 157 (top: Max Prugger, permit no. G 30/11066 of the Govt. of Upper Bavaria; center; bottom), 158, 159
Deutsches Theatermuseum 60 (center right)
Die Neue Sammlung 136 (top)
Drave, Erika 10 (4th from top), 12 (2nd from top), 13 (top, 2nd from top), 14 (3rd from top), 37 (center left), 39, 41 (bottom), 44 (bottom), 45, 47 (bottom), 49 (bottom left), 57, 63, 68 (bottom), 91, 93 (top), 101 (bottom right), 124, 149, 168 (top), 173 (bottom), 182, 199 (bottom), 200 (top left), 203, 213 (top), 221 (bottom), 222 (top), 223, 238
Fremdenverkehrsamt Ostbayern (Regensburg) 227
Glyptothek 97 (bottom)
Goertz, Ev 38 (bottom)
Hardt, Barbara 120 (top)
Hetz, Robert front flap, 10 (top; 2nd, 3rd, and 5th from top; bottom), 11 (top, 3rd from top), 12 (top, 3rd and 4th from top), 13 (5th from top), 14 (2nd from top, bottom), 15 (4th from top), 31 (bottom), 36 (bottom), 37 (bottom right), 38 (top), 46 (bottom left), 49 (bottom right), 60 (bottom), 67 (top), 71 (top), 78 (bottom), 86 (top), 92 (top, bottom left), 93 (bottom), 94 (top), 95 (center), 110 (top), 111 (top), 117 (top, bottom), 118 (bottom), 123 (bottom), 128 (top), 141 (bottom), 147, 152 (top left), 154 (top left), 155 (top), 161 (bottom), 163, 164 (top), 165 (bottom right), 167 (center right), 168 (bottom), 180 (bottom), 195 (bottom left), 201 (bottom), 205 (top left), 207 (bottom), 211 (bottom), 216, 217, 219, 220, 221 (top, center, bottom right), 224, 225
Hirmer, Albert 40 (bottom)
Hotel Bayerischer Hof 218 (bottom)
i-team, Bernd Glocke KG back flap (top)
Klammet & Aberl 2 (permit no. G 42/371 of the Govt. of Upper Bavaria)
Langemann, Peter 115 (bottom), 126 (top, center), 164 (center)
Mader, Fritz (Hamburg) 9
Mayer, Richard F.J. 6/7, 11 (5th from top), 15 (top), 178 (center), 179 (top), 195 (bottom right)
Mineralogische Staatssammlung 114 (top)
Moses, Stefan 5, 18 (bottom right), 30 (left), 37 (top), 61 (bottom), 140 (bottom right), 148 (top), 167 (bottom left), 205 (top right), 214 (bottom), 222 (bottom), back cover (bottom right)
Mülbe, Wolf-Christian von der front cover, 29, 33 (top), 34 (center), 35, 36 (top), 51, 52, 53 (top), 55, 62 (bottom), 64 (top), 65 (bottom), 66, 69, 72 (bottom), 73 (top), 76/77, 79, 80 (top), 81 (top), 82 (top left, center left and right, bottom right), 83, 84, 85, 102 (top), 119, 138 (top), 144 (top left), 145, 154 (top left, bottom), 165 (center), 169 (top), 173 (top), 174 (top), 175, 180 (top), 181 (top, bottom right), 186, 193 (top), 194 (bottom

left), 195 (top), 202, 204, 230 (right), 231 (bottom), back cover (left)
Münchener Messe- und Ausstellungsgesellschaft mbH 169 (bottom)
Münchener Feuerwehrmuseum 86 (bottom)
Münchener Rennverein e.V. 13 (bottom)
Münchner Tierpark Hellabrunn AG 197, 198 (bottom)
Münchner Olympiapark GmbH 15 (3rd from top)
Münchner Stadtmuseum 17 (top), 20, 21, 87 (center right), 88, 89, 90
Münchner Verkehrs- und Tarifverbund GmbH back flap (bottom)
Museum Villa Stuck 142
Neumann, J. H., BILDARCHIV BUCHER 232/233
Neumeister, Werner 11 (4th from top), 13 (3rd from top), 14 (4th from top), 15 (bottom), 28, 31 (top), 32 (right), 41 (top), 42, 44 (top), 46 (bottom right), 59, 61 (top), 65 (center), 67 (center, bottom), 70 (center, bottom), 71 (bottom), 74 (top), 75, 87 (top), 94 (bottom), 97 (top), 99 (top), 100, 102 (bottom left), 106 (top), 114 (bottom), 116, 121, 122 (top), 125, 128 (bottom), 129 (top), 131, 138 (bottom), 148 (bottom), 150 (top), 153 (top), 160, 161 (top), 164 (bottom), 167 (top), 171 (top), 176, 184, 185 (top), 212 (bottom)
Obermayer, Gustav 181 (bottom left), 205 (bottom left), 207 (top)
Ott, Klaus 191 (permit no. GS 300/9240/82 of the Govt. of Upper Bavaria)
Peras, Hans 49 (top right), 92 (bottom right), 114 (center left), 153 (bottom left), 155 (bottom)
Prähistorische Staatssammlung 136 (bottom), 137
Presse- und Informationsamt der Stadt München 27 (center)
Prestel-Archiv 14 (top, 5th from top), 16 (top right, bottom), 18 (bottom left), 22, 30 (top right), 34 (top), 96, 120 (bottom), 140 (left), 143 (bottom), 162 (bottom), 199 (top), 200 (bottom), 205 (bottom right), 206 (bottom)
Private collections 33 (bottom), 40 (top), 46 (top left), 62 (top), 70 (top), 72 (top), 73 (bottom), 78 (top), 81 (center), 122 (bottom), 143 (top), 144 (right), 152 (right), 166, 170 (center), 193 (bottom)
Prugger, Max 208
Ruelius, Elisabeth 30 (bottom), 153 (bottom right)
Schleich, Erwin 82 (bottom left)
Siemens Museum 68 (top)
Spielzeugmuseum im Alten Rathaus 32 (left)
Staatliche Antikensammlungen 101
Staatliche Münzsammlung 223 (top)
Staatliche Sammlung Ägyptischer Kunst 58
Staatliches Museum für Völkerkunde 150 (bottom left, center), 151
Stadtarchiv München 24 (top right, bottom)
Städtische Galerie im Lenbachhaus 102 (bottom right), 103, 104 (top, bottom), 105
Städtisches Fremdenverkehrsamt (Augsburg) 226 (left)
Stepan, Peter 98, 99 (bottom), 104 (center), 206 (top)
Tanzschule im Deutschen Theater 11 (2nd from top)
Toepffer, Sabine 43
Ullstein Bilderdienst 24 (top left)
Verlag Schnell & Steiner GmbH & Co 65 (top), 196 (bottom), 200 (center)
Walz, Tino 12 (5th from top)
Widmann, Thomas P. 155 (top)
Zähler-Museum 126 (bottom)
Zaigler, Robert 64 (bottom), 141 (top), 179 (bottom)

Map of the City of Munich

The map shows the areas covered by separate plans in the guide, with the exception of the Old Town (plan **1**, inside front cover). Items mentioned on pages 202-07, but not included in the individual plans, appear in blue type.

The plans

2 Maxvorstadt, the Pinakotheks, Ludwigstrasse *page 95*
3 English Garden, Schwabing *123*
4 Prinzregentenstrasse, Lehel, Bogenhausen *127*
5 Maximilianstrasse, Gasteig, Deutsches Museum *146*
6 Central Station, South Cemetery, Theresa Meadows *162*
7 Neuhausen, Nymphenburg, Blutenburg, Pipping *170*
8 Olympic Park, BMW Museum, Luitpold Park *182*
9 Schleissheim and Lustheim Palaces *186*
10 Neu-Bogenhausen, Berg am Laim, Ramersdorf, Perlach *192*
11 Thalkirchen, Forstenried, Geiselgasteig, Grünwald *196*

Public Transport

Munich and the outlying areas within a twenty-mile radius of the city are served by the Münchner Verkehrs- und Tarifverbund (MVV for short), a combined transport system that covers about 2,100 miles of bus, tram, U-Bahn (subway), and S-Bahn (suburban railroad) routes. The plan on the back flap of this guide shows the various U-Bahn and S-Bahn lines. It does not include buses and trams, since these routes are subject to a certain amount of change. A full, up-to-date plan of the network is displayed at all stops and stations within the area covered by the MVV, and is also published in the official timetables issued twice a year by the MVV and obtainable from most kiosks in town.

Here are some general tips on how to use the MVV transport system (detailed information is available from the below-ground Stadtinformation bureau on Karlsplatz [Stachus], which is open on weekdays from 9 a.m. to 5 p.m.).

All MVV **tickets** are valid for buses, trams, U-Bahn, and S-Bahn, so there is no need to buy a separate ticket if your journey involves more than one type of transport; unlimited transfers are allowed as long as you travel in one direction. Tickets can be bought from the blue machines located at all U-Bahn and S-Bahn stations, at some bus and tram stops, and in the trams themselves, as well as from about 300 tobacconists and stationers around town. All places where tickets can be bought display a white "K" on a green background.

Single tickets are available, but it is usually more economical to buy a strip ticket – a *Kurzstrecke* (short journey) strip ticket (red) or a *Langstrecke* (long journey) strip ticket (blue). All these tickets must be canceled at the **canceling** machines found at the entrance to U-Bahn and S-Bahn stations and inside the buses and trams. The number of strips to be canceled varies according to the number of zones you will be traveling across – zone plans are posted at every U-Bahn and S-Bahn station, at all bus and tram stops, and in the buses and trams themselves.

The best bet for those intending to travel a lot is to buy a **twenty-four-hour ticket,** which can be obtained from the City Tourist Office (details on page 219 of this guide), at all ticket offices, and at the blue ticket machines.